NEW EXPLORATIONS IN THEOLOGY

To Newell & Mary

THE MAKING OF
STANLEY HAUERWAS

BRIDGING BARTH AND POSTLIBERALISM

DAVID B. HUNSICKER

FOREWORD BY STANLEY HAUERWAS

ivp
Academic
An imprint of InterVarsity Press
Downers Grove, Illinois

InterVarsity Press
P.O. Box 1400, Downers Grove, IL 60515-1426
ivpress.com
email@ivpress.com

InterVarsity Press® is the book-publishing division of InterVarsity Christian Fellowship/USA®, a movement of
students and faculty active on campus at hundreds of universities, colleges, and schools of nursing in the United
States of America, and a member movement of the International Fellowship of Evangelical Students. For
information about local and regional activities, visit intervarsity.org.

Cover design: Cindy Kiple
Interior design: Beth McGill

ISBN 978-0-8308-4916-1 (print)
ISBN 978-0-8308-6666-3 (digital)

Printed in the United States of America ♾

InterVarsity Press is committed to ecological stewardship and to the conservation of natural resources in all our
operations. This book was printed using sustainably sourced paper.

Library of Congress Cataloging-in-Publication Data

A catalog record for this book is available from the Library of Congress.

P	23	22	21	20	19	18	17	16	15	14	13	12	11	10	9	8	7	6	5	4	3	2	1
Y	38	37	36	35	34	33	32	31	30	29	28	27	26	25	24	23	22	21	20	19			

To Barbara

whose love and commitment

made this work possible

and to Felicity

who has made me happy beyond belief

Contents

Foreword

STANLEY HAUERWAS

IT IS ENOUGH TO MAKE ME THINK there is a conspiracy afoot by intelligent young theologians to embarrass me. Robert Dean recently wrote a wonderful book, *For the Life of the World: Jesus Christ and the Church in the Theologies of Dietrich Bonhoeffer and Stanley Hauerwas*, in which he developed a very interesting comparison between Bonhoeffer's and my theology. Dean's treatment of my work was positive and constructive. In particular, he called attention to the christological commitments that are at the heart of everything I do but critics of my work usually ignore. But who wants to be compared with Bonhoeffer? Bonhoeffer was a great theologian. I am an American academic.

Being put up against Bonhoeffer is one thing, but now I have to face David Hunsicker's investigation of my claim to be a Barthian. Barth, too, was a great theologian. I follow at a great distance. Barth was not only more learned than I could ever hope to be, but he had a theological imagination that was without compare. From my perspective, Barth is a miracle. He seems to have come from nowhere to help us recover the magic of the gospel. Hunsicker is, of course, right to hold my feet to the fire because I have claimed to be a "Barthian," but as he also indicates I have never claimed to be a Barth scholar. Nonetheless, to be put up against Barth, if only to suggest there is something to be said for my claim to be a Barthian, is profoundly humbling.

What then am I to make of the fine books Dean and Hunsicker have written? Why should anyone care if I am a Barthian? Little seems to hang on an answer to that question. Yet the care with which Hunsicker pursues that question means that it might matter not because there is a definitive answer but because the pursuit of an answer can tell us something about how theology needs to be done. In short, theology is best done in conversation with other theologians. Barth's *Church Dogmatics* is one long conversation with Scripture, the Christian tradition, contemporary theologians, and philosophers. What one learns from watching Barth carry on his conversations is how well he listens to his friends . . . and his foes.

I cannot claim to listen as well as Barth, but I hope even at this late time in my life that I can listen to the kind of critiques of what I have tried to do offered by Hunsicker (and Dean). Hunsicker develops criticisms that matter because he has done me the favor of reading me sympathetically but critically. That is a gift I cherish, and I can only hope that Hunsicker's book will attract others to the conversation. For if he is right, as I take him to be, that in some ways I am a pragmatist, then we will know we are on to something by attending to the work done because someone listened.

Acknowledgments

ONLY AFTER THE TOIL of one's labor is finished is it possible to look back and to acknowledge that the work was not done alone. Along the way, there have been many people who have helped to nurture and prune the ideas that became this book. Although it seems far too small a way to give thanks, it is nevertheless right that I should mention them here at the outset. To anyone I have overlooked, I apologize in advance.

The seeds of this book were planted in Durham, North Carolina, where I was simultaneously studying at Duke Divinity School and serving in ministry with my friend and mentor, Jeff McSwain. Jeff introduced me to the work of T. F. Torrance and, therefore, to Karl Barth. At the same time, I was taking classes with Douglas Campbell, a kindred theological spirit. In the following year, I began my first in-depth reading of Karl Barth's theology with Willie Jennings at the same time I was taking Stanley Hauerwas's Introduction to Christian Ethics course. I began to see connections that seemed natural to me. Only later would I discover that those connections were not widely acknowledged.

The seeds began to sprout at St. Mary's College, University of St. Andrews. There, I began to develop the idea that if you take Barth's rejection of natural theology seriously, then you must end up with something like Hauerwas's theological ethics. At that point in time, comments from Alan Torrance and Stephen Holmes helped me to clarify my thought.

The tree reached maturation and began to bear fruit at Fuller Theological Seminary in Pasadena, California. My time at Fuller was marked by wonderful conversation and collaboration with a number of people. I can only mention a few here: Howard Loewen, Veli-Matti Kärkkäinen, Oliver Crisp, Nancey Murphy, Tommy Givens, and Daniel Lee. I am also grateful for the regular participants in the Karl Barth Reading Group and Eric Mulligan for facilitating that group. Among my peers, no one provided more feedback to early drafts of the work than Tom Bennett. Finally, I am thankful to my church family, First Presbyterian Church of Hollywood, and the Fraser Fund, without which I could not have afforded the time to pursue this inquiry.

The book was pruned and brought to harvest by Brian Brock and Stanley Hauerwas, who took interest in the project. But it is David McNutt who helped me to see how the development from dissertation to book should occur. IVP has been the perfect nursery for this little book, and I am grateful for the working relationship we have. Since St. Andrews, I have known David as a pastor, a theologian, a golfer, and a fantasy football commissioner. He was good at most of those things; he is an excellent editor.

Finally, the person who has the most sweat equity in the success of this book is my wife, Barbara, whose theological prowess and editorial acumen helped me to present the best possible manuscript to my editors. For Barbara, for our daughter, Felicity, and for our families, who gave us generous and unending support, I am thankful.

At this point, an author will often say something like, "If anything I have written here is wrong, the error is mine alone" in order to absolve one's dialogue partners and friends. That is mostly true; however, you can blame Stanley Hauerwas for anything here you don't much like. Stanley likes to say that it is his job to indoctrinate his students and that he wants them to think like him. I began as a dubious student in his intro to ethics course but grew over time to see the logic of his thinking. No doubt, that is at least partly Stanley's fault.

David B. Hunsicker
Pasadena, CA
On the fiftieth anniversary of Karl Barth's death, December 10, 2018.

Abbreviations

AC	Hauerwas, *After Christendom*
AE	Hauerwas, *Approaching the End*
AN	Hauerwas, *Against the Nations*
B	Brock and Hauerwas, *Beginnings*
BCCE	Hauerwas and Wells, *The Blackwell Companion to Christian Ethics*
BH	Hauerwas, *A Better Hope*
CC	Hauerwas, *A Community of Character*
CCL	Hauerwas, *Character and the Christian Life*
CD	Barth, *Church Dogmatics*
CDRO	Hauerwas and Coles, *Christianity, Democracy, and the Radical Ordinary*
CET	Hauerwas, *Christian Existence Today*
CSC	Hauerwas, *Cross-Shattered Christ*
CSH	Hauerwas, *A Cross-Shattered Church*
DF	Hauerwas, *Dispatches from the Front*
DT	Hauerwas, *Disrupting Time*
HC	Hauerwas, *Hannah's Child*
HR	Hauerwas, *The Hauerwas Reader*
HS	Hauerwas and Willimon, *The Holy Spirit*
IGC	Hauerwas, *In Good Company*
M	Hauerwas, *Matthew*
MW	Hauerwas and Dean, *Minding the Web*
NT	Brunner and Barth, *Natural Theology*

PF	Hauerwas, *Performing the Faith*
PK	Hauerwas, *The Peaceable Kingdom*
RA	Hauerwas and Willimon, *Resident Aliens*
STT	Hauerwas, *Sanctify Them in the Truth*
SU	Hauerwas, *The State of the University*
TT	Hauerwas, *Truthfulness and Tragedy*
US	Hauerwas, *Unleashing the Scripture*
VV	Hauerwas, *Vision and Virtue*
WAD	Hauerwas, *War and the American Difference*
WGU	Hauerwas, *With the Grain of the Universe*
WRAL	Hauerwas and Willimon, *Where Resident Aliens Live*
WT	Hauerwas, *The Work of Theology*
WW	Hauerwas, *Wilderness Wanderings*
WWW	Hauerwas, *Working with Words*

Introduction

Stanley Hauerwas is a Barthian. At least, that is what he claims.[1] He may very well be in some respects; nevertheless, a number of Barth's contemporary interpreters bristle at the suggestion. For some interpreters, like Bruce McCormack, Hauerwas belongs to a group of scholars who misunderstand Barth. Barth influences these scholars *indirectly*, but they are not really Barthian. For McCormack, Hauerwas is a postliberal—an offshoot of neo-orthodoxy that caricatures Barth's work in a manner that has been described by Francesca Murphy as "story Barthianism."[2] According to McCormack, the postliberal "narrative theology" interpretation of Barth neuters his realism. Others, like Nigel Biggar and Nicholas Healy, argue instead that Hauerwas's theology is ecclesiocentric, replacing God-talk with church-talk. On these terms, Hauerwas is actually a Protestant liberal, the very thing against which Barth railed in his theology! Common to both of these perspectives is the assumption that Hauerwas is either disingenuous or deeply mistaken to locate his own work within a Barthian perspective.

This book critically investigates Hauerwas's claim to be a Barthian over and against these alternative suggestions. Against these scholars, I will argue that Hauerwas is both *Barthian* and *postliberal*. Hauerwas's theology is the continuation of a basic theological lesson he learned from Barth: to reject Protestant liberalism. Where it appears that Hauerwas breaks with Barth's

---

[1]*HC*, 87.
[2]Francesca Aran Murphy, *God Is Not a Story: Realism Revisited* (Oxford: Oxford University Press, 2007), 6.

christocentrism, I argue that it is actually a chastened return to a theology of the third article after Barth—a possibility that Barth himself considered at the end of his life.[3] Thus, while Hauerwas's theological ethics bears strong resemblances to the ecclesiocentricity of Protestant liberalism, he presupposes some basic Barthian convictions that prevent him from simply resuming the liberal Protestant project without Barth's insights. In this sense, Hauerwas is a *Barthian postliberal.*

THE IMPORTANCE OF KARL BARTH

Stanley Hauerwas (b. 1940) has been the subject of a number of dissertations and theological monographs. Best in class is surely Samuel Wells's *Transforming Fate into Destiny*, a work that Hauerwas himself compliments.[4] Published in 1994, *Transforming Fate* is a bit dated. Since that time, Hauerwas's career has changed in a number of significant ways. To be precise: he delivered the prestigious Gifford Lectures at the University of St. Andrews in 2001; he reflected on and responded to the September 11 terrorist attacks and the subsequent wars in Iraq and Afghanistan; and he published over two dozen new books, and countless essays and sermons. Moreover, *Transforming Fate*—like most other works on Hauerwas—fails to explore the influence that Barth has on him. Scholars of Hauerwas's work tend to skirt the topic, either taking Hauerwas at his word or ignoring the influence altogether. In my estimation, this is a significant mistake.

Michael Cartwright once described Hauerwas's theology as a constellation.[5] I think that image is especially helpful for thinking about the theologians and philosophers who influence Hauerwas. The intellectual stars in Hauerwas's constellation include Alasdair MacIntyre, John Howard Yoder,

---

[3]In a late reflection on his relationship to Schleiermacher, Barth wrote, "What I here and now . . . have casually taken into consideration concerning material clarification of my relationship to Schleiermacher and here and there already indicated among good friends, is the possibility of a theology of the third article, dominating and decisively of the Holy Spirit" (Karl Barth, "Nachwort," in *Schleiermacher-Auswahl: mit einem Nachwort von Karl Barth*, quoted in Aaron T. Smith, *A Theology of the Third Article: Karl Barth and the Spirit of the Word* [Minneapolis: Fortress, 2014], 52). As I will make clear, I intend the term slightly differently, expanding "third article" to necessarily include its ecclesiological dimension in tandem with its pneumatological.

[4]Samuel Wells, *Transforming Fate into Destiny: The Theological Ethics of Stanley Hauerwas* (Carlisle, UK: Paternoster, 1998; repr., Eugene, OR: Cascade, 2004).

[5]Michael G. Cartwright, "Afterword: Stanley Hauerwas's Essays in Theological Ethics: A Reader's Guide," in *HR*, 624.

and Ludwig Wittgenstein, among others. While scholars have trained their telescopes on the bright stars of each of these thinkers, no one has focused on Barth's role in the constellation of Hauerwas's thought. To my mind, this is like studying Orion yet ignoring Betelgeuse—one of the oldest and brightest stars in the constellation.

This is not to say, however, that no scholar has ever engaged Hauerwas and Barth in conversation. Indeed, a number of scholars have seen enough similarity to work constructively between both thinkers.[6] Nor is it to say that no one has ever considered the matter of influence at all. Nicholas Healy's recently published *Hauerwas: A (Very) Critical Introduction* is a critical treatment of Hauerwas that intends to lay bare Hauerwas's liberal tendencies in a manner that undercuts his Barthian claims.[7] Between these works, however, there is a lacuna in the literature regarding the exact nature and extent of influence that Barth has on Hauerwas. Can we take Hauerwas's claim to be Barthian at face value? Or are his critics correct that his work moves in an opposing direction to Barth's? To answer these questions is to understand Hauerwas on his own terms, that is, to understand him as a Barthian postliberal.

WHAT IS A BARTHIAN?

To claim that Hauerwas is a Barthian postliberal invites the more basic questions, What is a Barthian? and, What is a postliberal? Regarding the first question, there are some provisional typologies in the literature.[8] For my purposes, McCormack's basic distinction between two different types of Barthian scholarship is most helpful. For McCormack, the simple litmus test for determining a scholar's Barthian bona fides is to ask whether a scholar has a "genuine understanding" of Barth's thought. If the answer is yes, then that scholar falls into a type of Barthian that McCormack describes as

---

[6]Among those worth mentioning are: Reinhard Hütter, *Evangelische Ethik als kirchliches Zeugnis: Interretationen zu Schlüsselfragen theologischer Ethik in der Gegenwart* (Neukirchen-Vluyn: Neukirchener, 1993); John B. Thomson, *The Ecclesiology of Stanley Hauerwas: A Christian Theology of Liberation* (Aldershot: Ashgate, 2003); and Joseph L. Mangina, *Karl Barth: Theologian of Christian Witness* (Louisville, KY: Westminster John Knox, 2004), chap. 4 especially.
[7]Nicholas M. Healy, *Hauerwas: A (Very) Critical Introduction* (Grand Rapids: Eerdmans, 2014).
[8]The broadest example being Richard H. Roberts, "The Reception of the Theology of Karl Barth in the Anglo-Saxon World: History, Typology and Prospect," in *Karl Barth: Centenary Essays*, ed. S. W. Sykes (Cambridge: Cambridge University Press, 1989), 142-55.

"directly influenced" by Barth; in contrast, if the answer is no, then the scholar falls into a category that McCormack calls "indirect influence." In McCormack's thinking, "genuine understanding" requires one to conform to McCormack's interpretation of Barth as a "critically realistic dialectical theologian."[9] McCormack himself coined this term. He means it to simultaneously communicate three things about Barth's theology. First, in contrast to early English interpreters of Barth, McCormack insists that Barth's theology remains dialectical from his early work through his mature work. Second, that Barth's theology maintains that God is real, that is, that God exists beyond the bounds of human thought. Third, that Kant was right in his *Critique of Pure Reason* to suggest that humans cannot have knowledge of God's very being because God exists beyond the bounds of human knowledge.[10]

Ever since the publication of McCormack's magisterial *Karl Barth's Critically Realistic Dialectical Theology*, Anglo-American Barth studies has turned to a reading of Barth that is closer to his German interpreters and, therefore, more attentive to Barth's dialectical thinking, as well as the political and ethical dimensions of his work. This move undercuts a number of neo-orthodox assumptions about Barth's theology, not least of which is the assumption expressed by H. Richard Niebuhr, James Gustafson, and others that Barth's ethics have no room for human agency. Thus "critically realistic dialectical theology" positions itself over and against earlier Anglo-American interpretations of Barth as a "neo-orthodox" theologian.

McCormack is particularly hard on a group of theologians that operates under the label "postliberal." According to him, postliberalism tends to read Barth in two mistaken directions. The first is exemplified by Hans Frei and the second by George Lindbeck. Although Frei was the best early English interpreter of Barth, he tended to read Barth as a nonfoundationalist. Nonfoundationalism is a postmodern rejection of an epistemological position called "foundationalism" usually attributed to modern philosophy after Descartes. According to Descartes, the acquisition of knowledge about anything is like building a house. You begin with a strong foundation, in this case basic propositions, and then you logically build the structure of knowledge

---

[9]Bruce McCormack, *Orthodox and Modern: Studies in the Theology of Karl Barth* (Grand Rapids: Baker Academic, 2008), 164.
[10]McCormack, *Orthodox and Modern*, 158-59.

from deducing further truths from the foundations up.[11] As Nancey Murphy notes, for non- and postfoundationalists, an apt metaphor for epistemology is not a house but a web. No truth claim is obviously more basic than another. Depending on the distance between two particular truth claims in the web of knowledge, one might be perceived as more basic to the other. What makes them both true is that they both cohere within a web of knowledge that remains consistent.[12] For McCormack, it is not that Barth is committed to philosophical foundationalism itself; indeed, nonfoundationalist or post-foundationalist theologians can still find much in Barth's canon that is compatible with their agenda. Yet to suggest that Barth himself was engaged in a nonfoundationalist project is to read him anachronistically.[13]

Lindbeck's misreading of Barth is far more severe, according to McCormack. Lindbeck argues that theology is "a highly contextual exercise in communal self-description."[14] He reads Barth as a theologian who is doing a type of intratextual theology that eschews metaphysics and focuses instead on the internal coherence of Scripture. By reading Barth in this way, McCormack argues, Lindbeck returns to the neo-orthodox interpretation of Barth that he learned from his teacher, H. Richard Niebuhr. Thus postliberalism is nothing more than a revival of the neo-orthodox reading of Barth, which "made sweeping use of the biblical language without committing itself to the ontology and cosmology which such language presupposed."[15]

Hauerwas, a student of Niebuhr via Frei and Gustafson (the latter was his doctoral supervisor), inherits the neo-orthodox interpretation of Barth. As such, according to McCormack's typology, Hauerwas slots into the group of postliberals "indirectly influenced" by Barth who tend to misread him in a manner that ignores his dialectical thinking and his critical realism. While Hauerwas has never pretended to be a Barth scholar—and therefore has never felt the need to conform to prevailing interpretations of Barth—he is deeply interested in the question of whether he "understands" Barth. For

---

[11]For a helpful summary of foundationalism, see C. Steven Evans, *A History of Western Philosophy: From the Pre-Socratics to Postmodernism* (Downers Grove, IL: IVP Academic, 2018), 250-52.

[12]Nancey Murphy, *Anglo-American Postmodernity: Philosophical Perspectives on Science, Religion, and Ethics* (Boulder, CO: Westview, 1997), 27.

[13]McCormack, *Orthodox and Modern*, 124-27.

[14]McCormack, *Orthodox and Modern*, 114.

[15]McCormack, *Orthodox and Modern*, 135.

this reason, I will subject his claim to be a Barthian to McCormack's criteria, rigorously investigating the suggestion that his work is plagued by its enduring relationship with Niebuhr and Lindbeck.

Although Hauerwas's early work is heavily dependent on neo-orthodox interpretations of Barth, his understanding of Barth's theology grows and adapts with the guild itself. This suggests that Hauerwas is at least interested in understanding Barth. Where Hauerwas chooses to "go beyond" Barth will be the place where we see most clearly the degree to which we can call Hauerwas a Barthian. Does his "going beyond" Barth demonstrate that he understands him enough to warrant a break with the Swiss theologian's work? Or does he misunderstand Barth, and therefore fail to grasp the manner in which Barth's own theology resolves the perceived problems that lead Hauerwas "beyond"?

I will argue that when I say Hauerwas is a Barthian, I mean that he at least understands the basic impulse that set Barth's theology in motion: the rejection of Protestant liberalism. Such an understanding leads directly to a theological ethics that moves with the grain of Barth's rejection. As such, Hauerwas ought to be considered "directly influenced" by Barth even though he will never fit the mold of a "critically realistic dialectical theologian." At the very least, we must acknowledge that McCormack's definition of "direct influence" is overly narrow, and that Barth's influence on Hauerwas is certainly something more than "indirect."

One difficulty noted by McCormack's distinction between directly and indirectly influenced Barthians is his argument that postliberalism represents a misunderstanding of Barth's theology insofar as it perpetuates some of the problems of the "neo-orthodox" Barth. Can one be—as I argue Hauerwas is—both Barthian, in a direct sense, and postliberal? In order to answer this question, we must attend to what it means to call someone a "postliberal."

What Is a Postliberal?

If the term *Barthian* is hard to nail down, the term *postliberal* is at least equally so. It first appeared in an essay by H. Richard Niebuhr, as a description for a type of theology that sought "to recover the Christian theological heritage and to renew modes of thought which the anti-traditional pathos of liberalism depreciated."[16] For a time, *postliberal* operated in a slippery fashion, referring to a number of generic postmodern theological projects. Eventually, its meaning became fixed to the school of theologians that emerged out of Niebuhr's students. For this reason, postliberalism is also sometimes called "the Yale school" or "narrative theology."

In the first case, "the Yale school" moniker is used to set postliberalism over and against the liberalism of "the Chicago school" at the University of Chicago. William Placher explains: at Yale, "students studied Christianity or Judaism or Buddhism, but not 'religion'"; at Chicago, students studied religion "as a universal phenomenon whose themes and symbols manifest the experience of the sacred in different but related ways in different cultures."[17] Thus postliberalism is a counter to the modern liberal penchant for running roughshod over the particularities of religious traditions.

In the second case, postliberalism is sometimes called "narrative theology" because of its relationship to Yale theologians George Lindbeck and Hans Frei. The term *postliberalism* comes from Lindbeck, who is credited with coining the term in his famous book, *The Nature of Doctrine*.[18] Whether or not he had his teacher H. Richard Niebuhr's call for a "post-liberal" theology in his mind is hard to say. Regardless, the continuity between Niebuhr's neo-orthodoxy and Lindbeck's postliberalism is hard to deny. The name "narrative theology" comes from Lindbeck's dependence on and association with Hans Frei's landmark work *The Eclipse of Biblical Narrative*. Therein Frei argued that modern liberal Christianity distorted the biblical narrative by reading it with prior foundational commitments. Thus Scripture required an act of translation into a contemporary worldview that was prioritized over the worldview of Scripture itself. To the contrary, Frei argued that the theological task must allow the worldview of Scripture to encounter the reader on its own terms. In the first instance, then, theology must attend to the narrative dimensions of Scripture itself.

---

[16]H. Richard Niebuhr, "The Doctrine of the Trinity and the Unity of the Church," *Theology Today* 3, no. 3 (1946): 371. Here the term is hyphenated: "post-liberal."

[17]William C. Placher, "Postliberal Theology," in *The Modern Theologians: An Introduction to Christian Theology in the Twentieth Century*, ed. David F. Ford, 2nd ed. (Cambridge, MA: Blackwell, 1997), 343-44.

[18]George A. Lindbeck, *The Nature of Doctrine: Religion and Theology in a Postliberal Age* (Philadelphia: Westminster, 1984).

To this Lindbeck added a "cultural-linguistic" approach to the study of religion. Instead of grounding theology in commitments to foundational propositional truths or precognitive human experiences, postliberal theology begins with the language that is used to render the narrative and the thought-world of Scripture coherent. Christianity is a living tradition—a linguistic community that extends through time and space—with its own language that is coherent in its own cultural context. To translate it into a different idiom or to extrapolate foundational truths or experiences from it is to render it incoherent. Christian doctrines function as grammatical rules that teach us how the language of Scripture and the Christian community functions. In the second instance, then, theology must regulate the grammar of the Christian community in order to make sure it does not betray its own central narrative.

Postliberalism is grounded in these basic narrative and linguistic sensibilities. From there, however, it multiplies into an ever-growing number of theological agendas. Paul DeHart famously argues that postliberalism is like a river delta:

> Like a powerful and clear stream which gradually disperses into smaller branches, the characteristic ideas associated with Frei and Lindbeck have spread in several directions, watering a greater area but also becoming more shallow and indistinct as they are simplified and abstracted from their original contexts and mingled with other intellectual sources.[19]

As a result, "there is no such position" as postliberalism.[20]

I think that DeHart is basically right. Consider the difference between essays on postliberalism published in different editions of David F. Ford's volume *The Modern Theologians*. William Placher's contribution to the 1997 edition claimed that postliberalism has four distinct characteristics: a non-foundationalist epistemology, an unapologetic theology, an emphasis on the particularity of a religious tradition, and a narrative-communal approach to Scripture.[21] By the publication of the 2005 edition, Jim Fodor felt it necessary to list nine characteristics: the retrieval and redeployment of premodern

---

[19]Paul J. DeHart, *The Trial of the Witnesses: The Rise and Decline of Postliberal Theology* (Malden, MA: Blackwell, 2006), 45-46.
[20]DeHart, *Trial of the Witnesses*, 55.
[21]Placher, "Postliberal Theology," 344-45.

sources, a concern with the ecclesial nature of the theological task, the use of narrative, the grammar of Christian doctrine, the corrective role of theology, a distinct but ecumenical Protestantism, a nonessentialist approach to religion, a nonfoundationalist epistemology, and an unapologetic theology.[22] Since then, the Jewish theologian Peter Ochs has argued that a further distinct characteristic of postliberalism should be its emphasis on a "nonsupersessionist" theology.[23] DeHart's river delta image is indeed apt!

Nevertheless, I still find the term *postliberal* useful as a description of Hauerwas's theological sensibilities. To be sure, he obviously demonstrates affinity with a number of these theological commitments. Even more, however, I think his work is importantly characterized by one underappreciated aspect of postliberalism: pragmatism.

In his book *Transforming Postliberal Theology*, Chad Pecknold makes the compelling argument that the "complex relationship between scripture and pragmatism" is the "frequently neglected heart of postliberal thought."[24] Originally, the pragmatic nature of postliberalism was perceived as a weakness or a problem. Pecknold writes, "The early reception of *The Nature of Doctrine* either (1) ignored the pragmatic dimension of Lindbeck's book; or (2) criticized its 'pragmatism'; or (3) accused Lindbeck of not sufficiently thinking through his implicit pragmatism."[25] It is only recently, and largely on account of Hauerwas, that postliberalism's pragmatic bent has reemerged as a distinguishing feature.[26]

When I say that Hauerwas's theology is postliberal, I mean basically this: that Hauerwas's theology is pragmatic. Yes, Hauerwas's work is informed by his Yale school education; and yes, Hauerwas attends to the power of narrative to form disciples; but his work cannot be reduced to either of these

---

[22]James Fodor, "Postliberal Theology," in *The Modern Theologians: An Introduction to Christian Theology Since 1918*, ed. David F. Ford with Rachel Muers, 3rd ed. (Malden, MA: Blackwell, 2005), 230-31.

[23]Peter Ochs, *Another Reformation: Postliberal Christianity and the Jews* (Grand Rapids: Baker Academic, 2011), 18.

[24]C. C. Pecknold, *Transforming Postliberal Theology: George Lindbeck, Pragmatism and Scripture* (New York: T&T Clark, 2005), ix.

[25]Pecknold, *Transforming Postliberal Theology*, 11.

[26]James K. A. Smith turns to postliberalism as a resource for Christian pragmatism in *Who's Afraid of Relativism? Community, Contingency, and Creaturehood* (Grand Rapids: Baker Academic, 2014), 151-78. Indeed, Smith's larger project appears to be an attempt to apply the pragmatic lessons of postliberalism to a basically Reformed and Augustinian political theology.

labels. Instead, Hauerwas's theology is an exemplification of what postliberal theology is to the extent that he wants to clarify the relationship between Christian convictions and Christian practices. This is more than a simple regression to the anthropocentrism of Protestant liberalism because it always seeks to describe human agency as it relates to the God who is presupposed in the basic narratives of the Christian faith. Hauerwas's work connects philosophical impulses he learns from Wittgenstein with theological concepts of narrative and biography he gets from James McClendon and Lindbeck in order to generate a robust vision for how to speak about human agency after Barth. Or so I will argue.

BARTHIANISM OR ECCLESIOCENTRISM?

In 1986, at a conference in Oxford celebrating the centenary of Karl Barth's birth, ethicist and Barth scholar Nigel Biggar suggested to Hauerwas that his work lacked a sufficient doctrine of God. To be more precise, Biggar suggested that "God was . . . curiously missing" from Hauerwas's work. At least that is how Hauerwas remembers it.[27] Biggar remembers suggesting that Hauerwas has "a suspect tendency to talk about the church where Barth would talk about God."[28] According to both accounts, then, Biggar's main contention was that Hauerwas's work to that point was insufficiently theocentric. From Biggar's perspective, however, it is worth noting that not only did Hauerwas's work lack "God-talk," it actually refocused theological ethics on the locus of ecclesiology at the expense of the doctrine of God. Thus was born the charge that Hauerwas is "ecclesiocentric."

Biggar would later go on to characterize his problems with Hauerwas's theological ethics in tension with his interpretation of Barth's:

> With Stanley Hauerwas Barth agrees that the Bible contributes to Christian ethics through its basic "story." But whereas for Barth the biblical story is significant in its reference to the reality of the living God, for Hauerwas its importance lies immediately in its sociological function in forming the identity of the Christian community and thereby providing the rationale of its morality.[29]

---

[27]*STT*, 37.
[28]Nigel Biggar, *Behaving in Public: How to Do Christian Ethics* (Grand Rapids: Eerdmans, 2011), 94.
[29]Nigel Biggar, *The Hastening that Waits: Karl Barth's Ethics* (Oxford: Clarendon, 1993), 118.

Biggar subsequently argues that the difference between Barth and Hauerwas is the difference between a *theological* and a *sociological* account of human agency. That is, for Barth, human action is always framed by God's covenantal relationship with humanity. Therefore, to focus on human agency at the expense of divine agency is to allow the sociological to eclipse the theological.[30] This is Biggar's basic problem with Hauerwas's theology: ecclesiocentrism focuses on the church's agency at the expense of God's. In this sense, Biggar worries that Hauerwas lacks "ecclesial humility."[31]

Although Biggar was perhaps the first to express concerns of ecclesiocentrism, he is not alone. Indeed, it is open season on Hauerwas. In recent years, Hauerwas has been called an "onto-ecclesiologist,"[32] an "ecclesiological fundamentalist,"[33] and, most significantly, a liberal Protestant in the mold of Schleiermacher or Ritschl. As I've already indicated, I think the accusation that Hauerwas's work is a continuation of the liberal Protestant project is the one that poses the greatest threat to his legitimacy as a Barthian. Any attempt to read Hauerwas in relationship to Barth will have to prove that these charges are false, or at least articulate how Hauerwas's theology avoids any easy assimilation to Protestant liberalism. In my mind, two very specific charges must be addressed.

The first is what I am calling "the Schleiermacher thesis." The Schleiermacher thesis is expressed by Healy, who argues in *Hauerwas* that Hauerwas's "ecclesism" reduces theology to ecclesiology in a manner that is similar to Schleiermacher's reduction of theology to the believing subject in *The Christian Faith*.[34] Although Healy concedes that Hauerwas avoids some of

---

[30]Biggar, *The Hastening that Waits*, 142-45.

[31]Biggar, *Behaving in Public*, 93.

[32]Ry O. Siggelkow, "Toward an Apocalyptic Peace Church: Christian Pacifism *After* Hauerwas," *Conrad Grebel Review* 31, no. 3 (2013): 274-97.

[33]Theo Hobson, "Ecclesiological Fundamentalism," *Modern Believing* 45, no. 4 (2004): 53-55.

[34]Healy, *Hauerwas*, 40. Healy is not alone in making this charge. Siggelkow demonstrates how Hauerwas's concrete ecclesiology pushes toward Schleiermacher's emphasis on the "empirically visible form" of the church and ignores Barth's emphasis on the church's hiddenness with God in Christ (Ry O. Siggelkow, "A Response to Doerge on Barth and Hauerwas," in *Karl Barth in Conversation*, ed. W. Travis McMaken and David W. Congdon [Eugene, OR: Pickwick, 2014], 127). Gerald McKenny argues that Schleiermacher's legacy is seen in "a widespread tendency" in contemporary theology "to assert the primacy of ethics by articulating the rest of theology in ethical terms" and continued by those "treating Christian ethics as the description of the ethical life of the church as a historical community, while . . . dispensing with universal morality altogether" (Gerald McKenny, *The Analogy of Grace: Karl Barth's Moral Theology* [Oxford: Oxford University Press, 2010], 138-39).

Schleiermacher's pietism and individualism, the basic problem is the same for both theologians. Both theologians emphasize a primarily "social-philosophical" account of the church; both suggest the church is the superior form of human community based on its special relationship with Jesus; both turn the church into an apologetic; and finally, both redirect doctrine from being about God to being about the church.[35]

At its heart, then, the Schleiermacher thesis is the claim that Hauerwas reproduces some of the very aspects of Protestant liberalism that he opposes. In turning to the church, his theology ends up talking about human agency—albeit in the form of church practices—instead of divine agency, and therefore collapses theology into anthropology. All of this obtains despite his strong insistence that he follows Barth in rejecting the anthropocentrism of Protestant liberalism. I think Halden Doerge explains it best when he argues that Hauerwas's ecclesiocentrism "loops back *behind* Barth's critique of liberal Protestantism"—meaning that Hauerwas recommences a liberal theological program after a Barthian interlude.[36] An unasked question for Doerge is whether this "looping back" is of an anti-Barthian or a post-Barthian variety. I will argue that it is post-Barthian to the extent that it is Hauerwas's postliberalism bringing him back to some of the key questions of liberal theology—*not* over and against Barth *but* with the grain of Barth's thought.

The second charge that must be addressed is what I'm calling "the Ritschl thesis." This charge takes its name from ethicist and Barthian theologian John Webster's suggestion that Hauerwas's work is not so much reminiscent of Schleiermacher but of Ritschl. In many ways, this charge is an intensification of the claim that Hauerwas is a Protestant liberal. Barth, after all, holds a great critical appreciation for Schleiermacher; the same cannot be said for Ritschl. When Barth turned from the theology of his teachers Harnack and Herrmann, he made a decisive break with the Ritschl school.

Ritschl famously described his own theology as an ellipsis with two focal points: personal salvation and the kingdom of God.[37] The first has to do with

---

[35]Healy, *Hauerwas*, 48-51.

[36]Halden Doerge, "Dueling Ecclesiologies: Barth and Hauerwas in Con-verse," in McMaken and Congdon, *Karl Barth in Conversation*, 121.

[37]Albrecht Ritschl, *The Christian Doctrine of Justification and Reconciliation: The Positive Development of the Doctrine*, trans. and ed. H. R. Mackintosh and A. B. Macaulay, 2nd ed. (Edinburgh: T&T Clark, 1902), 11.

Jesus himself and the freedom from sin that his life embodies, while the second has to do with the community he established where such freedom is experienced. Thus the two focal points of the ellipsis are christological and ecclesiological respectively. Historically, we come to the Christian faith from a perspective weighted toward the second focal point; the church is the precondition for understanding Christianity as a whole. On the one hand, the church historically and logically precedes the redemption of an individual believer.[38] On the other hand, the church is a community of forgiveness founded by Jesus where people truly experience their Christian freedom in spite of the continued presence of sin in their lives.[39]

All of this means that Ritschl's theology is ecclesiocentric in a twofold sense. First, the church is the historical and logical precondition for coming to a saving knowledge of our redemption by God through Christ. Second, the church is the place where we live out our freedom in God in such a manner that we further the transformation of the world around us into the kingdom of God. From the ecclesiological focal point, Christians look back toward the message of freedom proclaimed by Christ and look forward to the establishment of a perfect community of freedom in the world.

Webster reminds us that Ritschl is *the* great theologian of liberal Protestant ethics, with "his repudiation of metaphysics, his fear that preoccupation with *fides quae* is a speculative distraction from viewing the world in terms of moral value, and his conviction that Christian faith is principally a mode of active moral community."[40] In particular, Webster worries that (1) Ritschlian theologies abandon Nicaean Christology and attend to the moral example of Jesus' earthly life,[41] (2) collapses Christ into the moral community in the form of "the kingdom of God,"[42] and (3) reduces Scripture to "the church's book" giving undue "prominence to anthropological concepts such as 'practice' and 'virtue.'"[43] For Webster, these unmistakably Hauerwasian themes amount to

---

[38]Ritschl, *Christian Doctrine*, 549.

[39]Ritschl, *Christian Doctrine*, 543.

[40]John Webster, "Ecclesiocentrism: A Review of *Hauerwas: A (Very) Critical Introduction* by Nicholas M. Healy," *First Things*, October 2014, 55.

[41]John Webster, *Word and Church: Essays in Christian Dogmatics* (London: Bloomsbury T&T Clark, 2016), 144.

[42]Webster, *Word and Church*, 229.

[43]John Webster, *Holy Scripture: A Dogmatic Sketch* (Cambridge: Cambridge University Press, 2003), 43.

"a highly sophisticated hermeneutical reworking of Ritschlian social mor-
alism" that shifts theological accounts of Scripture away from God and
toward the church. In this regard, Webster joins Biggar in locating Hauerwas's Protestant liberalism in his treatment of Scripture. This is really the crux
of what I am calling the Ritschl thesis. For these Barthians, Hauerwas vacates
Scripture of its ability to witness to God's activity, reducing it instead to a
guidebook for the church's activity and Jesus to little more than the guide
whose life becomes paradigmatic for the church. He introduces a second,
ecclesial, theological loci to his theology that distorts any possible christocentrism and weights the center of gravity toward ecclesiology.

The Argument in Overview

As we've just seen, the case against Hauerwas's claim to be a Barthian unfolds
in two parts. First, Hauerwas's theology is obviously ecclesiocentric. Second,
this ecclesiocentrism repeats the basic habits of Protestant liberalism.
Therefore, Hauerwas's work actually represents a retrieval of the type of theology that Barth rejected when he broke with Protestant liberalism. Ergo,
Hauerwas is not a Barthian. I think the Ritschl thesis overstates its case when
its advocates suggest that Hauerwas is not concerned with metaphysics, but
I admit that there is something to the suggestion that Hauerwas resembles
Ritschl to the extent that he attends to the social dimension of the Christian
faith, particularly as it relates to Scripture and salvation.[44] In general, I think
the Schleiermacher thesis has more explanatory power, arguing that Hauerwas's theology is "liberal" because it replaces divine agency with human
agency and/or collapses the two in his ecclesiology.

I will argue, over and against Healy and others, that Hauerwas is Barthian
exactly to the extent that he learns from Barth to reject Protestant liberalism.
Indeed, his whole theological project is an attempt to mount a Barth-like
rejection of Protestant liberalism in his own American context. This requires him to work "after Barth" in some ways that push beyond difficulties

---

[44]Hauerwas does not reject metaphysics; he simply refuses to engage in something called "metaphysics" because he worries that metaphysical claims often are abstract "explanations" about
reality that threaten to undermine the uniqueness of Christian convictions about the world.
Hauerwas prefers to speak of doing "metaphysics by way of indirection," a move he thinks he
learns from Barth (*HC*, 157). All in all, Hauerwas's work depends on a deep-seated conviction
that Christianity is in and of itself a metaphysical claim about reality.

he finds in Barth's work. This "after Barth" is best understood by Hauerwas's commitment to postliberal theology as the means by which Barthian convictions actually inform Christian practice. This is what I mean when I argue that Hauerwas is a Barthian postliberal.

In part one I will develop my argument that Hauerwas is a Barthian postliberal. I will do this primarily by attending to Hauerwas's biography, with special attention to Hauerwas's intellectual influences. In chapter one I provide an overview of Barth's influence on Hauerwas, from Hauerwas's first encounters with Barth's theology to his mature application of Barthian themes in his own theological ethics. In particular, I will pay attention to two narratives that shape Hauerwas's theological ethics: the story of how ethics became divorced from doctrine and the story of how Christian ethics in America became about America instead of Christianity. These are the basic narratives of Protestant liberalism and how Hauerwas learns to reject it by attending to Barth's claim that dogmatics and ethics are inseparable.

In chapter two I will sympathetically introduce Hauerwas's claim to be a Barthian by attending to Hauerwas's self-understanding of Barth's influence on his work. I will argue that the basic theological lesson Hauerwas learns from Barth is to reject Protestant liberalism. For Hauerwas, learning this lesson means repeating this move in his own American Protestant context, a move that requires Hauerwas to go "beyond" Barth in some ways. Then in chapter three I will use abortion to demonstrate how Hauerwas's theological ethics are both dependent on and go beyond Barth. Particularly, I will show how Hauerwas (1) leverages Barth's rejection of natural theology into a rejection of ethical claims that are grounded in universal reason, and then (2) goes beyond Barth by asking the question from the third article of the creed, namely, ecclesiology.[45]

In chapter four I will pick the story back up at this point: that Hauerwas sees his own work as an attempt to "fix" deficiencies in Barth's ecclesiology. Where Hauerwas appears to break with Barth's own understanding of

---

[45]When I speak of the third article, I am nodding to Barth's final reflections on Schleiermacher and the possibility of holding Barth's christological commitments while beginning theology from a different doctrinal locus. But I am also indicating the creedal tradition of speaking of the church in tandem with the Holy Spirit, suggesting that to speak of the church is not to occlude God-talk. In Hauerwas's case, I will argue that his ecclesiology presupposes both the priority of his christological commitments and the ongoing work of the Spirit in the life of the church.

theological ethics by attending to the church's centrality as a community of moral formation, Hauerwas understands himself to be improving on Barth by reading him in a postliberal trajectory. In order to make sense of this claim, I will go back into Hauerwas's biography in order to understand how the postliberal impulses in his thought develop and what purpose they serve. In chapter five I will conclude part one with the argument that Hauerwas's postliberal reading of Barth is a legitimate interpretation to the extent that he really understands the manner in which Barth thinks theology should work and the type of work it should accomplish. In this regard, I take Hauerwas to be more than "indirectly influenced" by Barth, warranting an expanded understanding of what it means to be a Barthian beyond McCormack's narrow definition. Thus the story of how Hauerwas became a Barthian postliberal concludes.

Part two will be the first of two parts that raise important counterarguments to the story that I tell in part one. Specifically, in parts two and three I will continue the line of criticism developed by those who claim Hauerwas is a Protestant liberal. In part two I will develop the argument raised by the Schleiermacher thesis, interrogating Hauerwas's claim that he learns to keep dogmatics and ethics together from Barth. In chapter six, I will argue that for Barth, keeping dogmatics and ethics together obtains in his reversal of the priority of the relationship between the law and the gospel and his rejection of casuistry, or the application of abstract ethical principles to concrete cases. Both moves require a deep theological commitment to the idea that dogmatics and ethics are grounded in the doctrine of God proper. In chapter seven I will then demonstrate that Hauerwas's theology, to the contrary, holds the connection between dogmatics and ethics to obtain in ecclesiology, in particular through a revised use of casuistry. On the surface, then, Hauerwas's theology seems anti-Barthian. Finally, in chapter eight, I will show how Hauerwas's postliberalism allows him to sidestep this criticism in a way that both honors Barth's theology and goes beyond it.

In part three I will attend to the argument made by advocates of the Ritschl thesis, namely, that Hauerwas's use of Scripture is sociological in nature while Barth's is theological. I will test this thesis by attending, in chapter nine, to the formal relationship between Scripture and the church in Barth and Hauerwas and, in chapter ten, to the manner in which each theologian actually reads Scripture. I will argue that the Ritschl thesis holds to the extent that where Barth talks about God, Hauerwas talks about the church. In chapter eleven, I will again show how Hauerwas's postliberalism sidesteps the problem by moving in a manner that is not contrary to Barth. In this case, Hauerwas's ecclesiocentrism is not contrary to Barth's rejection of liberalism because Hauerwas's turn to the church is a re-turn to the church from a Barthian perspective.

In the conclusion, I will suggest a few ways that Hauerwas could make his Barthian influence more transparent. First, I will use Kimlyn Bender's work on Barth's ecclesiology to show how it is possible to read Hauerwas's ecclesiology as an extension of Barth's basic christological commitments. This will put to bed the concerns of those who espouse the Ritschl thesis, that Hauerwas's theology operates with a second ecclesiological focal point. Second, I will draw on the resources of the missional theology movement in order to show how a number of Hauerwas's concerns are being addressed in similar ways from a more explicitly Barthian framework. The result will be an affirmation of Hauerwas's diagnosis of the problems facing the church and an alternative construal of the solution that is more obviously Barthian.

PART ONE

The Making of a
Barthian Postliberal

THE BASIC ARGUMENT I MAKE in this book is that in order to understand Hauerwas's theological ethics, you have to understand how he is influenced by Karl Barth and postliberalism respectively. For therein lies the theological convictions that make his ethical arguments intelligible. Central to this point is the claim that one cannot simply reduce Hauerwas's Barthianism to his postliberalism. Scholars who do so tend to assume that he is a bad interpreter of Barth, at the least, or part of a type of Protestant liberalism that is incommensurable with Barth's theology.

In the first part of this book, I develop the argument that Hauerwas is a Barthian postliberal. I do this by first attending to the way Hauerwas understands modern Protestant theology in general and the development of Christian ethics in American theology specifically. First, Hauerwas argues, Protestant liberalism is plagued by a particular Christian response to Enlightenment rationalism: namely, that God was a subject that was beyond the possibility of empirical knowledge and, therefore, theology should be about morality. Second, it was subsequently determined that morality was a topic that could be established without respect to any particular religious convictions. With regard to how this plays out in the discipline of Christian ethics, Hauerwas notes that by the middle of the twentieth century, Christian ethicists were asking themselves if they really needed to be "Christian" to arrive at the conclusions they made.

I follow both of these suggestions as they work themselves out in Hauerwas's thought. First, the story of Protestant liberalism is the story of how ethics, or morality, becomes divorced from theology. For Hauerwas, the problem of reducing theology to morality is resolved by Barth, who rejected any attempt to reason theologically from any starting point other than God. This includes Barth's famous rejection of natural theology, which Hauerwas adopts and extends in his own rejection of rationalist appeals to universal law. We see this especially in the similarities between Barth's and Hauerwas's treatments of abortion.

Next, the story of Christian ethics in America is the story of how ethics ceased to be Christian, or how the church lost its distinctiveness in American culture. This problem is solved by a fusion of influences from John Howard Yoder and postliberalism. In the first instance, it is Yoder who—influenced by Barth—rejects the entire tradition of Christian ethics and grounds his own theological ethics in Scripture. This emboldens Hauerwas to break with the liberal Protestant Christian ethics of his Yale teachers. In the second instance, it is the development of a new type of postliberal theology that emphasizes practical reasoning that points a way forward for a theological ethics that at once speaks about God and human moral action in correspondence to what Christians have to say about God. For Hauerwas, this means learning from Barth how to ground his ethics christologically, from Yoder how to work out the ecclesiological implications of such a Christology, and from postliberalism how Christians "perform their faith" in light of these christological and ecclesiological convictions.

These two streams of theological influence come together in Hauerwas's thought to produce Barthian postliberalism. For the vast majority of English-speaking interpreters of Barth, such a reading of Barth is problematic on its face. To the contrary, I argue, Hauerwas's attention to performance, and particularly to how Barth's theology performs its task, enables him to work with the grain of Barth's theology in order to develop surprising but consistent theological impulses in his own American theological context.

1

The Stories That Made
Stanley Hauerwas

STANLEY HAUERWAS ALTERNATIVELY calls himself a theologian and an ethicist. Early in his career, he was apt to identify himself as a Christian ethicist;[1] however, over time, he came to describe himself predominantly as a theologian. There is some fluidity between these terms in Hauerwas's thought to the extent that theology cannot be divorced from ethics.[2] Nevertheless, the shift represents a subtle, albeit significant, development in Hauerwas's work: over time he has learned to speak about God.[3] Indeed, in Hauerwas's later work he jokes that his colleagues do not consider him an ethicist and that he prefers to think of himself as a "theologian."[4]

That Hauerwas prefers to think of himself as a theologian instead of an ethicist has everything to do with the critical stance he takes against Protestant liberalism. "Ethics" is what remains of Christianity after the retreat of theological convictions from the public square. For Hauerwas, this retreat is synonymous with the name Immanuel Kant.[5] In this regard, "Christian

---

[1]See, for example, Stanley Hauerwas, "The Ethicist as Theologian," *Christian Century*, April 23, 1975, 408.

[2]*WGU*, 17.

[3]*HC*, 277. This is Samuel Wells's insight and a notable contribution to Hauerwas's own self-understanding. Samuel Wells, *Transforming Fate into Destiny: The Theological Ethics of Stanley Hauerwas* (Carlisle, UK: Paternoster, 1998; repr., Eugene, OR: Cascade, 2004), 42-43, 52-61.

[4]*CSH*, 145. See also Stanley Hauerwas, "Between Christian Ethics and Religious Ethics: How Should Graduate Students Be Trained?," *Journal of Religious Ethics* 31, no. 3 (2003): 399.

[5]*WT*, 59.

ethics" is the means by which Christian theologians seek to legitimize their existence in modern research universities and hospitals. Quoting his doctoral advisor, James Gustafson, Hauerwas writes, "The term 'ethicist' is popular because it provides an identity for former theologians 'who do not have the professional credentials of a moral philosopher.'"[6]

In order to understand why Hauerwas prefers to think of himself as a theologian and insists on keeping theology and ethics together, one must understand two important stories that Hauerwas tells about the history of theological ethics: The first is about the rise of Protestant liberalism as the end of theological ethics, while the second is about the continuation of the liberal Protestant project as "Christian ethics" in America. In this chapter, I will introduce each story—first, the divorce of ethics from theology, and second, the development of Christian ethics in America. Then I will tease out how Hauerwas conceives of his own theological ethics as parallel to Karl Barth's insistence that dogmatics and ethics are inseparable. All of this will set the stage for chapters two and three, where I will attend specifically to the stories of how Hauerwas came to be influenced by Barth and postliberalism respectively.

ONCE THERE WAS NO CHRISTIAN ETHICS

The first story Hauerwas tells is a story about how ethics became divorced from theology. This story begins with the early church and ends with the Enlightenment. Its basic thesis is that current conceptions of Protestant social ethics are contingent, not necessary. In fact, earlier expressions of the Christian life better exemplify Christianity as the integration of belief and practice. The punch line to the first story is that theologians began by talking about God but, over time, ended up talking about humanity. This story is worth retelling briefly because it gives concrete expression to Hauerwas's claim that he follows Barth in rejecting liberalism.

For Hauerwas, "Once there was no Christian ethics simply because Christians could not distinguish between their beliefs and their behavior."[7] Indeed, early Christianity was predominantly focused on how Christians should live. Theology simply was "pastoral direction" for how to live a

---

[6]Stanley Hauerwas, "Can Ethics Be Theological?," *The Hastings Center Report* 8, no. 5 (1978): 47.
[7]*STT*, 20; *BCCE*, 28.

morally substantial life.[8] This changed somewhat with the rise of Christendom, or "Constantinianism," as Hauerwas sometimes calls it.

Constantinianism is a term used by John Howard Yoder to describe the manner in which Christianity changes as it transitions from a persecuted minority to an established majority in the Roman Empire.[9] Hauerwas and Wells explain, "Prior to Constantine, it took courage to be a Christian. After Constantine, it took courage to be a pagan. Before Constantine, no one doubted that Christians were different. After Constantine, it became increasingly unclear what difference being a Christian made."[10] In other words, before Christianity became established, what Christians believed made all the difference for how they lived; and how they lived, therefore, distinguished them from everyone else. With Constantinianism, everyone became Christian by being born in a "Christian" society. Meanwhile, moral behavior became secondary to theological belief. When this happened, ethics became about inward dispositions because outwardly everyone was already Christian.[11]

Even so, Christians developed a variety of theologically robust moral traditions. The most prominent is that of Augustine, who represents the mainstream of Western theological tradition. Two aspects of Augustine's work are worth noting. First, Augustine argues that pagan conceptions of virtue (temperance, fortitude, justice, prudence) find their proper telos when they are understood as "forms of love whose object is God."[12] The priority of love for God has direct implications for how Christians imagine the social order.[13]

Secondly, as seen in *City of God*, Augustine distinguishes between the earthly city, which does not know God and is "characterized by order secured only through violence," and the heavenly city, which is peacefully ordered by

---

[8]*STT*, 23; *AN*, 27.

[9]Samuel Wells highlights four main changes that occur with Constantinianism: (1) Christians go from being persecuted to persecuting, (2) claims of Christ's lordship transfer from eschatology to ecclesiology, establishing the church as God's rule on earth, (3) the state replaces Christ as the norm for Christian ethics, and (4) a series of dualisms becomes normative for how Christians understand the world—visible/invisible, personal/structural, natural/revealed, and justice/gospel. Wells, *Transforming Fate*, 108-9.

[10]*BCCE*, 42.

[11]*CET*, 181.

[12]*STT*, 24.

[13]*BCCE*, 44.

the worship of the one true God.[14] While many see the Augustinian tradition as one that, for the most part, embraces Constantinianism—emphasizing the moral life as the pursuit of virtue while maintaining a sort of realpolitik with regard to the inherently sinful nature of worldly existence—Hauerwas maintains that Augustine's argument in *City of God* is that true worship founds true politics. In this regard, Augustine refuses to compromise the essential link between Christian convictions and the moral life.

A second substantial response to Constantinianism comes from the monastic tradition. Monasticism maintained the distinctiveness of Christian convictions by recovering some of the effects of persecution and martyrdom with vows of poverty, chastity, and obedience. Such lives became exceptional witnesses to the radical demands of the gospel that more "worldly" Christians could aspire toward.[15] Although it began as a countercultural movement within Christianity, monasticism came to have a lasting influence on mainstream Christianity through the development of penance.

Sometime around the fifth century, monks in Ireland began to hear confession from the laity. This practice became formalized with the development of penitentials (books that correlated particular sins with acts of penance meant to strengthen virtue as counteraction to sin).[16] With the practice of penance, the church developed a rich and sophisticated casuistical approach to moral formation that simultaneously took seriously the call for Christians to pursue holiness and the importance of communal practices in such a pursuit. Casuistry, remember, is the case-by-case application of general ethical principles. In this case, it meant that the church developed a rich moral reasoning that prescribed certain acts of penance in correspondence with particular sins. The basic idea was that Christians could be trained to pursue virtuous action and avoid vicious action by practicing acts that refocused their desire away from sin and toward God. Thomas Aquinas's *Summa Theologica* demonstrates the enduring influence of casuistry on Christian moral theology.

---

[14]*STT*, 24.
[15]*BCCE*, 43. For Hauerwas, monasticism does not represent "withdrawal"; instead, it represents a faithful response to Constantinianism. See Stanley Hauerwas and Samuel Wells, "Theological Ethics," in *God's Advocates: Christian Thinkers in Conversation*, ed. Rupert Shortt (London: DLT, 2005), 188.
[16]*BCCE*, 44-45; *STT*, 24-25.

Aquinas's moral theology is particularly exemplary for Hauerwas because Aquinas avoids the risk of reducing casuistry to legalism by underscoring the unity that exists between theology and ethics.[17] Aquinas's *Summa* has a three-part structure: part one explores God's creative activity in divine freedom, part two describes creation's return to God, and part three elaborates the means by which creation is able to return to God. A large part of the third section is devoted to casuistry. By considering questions regarding the moral life within the larger context of the story of creation and redemption, "the *Summa*, rather than being an argument for the independence of ethics, as it is sometimes characterized, is concerned to place the Christian's journey to God squarely within the doctrine of God."[18] Aquinas is often misread in this regard as a natural law ethicist. To the contrary, his moral theology is best understood as a description of communal practices of discernment that have friendship with God as their ultimate aim.

To Hauerwas, it is not surprising that monasticism began with the intention of developing exemplary moral lives and ended up changing the confessional practices of the whole church. Theological convictions are best exemplified by the lives of saints who bear witness to their truthfulness through performance. Central to the development of such lives is the sort of casuistry that we see developed in both the Augustinian and the Thomist streams of Catholic moral theology.

According to Hauerwas, the Protestant Reformation marks the beginning of the modern fragmentation of theology from ethics. To be sure, the magisterial reformers were keen to keep theology and ethics together. After all, the Reformation vision was centered largely on the goal of church renewal. For Hauerwas, Luther's treatment of the Decalogue in the *Shorter Catechism*, along with Calvinist and Wesleyan emphases on holiness, indicate that theology was inherently practical for the reformers.[19] Even so, Hauerwas marks the Reformation as the beginning of the split of theology from ethics for two reasons: the Lutheran distinction between law and gospel and the fragmentation of Christendom. Both are worth exploring briefly.

---

[17] *BCCE*, 45.
[18] *STT*, 26; See also *PK*, 53.
[19] *BCCE*, 48.

First, Luther's polemic against Roman Catholicism overdetermines the distinction between faith and works: "Faith, not works, determines the Christian's relationship to God. Moreover works became associated with 'ethics,' . . . the way sinners attempt to secure their standing before God as a means of avoiding complete dependence on God."[20] In other words, *faith* becomes about salvation by God's grace and *works* become about human obedience or disobedience to the law. Here, Hauerwas is concerned with two particular aspects of Lutheran theology: the law-gospel distinction and the two kingdoms doctrine.

The law-gospel distinction means, according to Hauerwas, that the gospel has to do with theological claims about who God is and soteriological claims about how God saves while the law has to do with how humans are expected to live and the manner in which they fall short of those expectations. Meanwhile, the two kingdoms doctrine socializes the law-gospel distinction by suggesting that the earthly kingdom is under the rule of law while the heavenly kingdom is under the rule of grace. Christians live a twofold existence, submitting to the gospel alone with regard to spiritual things and to the law with regard to things of the flesh. This twofold existence corresponds to the command to love God and neighbor. Thus submission to the law in accordance with the "orders of creation"—marriage, the state, and the church—is a form of neighbor love and constitutes the subject matter of ethics.[21]

Second, for Hauerwas, the Reformation destroyed the unity of Western Christendom.[22] Christians discovered that they had theological differences worth killing each other over. As such, theology could no longer provide a foundation for moral behavior to the extent that competing theological claims led to violence. While initially the magisterial reformers were deeply concerned with the practical nature of theological convictions, over time the search for a common foundation for ethics led to a self-conscious separation of ethics from theology. If theology creates division, then ethics must be partitioned off from theology so that people with great theological differences can find ways to coexist in peace. The name for this project is the

---

[20]*STT*, 27.
[21]*STT*, 28.
[22]*BCCE*, 48.

Enlightenment, and the figure that represents the formal divorce of theology from ethics is Immanuel Kant.

Kant famously distinguished between the *noumenal* and the *phenomenal*. The difference between the two is the difference between a thing in itself and our experience of it. On these terms, the transcendent world is unknowable as such and is the domain of metaphysics. Meanwhile, the immanent world is knowable through experience and observation and is the domain of mathematics and the natural sciences. For Kant, this distinction is equally true with regard to knowledge of God and knowledge of the created order. Statements about God are dogmatic and speculative in nature, while statements about humanity are ethical and empirical in nature.[23]

Since theology is speculative and we can never have certain knowledge of God, Kant redirected the study of religion to questions of morality.[24] In so doing, he thought he was saving Christianity from philosophical criticism by showing how the historical figure of Jesus Christ represents a true embodiment of the moral law. For Kant, the moral law is best summarized by what he called the categorical imperative: "Act only according to that maxim by which you can at the same time will that it should become a universal law."[25] On these terms, ethics have "a law-like character that makes possible cooperative forms of life between people who may not share common beliefs or history."[26] According to Hauerwas, Kant's great achievement is "to free morality from the arbitrary and the contingent, in order to secure at least minimal agreement between people of differing beliefs and societies." An approach to ethics based on well-reasoned universal laws means that ethics can be done "from the perspective of anyone."[27]

With Kant, the Lutheran law-gospel distinction becomes a formal ethical program that allows people with differing conceptions of what the "gospel" is to find common ground in the twin ideas of a universal moral law and the innate human capacity to discern the law by reason alone. Writing one hundred years after Kant's death, Ernst Troeltsch noted, "The Lutheran ethic

---

[23]*BCCE*, 4.
[24]*AN*, 27.
[25]Immanuel Kant, *Groundwork to the Metaphysics of Morals*, trans. with an intro. by Lewis White Beck (New York: Liberal Arts Press, 1959), 39, cited in *BCCE*, 30.
[26]*BCCE*, 30.
[27]*PK*, 10-11.

is summed up in the following characteristic features: confidence in God founded on His grace, and love of one's neighbor which is exercised in the social duties of one's calling, combined with an obedient surrender to the orders of society created by the Law of Nature."[28] The sort of things that constitute neighbor love—calling, given social orders, the law of nature—are theoretically discernible for Kant without confidence in God's grace.

This move, however, divides dogmatics from ethics. For instance, by the time Schleiermacher determined the order of the theological encyclopedia for the University of Berlin, he was able to put dogmatics before moral theology because he presumed that dogmatics was about metaphysical propositions and moral theology was the science of applying those same propositions to life.[29] Or again, when Ritschl and his students tried to find the essence of Christianity, they decided that they had to shuck away the husks of dogma in order to find the kernel of true Christianity that is the historical Jesus and his ethical teachings about the kingdom of God.[30]

The end result of the division of theology from ethics was that Protestant liberalism became increasingly focused on what we can know about human nature and human behavior. Whereas early Christian morality was the outworking of basic Christian convictions about God, post-Enlightenment Christian morality was an attempt to demonstrate that human moral consciousness was independent of and more basic than any particular theological convictions a person might have, Christian or otherwise. On these terms, theology best serves society by translating key concepts of the Christian faith "into terms that are meaningful and compelling for those who do not share Christianity's more particularistic beliefs about Jesus of Nazareth."[31]

---

[28]Ernst Troeltsch, *The Social Teachings of the Christian Churches*, trans. Olive Wyon (New York: Macmillan, 1931), 2:509-10, cited in *WT*, 60.

[29]*STT*, 30-32. For a detailed outline of the three-year theology program offered at Berlin in the early 1800s, see Thomas Albert Howard, *Protestant Theology and the Making of the Modern German University* (Oxford: Oxford University Press, 2006), 190.

[30]With the language of "kernel" and "husk," I am, of course, alluding to Adolf von Harnack, who once famously argued that to find the essence of Christianity, one had to remove the husk of historical Christianity in order to arrive at the kernel that was Jesus' original teachings about the kingdom of God (*What Is Christianity?*, trans. Thomas Bailey Saunders [1901; repr., Minneapolis: Fortress, 1986], 12).

[31]*AN*, 24.

CAN ETHICS BE CHRISTIAN?

Ritschl and Troeltsch are the names of the bridges by which Protestant liberalism traveled across the Atlantic Ocean and shaped Christian ethics in
America. Ritschl grounded the essence of true Christianity in the ethos of
Jesus' earthly teachings about the kingdom and the early church that
gathered around it. Similarly, Troeltsch's work *The Social Teachings of the
Christian Churches* was the first to document the ethos of Christian communities throughout history. Even before these theologians were translated
into English, they influenced the study of Christian ethics in America
through German-speaking American theologians like Walter Rauschenbusch and H. Richard and Reinhold Niebuhr.[32] And that is where our
second story begins.

The second narrative that Hauerwas tells developed as a lecture series called
Christian Ethics in America.[33] The course began with Walter Rauschenbusch's
"Christianizing the Social Order" and culminated with James Gustafson's "Can
Ethics Be Christian?"[34] The basic plot of the semester-long story is that
Christian ethics began with the hope of making the twentieth century into a
"Christian century" and ended with the presumption that Christian ethicists
should check their faith at the door.[35] As Hauerwas puts it, "Protestant Chris-
tians set out to make America Christian and ended by making Christianity
American."[36] Careful attention to the manner in which Hauerwas narrates this
story transposes his earlier criticisms of Protestant liberalism into a distinctly
American key, setting the stage for his own postliberal theological program to
recover the unity between theology and ethics in American Christianity. The
story goes something like this.

Walter Rauschenbusch was born to German Lutheran missionaries in
Missouri and grew up in Rochester, New York, where his father, now Baptist,

---

[32]*BH*, 67.

[33]Hauerwas, "Between Christian Ethics and Religious Ethics," 405.

[34]*BH*, 64; See also Stanley Hauerwas, "Christian Ethics in America: A Promising Obituary," in
Introduction to Christian Theology: Contemporary North American Perspectives, ed. Roger A. Badham (Louisville, KY: Westminster John Knox, 1998), 104. This essay, combined with a few
chapters in *BH*, were originally intended to be a textbook on Christian ethics in America to
match the taught course.

[35]This was indeed the theme of the inaugural issue of *Christian Century* in January of 1900. See
Stanley Hauerwas, Robin W. Lovin, and Emilie Maureen Townes, "Ethics in Our Time: Social
Witness for the New Century," *Christian Century*, September 27, 2000, 952.

[36]Hauerwas, "Christian Ethics in America," 111.

taught German at Rochester Theological Seminary. Walter was subsequently educated in Germany and at the seminary in Rochester. Thus he was schooled in the progressive wing of the American Baptist Church and the pietist Protestant liberalism of nineteenth-century Germany.[37]

For Rauschenbusch, Jesus Christ radically democratized religion in two distinct but important ways. First, he democratized the concept of God by teaching us to address God as Father, making all humans God's children.[38] Second, he democratized the concept of salvation, making the kingdom of God an ideal for human society.[39] Indeed, for Rauschenbusch, democracy was the very nature of the gospel.[40]

Combining aspects of Ritschl's theological vision of the fatherhood of God and the brotherhood of humanity with Troeltsch's thick historicism,[41] Rauschenbusch developed a theological vision that cast Jesus Christ as the moral embodiment of the social teachings of Israel's prophets.[42] His message was about the kingdom of God, a kingdom that is initiated by Jesus himself and gradually realized here on earth. The atonement, on these terms, is not predominantly about the forgiveness of individual sinners; instead, it is the revelation of the triumph of love over sin and, therefore, "the symbol and basis of a new social order based on love and solidarity."[43] Salvation is voluntary participation in the progressive realization of the kingdom as the reign of love that simultaneously unifies humanity and maintains individual liberty; hence the name "the social gospel."

At its heart, the social gospel was a movement that sought to "christianize the social order" by transforming society into the kingdom of God. This meant bringing it into harmony with the ethical convictions of Jesus Christ.[44] Since the gospel was primarily about the liberation of human society into a democratic vision of the kingdom of God, the church figures awkwardly

---

[37] *BH*, 73-75.

[38] *BH*, 90.

[39] *CET*, 176.

[40] *BH*, 96.

[41] That is, Troeltsch's unrelenting attention to the historical development of Christian doctrine over time and in different historical contexts. For a helpful summary of historicism in Troeltsch's theological project, see H. Ganse Little Jr., "Ernst Troeltsch and the Scope of Historicism," *Journal of Religion* 46, no. 3 (1966): 343-64.

[42] Hauerwas, "Christian Ethics in America," 111.

[43] *BH*, 94.

[44] *BH*, 82-83.

into Rauschenbusch's theology.[45] The church's main contribution is to supply society with people who are trained for the task of transformation. Nevertheless, Rauschenbusch's social gospel places America and democracy at the center of the story. In the end, for Rauschenbusch, the subject of Christian ethics is America, not the church. Hauerwas writes, "Christian ethics accordingly was understood as that mode of reflection that helped churches develop policies to make American ideals of freedom and equality more fully institutionalized in American life."[46]

The idea that Christian ethics is about the realization of the kingdom of God on earth lost traction in the aftermath of World War I. After such tragedy, people began to question the social-gospel movement's optimistic assessment of human nature. This was particularly true for brothers H. Richard and Reinhold Niebuhr.

H. Richard was influenced by Troeltsch, and he spent his career normalizing the field of Christian ethics as an academic discipline at Yale Divinity School.[47] He is most famous for *Christ and Culture*, in which he famously argued that the enduring problem of how to relate Christ to culture has repeatedly produced five basic ethical types. Attentive to Troeltsch's concern for history, Niebuhr acknowledges that relative to different times and places, Christians have developed various ethical responses to culture in their attempts to follow Christ.[48]

H. Richard's brother, Reinhold, taught ethics at Union Theological Seminary in New York City and is often described as imminently more practical than his brother.[49] Reinhold is the epochal figure of twentieth-century Protestant social ethics. Such was his influence that *Time* magazine reported in 1943 that students at Oxford commonly shared the witticism "Thou shalt love the Lord thy Dodd with all thy heart, and thy Niebuhr as thyself."[50]

Reinhold Niebuhr, particularly, was critical of the utopian vision of "christianizing the social order." For Niebuhr, Christian ethics requires a

---

[45]*BH*, 94.
[46]*BH*, 25.
[47]*AN*, 33.
[48]H. Richard Niebuhr, *Christ and Culture*, 50th anniversary ed. (San Francisco: HarperSanFrancisco, 2001).
[49]Hauerwas, "Christian Ethics in America," 113.
[50]"Thy Dodd and Thy Niebuhr." *Time*, August 23, 1943, 88. Dodd refers to Oxbridge professor C. H. Dodd, who was the preeminent Pauline scholar of his day.

realistic acceptance of the inherent sinfulness of human nature. Dependent on descriptions of sinfulness from Augustine, Luther, and Kierkegaard, Niebuhr developed an ethical posture that became known as "Christian realism."[51] Christian realism accounts for the contradictory impulses of altruism and selfishness that coexist in sinful human nature. Niebuhr writes, "A valid moral outlook for both individuals and for groups, therefore, sets no limits to the creative possibility of concern for others, and makes no claims that such creativity ever annuls the power of self-concern or removes the peril of pretension if the force of residual egotism is not acknowledged."[52] The good that Christian ethics pursues in the social order is always a relative good, and perhaps even a lesser evil, but it is never the full realization of the kingdom.[53] In this regard, Niebuhr's Christian realism is a stoic acceptance of the given limits of our existence combined with a chastened sense of Christian hope.[54]

Reinhold Niebuhr's basic theological convictions were largely consistent with Rauschenbusch's. Jesus' life and death were the very embodiment of an ethic of sacrificial love.[55] This "law of love" governs the human condition, and the cross is its greatest symbolic expression.[56] The Christian life is a life of imitation whereby Jesus' love ethic is appropriated as a personal ethic. Between two individuals, self-sacrifice is the paradigm for love.[57] In this regard, Niebuhr, like Rauschenbusch and Troeltsch before him, began his work with anthropology—"human needs, human powers, human responsibilities"[58]—and assumed that the subject of Christian ethics was society (in this case, America), not the church.[59]

Where Niebuhr parted ways with Rauschenbusch concerns the manner in which these basic theological convictions translate into social ethics. Niebuhr

---

[51]*AN*, 29-30.

[52]Reinhold Niebuhr, *The Structure of Nations and Empires* (Fairfield, NJ: Augustus M. Kelley, 1977), 30-31, quoted in *WW*, 49-50.

[53]*VV*, 197.

[54]Hauerwas and Wells, "Theological Ethics," 184-85; see also *WGU*, 133.

[55]To be sure, Niebuhr pays a great deal more attention to maintaining the doctrine of the incarnation than Rauschenbusch does. But even this is in service to the idea that Jesus is the embodiment of love: "The incarnation remains useful, Niebuhr argues, as a way to express the necessary paradox that the perfect love exemplified in the life of Christ was in history yet remains suprahistorical" (*WGU*, 125).

[56]*AN*, 32-33; *WGU*, 126, 134; *BH*, 34.

[57]*WGU*, 108, 135.

[58]See also Hauerwas, "Christian Ethics in America," 112.

[59]*WGU*, 138.

was skeptical of institutional structures. His retrieval of classical conceptions of sin gave him the language to speak of human depravity and the limits of societal sanctification. Indeed, one of the lasting influences of Luther's theology on Niebuhr was the doctrine of justification by faith alone. For Niebuhr, the doctrine of justification spoke to the reality of human sinfulness and the need for the cross of Christ. He worried about idealist doctrines of sanctification that suggested church and society could make progress in holiness, and perhaps even become the kingdom of God here on earth.[60]

In this regard, Christian existence is best described by the Lutheran expression *simul justus et peccator* (simultaneously righteous and sinner).[61] Individually, this means that before God the Christian is justified and lives in freedom under the gospel. In themselves, however, Christians are sinners like all humans and must continually confess their sins and repent. For Niebuhr, the tension between being justified and sinful extends beyond the individual and describes social organizations. Organizations are sinful and must be kept in check with a realistic recognition of the sin that exists within them. For this reason, Niebuhr thought that once you introduce more than two people to the ethical equation, the ideal of sacrificial love must be tempered with "a rational estimate of conflicting needs and interests."[62]

In order to achieve his Christian realism, Niebuhr often employed a theological method that Hauerwas calls "translation" or "accommodation." Here, Hauerwas means something like Paul Tillich's method of correlation, where the deep existential questions of the modern world become the starting point for theological reflection.[63] The gospel, containing some "kernel" of truth, must be translated into contemporary idioms in order to meet the needs of the modern world. The basic presumption is that the gospel needs

---

[60]*WGU*, 136. Niebuhr is critical of a type of socialization of the Wesleyan notion of perfection that coalesces in the social-gospel movement with a progressivist reading of history. We see this particularly in his rejection of pacifism as a denial of the doctrine of justification (*WGU*, 94).

[61]Luther writes: "The saints in being righteous are at the same time sinners; they are righteous because they believe in Christ whose righteousness covers them and is imputed to them, but they are sinners because they do not fulfill the law and are not without sinful desires" (Martin Luther, *Lectures on Romans*, ed. and trans. Wilhelm Pauck [Louisville, KY: Westminster John Knox, 1961], 208).

[62]Reinhold Niebuhr, *The Nature and Destiny of Man* (Louisville, KY: Westminster John Knox, 1996), 2:248, cited in *WGU*, 135.

[63]Paul Tillich, *Systematic Theology* (Chicago: University of Chicago Press, 1951), 1:59-64. Tillich, of course, was Niebuhr's colleague at Union.

to change to fit the world and that the theologian is the one who can master-
fully extract the kernel from the husk, the truth of the gospel from its accidental historical context. This approach, for Hauerwas, betrays the very
nature of the gospel and accommodates Christianity to modern cultural
assumptions that are inconsistent with Christian convictions.[64]

Niebuhr's ethics demonstrate a similar accommodation to the extent that
his primary concern is to develop a social ethic according to the terms of
modernity. Hauerwas writes that Niebuhr's "theology sought to make
Christian belief intelligible within the naturalistic presumptions that he
thought were a prerequisite of modern science. His ethics sought to make
Christian belief intelligible and even useful within the presuppositions of
political liberalism."[65] "Sin" becomes a theological answer to the existence
of corruption and self-interest in the social sphere, while "Christian realism"
becomes a version of Hobbesian political realism.

Niebuhr did not give up the theological game altogether. In fact, much of
his ethical work is pragmatic in nature and often functions as a means to
validate some of his basic religious convictions.[66] Nevertheless, the very
process of translating Christian convictions into terms that are reasonable
to anyone (or any American) eventually pressed James Gustafson's question,
Can ethics be Christian? A number of scholars at Harvard were keen to
answer no, calling themselves "Atheists for Niebuhr." As his career waned,
Niebuhr tended to agree with them, regretting his use of "original sin" because it offended the modern mind and reworking much of his material in
an even more secular idiom.[67]

To be sure, Niebuhr repeats some of the basic habits of Protestant liberalism as Hauerwas sees it: the separation of theology from ethics, the translation of theological speech into a "universal language," and the reduction
of theology to anthropology. He is not, however, merely repeating these
liberal moves. Instead, he extends the project by attempting to redeploy

---

[64]*RA*, 20-24.
[65]*WGU*, 137.
[66]*WGU*, 96, 104.
[67]Gary Dorrien, *Social Ethics in the Making: Interpreting an American Tradition* (Oxford: Wiley-
Blackwell, 2009), 270. I think Gabriel Fackre fails to appreciate this late turn in Niebuhr's work
when he argues that Hauerwas has misconstrued Niebuhr as a naturalist and a humanist (Gabriel J. Fackre, "Was Reinhold Niebuhr a Christian?," *First Things*, October 2002, 25-27).

specific theological concepts in service to American society as a whole. Hauerwas writes, "Under Niebuhr's influence, theology . . . became ethics and ethics became the investigation of the conditions necessary to make a liberal social order work."[68]

With this, we have reached the climax of our second narrative. For Hauerwas, what ties Rauschenbusch and Niebuhr together is the manner in which both theologians pave the way for Christianity to be co-opted as a civil religion that aims to prop up the liberal democratic principles that fund American society.[69] Progressive American Christianity is the continuation of the liberal Protestant reduction of theology to ethics to the point of practical atheism. Faith is relegated to the private sphere, where it can then influence the public sphere only as it is able to translate itself into atheistic prescriptions for public morality. Hauerwas writes, "If you accept . . . that Christian theology can no longer tell you anything about God or God's relation to God's creation, then all you have left is 'ethics.'" And ethics is something that is discernible by any rational individual as an explication of natural law.[70]

This has two practical effects on American Christianity. First, Americans do not believe in God, they believe in belief.[71] The God Americans worship, according to Hauerwas, is a God who is characterized by vague notions of love and does not require discipleship to a crucified Lord.[72] Second, the nation replaces the church as the place where civil religion takes place. American Christians identify more with being "American" than they do with being "Christian," and America becomes the "new Israel," God's new chosen people who exist by divine providence in the world.[73] Anything that furthers the project of "America" is a moral good, and as it turns out, nothing furthers America like war.[74]

---

[68] *WGU*, 139.
[69] *PK*, 13.
[70] *BH*, 118-19.
[71] *WAD*, 15.
[72] *BH*, 35; *DT*, 58.
[73] *DT*, 52; *WAD*, 16. Nobody has worked out the logic of this American exceptionalism better than Tommy Givens, who argues that this way of thinking masks the modern propensity for humanity to project their own self-election as a divine election of sorts. See Tommy Givens, *We the People: Israel and the Catholicity of Jesus* (Minneapolis: Fortress, 2014), chap. 3.
[74] *WAD*, 4.

If the story of Protestant liberalism is the story of how humanity replaces God as the subject of theology, then the story of Christian ethics in America is the story of how America replaces the church as the community of moral formation, practicing war as its main liturgical act. Indeed, for Hauerwas civil religion is "the great danger" to the American church.[75]

For Hauerwas, both of these stories are related and produce similar outcomes. The current state of affairs in American Christianity is much as H. Richard Niebuhr described Protestant liberalism in 1937: "A God without wrath brought men without sin into a kingdom without judgment through the ministrations of a Christ without a cross."[76] That the problem with Christian ethics in America is a recapitulation and extension of the problem of the separation of theology from ethics suggests to Hauerwas that the solutions might also be similar.

A POSTLIBERAL THEOLOGICAL ETHICS

These two narratives—the story of how Protestant liberalism reduced Christianity to ethics and the story of how Christian ethics in America ended up being more American than Christian—set the context for Hauerwas's own work to the extent that they name two concerns he has with the discipline of Christian ethics. In telling these two stories, however, I have withheld the endings in the hope that telling them now will help the reader see the way that Hauerwas effectively leverages his polemic against liberalism into a constructive program of theological ethics.

The great hero of Hauerwas's first narrative is Karl Barth, who rejects the division of theology from ethics. For Barth, theology is much more than the articulation of a set of metaphysical givens; it is the church's investigation of its own language about God. Central to such an investigation is a discussion about whether the church's language and actions are consistent with its basic theological convictions. The task of ethics is not to secure a universal ground for moral knowledge; instead, the task of ethics is to

---

[75]Oliver O'Donovan, *The Desire of the Nations: Rediscovering the Roots of Political Theology* (Cambridge: Cambridge University Press, 1996), 224. This concern is articulated very clearly in Hauerwas's criticism of President Trump's inauguration. See Stanley Hauerwas, "Christians Don't Be Fooled: Trump has Deep Religious Convictions," *Washington Post*, January 27, 2017, www.washingtonpost.com/news/acts-of-faith/wp/2017/01/27/christians-dont-be-fooled-trump-has-deep-religious-convictions/?utm_term=.440c14a5eceb; see also *MW*, 113-126.

[76]H. Richard Niebuhr, *The Kingdom of God in America* (New York: Harper, 1959), 193.

provide a thick theological description of the moral space in which humans act. John Webster explains, "Barth's ethics tends to assume that moral problems are resolvable by correct theological description of moral space."[77] Such a description necessarily includes the triune God's self-revelation in Jesus Christ.[78] In this regard, Barth's genius lies in his redirecting theological speech away from the experience of the human agent and to the God from whom all things come. Theological ethics, on these terms, is a description of human agency as determined by and in relation to God. Thus, as Hauerwas puts it, "Theology is ethics all the way down."[79]

For Hauerwas, Barth's rejection of Protestant liberalism represents the way forward for Christianity in America. He reads the narrative of Christian ethics in America as a parallel to the narrative of the rise and fall of Protestant liberalism. Just as Kant attempted to save Christianity by suggesting that its intellectual powers lie in the realm of practical reason, so too Niebuhr sought to make Christianity intelligible as a powerful description of moral responsibility; just as Kant appealed to the law of nature, so too Niebuhr appealed to the law of love. The implication of such a reading is that just as Barth's recovery of the inseparable relationship between theology and ethics is the resolution to the narrative of Protestant liberalism, a similar move is required in the discipline of Christian ethics in America.

Could Barth himself have been the hero of the story of Christian ethics in America for Hauerwas? Possibly; however, early American reception of Barth's work muddied the waters, often suggesting he was Niebuhr's theological ally in an ill-formed project called "neo-orthodoxy."[80] Although Barth and Niebuhr were peers, Niebuhr remained critical of Barth's theology, calling it a "theology for the catacombs" because it failed to take seriously a scientific-naturalist worldview.[81] In contrast, Niebuhr remained committed

---

[77]John Webster, *Barth's Ethics of Reconciliation* (Cambridge: Cambridge University Press, 1995), 2.
[78]*STT*, 33.
[79]Hauerwas and Wells, "Theological Ethics," 179.
[80]On the "myth of Neo-orthodoxy," see Bruce L. McCormack, *Karl Barth's Critically Realistic Dialectical Theology: Its Genesis and Development, 1909–1936* (Oxford: Oxford University Press, 1995), 23-28.
[81]*WGU*, 128-129. Interestingly, O'Donovan suggests that Hauerwas's theology is a return to the catacombs. In this sense, O'Donovan is perhaps an ally in my attempt to draw connections between Barth and Hauerwas; although in O'Donovan's case it is clear that the similarity is not a good thing. O'Donovan, *Desire of the Nations*, 216.

to "liberal theology's presumption that theology must be grounded in anthropology."[82] The problems of society were problems that he had theological resources to address and, as the Atheists for Niebuhr rightly gathered, God was an unnecessary hypothesis in much of his answer. For Hauerwas, these differing trajectories in twentieth-century Protestant theology epitomize "the difference between a theology that has given up on its ability to tell us the way the world is and a theology that confidently and unapologetically proclaims the way things are."[83]

When Hauerwas looks for a hero to his second narrative, it is hard to find someone in American Protestantism like Barth who breaks so clearly and completely with Protestant liberalism. The search for a hero to this second narrative leads Hauerwas to consider Niebuhr's brother, H. Richard, and then subsequently his protégés Paul Ramsey and James Gustafson, and finally, his critic John Howard Yoder. Yoder gives Hauerwas the resources to conclude the narrative of Christian ethics in America with a return to the distinctiveness of Christianity.

The first figure that Hauerwas turns to is H. Richard Niebuhr, Hauerwas's earliest theological influence. He read Niebuhr's *The Meaning of Revelation* and *Christ and Culture* as a high school student and continued to reflect on these works throughout his college career.[84] When it came time to go to seminary, he chose to attend Yale—where Niebuhr taught—in spite of strong objections from Schubert Ogden that he would turn into a "Barthian."[85] In many ways, H. Richard Niebuhr seems a likely hero to the narrative of American Christian ethics. *The Meaning of Revelation* was an intentional attempt to synthesize Troeltsch's historicism with Barth's theology of revelation.[86] Thus Niebuhr seemed on the way to a Barthian solution to the problem. But Niebuhr's solution to keep theology and ethics together still operated with the sort of two-step process that Hauerwas rejects: first, philosophical underpinnings, then theological reflection on "what's going on."[87]

---

[82]*AN*, 31.
[83]*WGU*, 21.
[84]*HC*, 9, 14.
[85]*HC*, 14.
[86]H. Richard Niebuhr, *The Meaning of Revelation* (1941; repr., Louisville, KY: Westminster John Knox, 2006), xxxiv–xxxv.
[87]*AN*, 33-34; *PK*, 53.

Niebuhr's students took up the task of making Christian ethics theological, but they hardly fared better. One of his most successful students was Paul Ramsey, a Methodist who taught at Princeton University. Ramsey's work on just war theory and medical ethics represents the deterioration of American Christendom to the extent that Christians can no longer presume basic Christian moral commitments to be universal. Faced with a growing utilitarianism, Ramsey turned to Catholic moral theology in order to shore up a deontological Protestant social ethic.[88]

In Ramsey's work, just war is an apt example of how he appropriates the Catholic moral tradition. At the heart of the just war tradition is a process of moral reflection that seeks to answer the question, can war be just? on a case-by-case basis. For Ramsey, this means testing all cases of war against "the absolute norm of Christian love."[89]

For Hauerwas, this approach demonstrates great promise as a means of recovering the integration of theology and ethics; however, he worries that the Catholic moral theology tradition fails to truly integrate its casuistry with theology.[90] Instead, he sees a tradition that is largely legalistic and act-oriented in nature. Yes, it is based broadly on theological assumptions like the existence of God and the rational nature of the universe, but this is not enough for Hauerwas. One needs to look no further than the casuistry of just war to see Hauerwas's point. In practice, just war often operates more as a "public policy checklist" to legitimate the predetermined bellicose actions of the nation-state than as a deep process of moral discernment.[91]

Another H. Richard Niebuhr protégé, James Gustafson, is perhaps the one who most tried to adhere to Niebuhr's desire to make ethics theological. His work began where Niebuhr's *The Responsible Self* left off, focusing on questions of character. Later in his career, he became concerned to make ethics theological again. His magnum opus, the two-volume *Ethics from a Theocentric Perspective*, is a concerted effort to keep theology and ethics

---

[88]Hauerwas, "Christian Ethics in America," 114.

[89]James T. Johnson, "Just War in the Thought of Paul Ramsey," *Journal of Religious Ethics* 19, no. 2 (1991): 185.

[90]*HC*, 92. He does permit that this does shift in a positive direction after Vatican II (*AN*, 34-35).

[91]No one has made this point more effectively than Hauerwas's student Daniel M. Bell Jr. See *Just War as Christian Discipleship: Recentering the Tradition in the Church Rather Than the State* (Grand Rapids: Brazos, 2009), chap. 3 especially.

together, with volume one subtitled *Theology and Ethics* and volume two subtitled *Ethics and Theology*.[92]

Early in his career, Hauerwas saw himself working in Gustafson's footsteps. He wrote: "Following James Gustafson, I have taken as a central concern the task of finding the most appropriate means to articulate how Christians have understood . . . the relationship between Christ and the moral life."[93] With the publication of *Ethics in a Theocentric Perspective*, Hauerwas begins to worry that Gustafson, in the name of bringing together peoples of faith, downplays the uniqueness of Christ to the point where it is not obvious that Gustafson is speaking of the God Christians worship as Father, Son, and Holy Spirit.[94] In this regard, it seems that Gustafson answered his own question, Can ethics be Christian? with a resounding "maybe . . . sort of . . . not really."

The theologian who finally emerges as the hero of Hauerwas's second narrative is the Mennonite theologian John Howard Yoder. Hauerwas first came across Yoder's work as a graduate student at Yale, when he discovered Yoder's pamphlet *Karl Barth and the Problem of War* in the school bookstore.[95] He later connected with Yoder when he moved to Notre Dame.[96] Shortly thereafter, he began to articulate a vision for theological ethics that represents a radical break with the tradition of Christian ethics represented by the Rauschenbusch-to-Gustafson storyline.

For Hauerwas, Yoder is the hero because his "'ethics' is built on the assumption that Christian ethics is for Christians."[97] He brings about an end to the tradition of doing Protestant social ethics as a means to better society and the rediscovery that "the true subject of Christian ethics is not America, but the church."[98] Thus, whereas Barth's break with his liberal predecessors related to his conviction that their bankrupt support of Germany's war

---

[92]James F. Childress, review of *Ethics from a Theocentric Perspective*, vol. 1, *Theology and Ethics*, by James M. Gustafson, *Ethics* 94, no. 1 (1983): 136.

[93]Hauerwas, "Ethicist as Theologian," 409.

[94]Hauerwas, "Christian Ethics in America," 114; Wells, *Transforming Fate*, 8.

[95]*DT*, 236.

[96]*HC*, 116.

[97]Recently, the extent of Yoder's systemic sexual abuse of women in the Mennonite community has become public (Rachel Waltner Goossen, "Defanging the Beast: Mennonite Responses to John Howard Yoder's Sexual Abuse," *Mennonite Quarterly Review* 89, no. 1 [2015]: 7-80). This revelation, no doubt, problematizes Hauerwas's dependence on Yoder's theology.

[98]Hauerwas, "Christian Ethics in America," 104-6.

policy during World War I betrayed a bankrupt theology, Hauerwas's break with his liberal predecessors is related to his discovery that the church, not society, is the place where Christian moral formation takes place. This discovery is mediated by Yoder's work because it is a theological ethic that begins without the presupposition that the church serves the state.[99]

For Hauerwas, this realization is deeply Barthian at its core. Reflecting on this time of theological growth in his career, Hauerwas writes,

> What I had discovered in my teaching and writing at Notre Dame is the difference it makes when you refuse to ignore the eschatological character of the gospel, a discovery that Barth made in the second edition of his commentary on Romans and that Yoder made as he wrote pamphlets for display in the back of Mennonite churches. Barth's discovery, bound as it was by the possibilities of European Christianity in 1921, awaited and required rediscovery. And Yoder helped me see that God has freed the church from its cultural captivity to the world.[100]

Thus, for Hauerwas, Yoder's insistence that the church is free is a specifically American analogue and extension of Barth's theological break with liberalism.

In the final evaluation, Hauerwas's break with the Protestant liberalism represented by the Niebuhrs is mediated by two particular changes in his thinking that are represented by Ramsey and Yoder. Something of this twofold inheritance can be observed in *Against the Nations*, a book he dedicated to both Ramsey and Yoder. This odd couple fits together in *Against the Nations* as representing different critiques of nuclear armament in two different essays on the matter.

In the first essay, Hauerwas argues that the just war position exemplified by Ramsey has the virtue of presupposing an eschatology that limits the goods for which a Christian may go to war. Thus war for the sake of survival or self-defense is no longer reasonable. Instead, war may only be justified on the grounds that it defends the innocent. A Christian vision of the kingdom of God reorders views of war to the extent that it relativizes death for Christians by reminding them that death is not the end.[101]

---

[99]Wells, *Transforming Fate*, 10-11.
[100]*HC*, 136.
[101]*AN*, 135-40, 154.

In the second essay, Hauerwas ties Yoder's Christology to eschatology and argues, "Christians are a people who believe that we have in fact seen the end; that the world has for all time experienced its decisive crisis in the life and death of Jesus of Nazareth. . . . Through Jesus' cross and resurrection the end has come; the kingdom has been established."[102] For this reason, the Christian response of pacifism is one that is grounded, not in political effectiveness, but in hope. Pacifism is "not first of all an 'ethic' but a declaration of the reality of the new age." It is the fruit of a particular eschatology that claims that God's kingdom is already here.[103]

With Ramsey, Hauerwas's theological ethics develop along the line of the Roman Catholic tradition of casuistry, and with Yoder, they develop along the lines of an eschatologically oriented Christology with its concomitant commitment to pacifism. In both cases, the common theme is a break with the tradition of Christian ethics in America that works from the Protestant liberalism of Kant and Troeltsch and moves through Rauschenbusch, the Niebuhrs, and, finally, Gustafson. Ramsey, working somewhere between the Roman Catholic tradition and his mentor, H. Richard Niebuhr, represents something of a middle ground. Yoder, on the other hand, marks a radical break with the Christian ethics tradition and becomes the interlocutor who best represents Hauerwas's own break with the Niebuhrs.

Yoder represents the end of the tradition of Christian ethics in America in two senses. In the first sense, Yoder interrupts this tradition with the rediscovery of the inherent relation between theology and ethics. In an early examination of Yoder's work, Hauerwas admires its deep christocentrism. For Yoder, Jesus' life, death, and resurrection reveal something of God's very character: God is a peaceful God who would rather die on a cross than resist evil with violence. In the cross, God meets violence with nonresistant love; and in the resurrection, he demonstrates that evil is defeated by love. God's

---

[102] *AN*, 165. Hauerwas previously described eschatology using Yoder's own definition: "This is what we mean by eschatology: a hope which, defying present frustration, defines a present position in terms of the yet unseen goal which gives it meaning" (John Howard Yoder, *The Original Revolution* [Scottdale, PA: Herald, 1971], 56, quoted in *AN*, 160).

[103] *AN*, 194. Some might be inclined at this point to ask whether this is a "realized eschatology" or an "inaugurated eschatology." For Hauerwas, to do so would mean to offer an explanation for the claim "Jesus Christ is Lord" that becomes more determinative than the claim itself. In other words, such a question would immediately qualify the claim and limit its scope: Lord of what? For whom is he Lord?

action in Jesus Christ establishes his new kingdom here on earth. The Christian life is a call to imitate Christ's nonviolent life as an expression of the peaceable kingdom.[104] Yoder's ethical commitment to nonviolence is directly related to and a reflection of his deeper theological conviction that God in Jesus Christ reveals himself to be a nonviolent God.

In a second sense, Yoder represents the end of the Christian ethics tradition in that his work embodies all of the best aspects of his forebears while developing his own brand of theological ethics. With Rauschenbusch, he is concerned with the ethical implications of Jesus' life and ministry; with Reinhold Niebuhr, he is deeply committed to realism; with H. Richard Niebuhr, making ethics about God; with Ramsey, the moral implications of war; and with Gustafson, clarity and precision.[105] In short, Yoder is the hero to the story of Christian ethics in America because in Yoder Hauerwas sees someone who comes from outside of that tradition and speaks to all of the strengths of the tradition while also providing a Barth-like alternative that is able to fix some of its problems, especially the problem of how to keep Christian ethics Christian.

SUMMARY

Stanley Hauerwas intentionally locates his theological ethics in the context of two narratives about the relationship of theology and ethics. In the first narrative, Hauerwas is the inheritor of a liberal Protestant tradition that intentionally divorced theology from ethics for the sake of making ethics effective as a common discourse in a pluralist society. In the second narrative, Hauerwas is the inheritor of an intellectual tradition of Christian ethics in America that intentionally eschews the distinctiveness of Christianity in the name of providing moral support to a liberal democratic society. In both instances, the results are devastating to the extent that Christian theological convictions become first private and subsequently obsolete to many Christian ethicists. In his own work, Hauerwas tries to recover the inherent relationship between theology and ethics and the distinctiveness of Christianity. In so doing, he sees himself continuing the theological projects of Barth and Yoder—two projects that he understands to be largely commensurate with each other.

---

[104]*VV*, 201-3.
[105]*BH*, 67.

In the context of my larger project to discern if and how Hauerwas is a "Barthian," these insights establish aspects of Hauerwas's self-understanding that his work is a continuation of Barth's rejection of Protestant liberalism. I have identified this aspect of Hauerwas's project as postliberalism. Here, we see that as he tries to continue a Barth-like rejection of the Christian social ethics represented by Reinhold Niebuhr and others, he draws on Ramsey's turn to casuistry and Yoder's eschatological Christology.

Yoder is really the driving force in Hauerwas's break with Niebuhr. Samuel Wells is right to call Yoder the "watershed" in Hauerwas's theological development.[106] Prior to Yoder, Hauerwas thought that his Niebuhrian commitments and his Barthian commitments were commensurate with each other.[107] Afterward, he sees that he must make a Barth-like break with the Protestant liberalism of American Christian ethics. With this break, he prefers Barth's emphasis on the reality of the lordship of Christ over and against Niebuhr's emphasis on the reality of the persistence of sin this side of the eschaton.[108]

The positive move Barth made beyond liberalism, according to Hauerwas, was to reconnect dogmatics and ethics. Hauerwas attempts a similar move with his turn to the related themes of casuistry, narrative, and community in order to emphasize the church's liturgical practices as a means to form virtuous people. While these moves intentionally reconnect theology and ethics, it is hard to reckon how Hauerwas sees these moves as Barthian. Sure, Barth and Yoder share some similar christological assumptions, but Yoder seems more eager to develop an account of the moral life as *imitatio Christi* than Barth—a difference that is keenly felt in their diverging views regarding absolute pacifism. Ramsey, on the other hand, may share Barth's intuitions about remaining open to the possibility of war, but his theological ethics function casuistically in a manner that Barth would have rejected outright.

In other words, the main problem at this point is that Hauerwas claims to learn from Barth how to reject Protestant liberalism by keeping

[106]Wells, *Transforming Fate*, 10.

[107]*HC*, 67.

[108]Brandon Morgan captures this tension between Barth and Niebuhr by focusing on their 1948 exchange, which began at the Amsterdam assembly of the World Council of Churches and continued in the *Christian Century*. See Brandon L. Morgan, "The Lordship of Christ and the Gathering of the Church: Hauerwas's Debt to the 1948 Barth-Niebuhr Exchange," *Conrad Grebel Review* 33, no. 1 (2015): 49-71.

dogmatics and ethics together, and yet he deploys methods that Barth explicitly rejects. In order to determine if this break with Barth over casuistry places Hauerwas at complete odds with Barthianism, we must explore, first, how Hauerwas understands his own theological ethics to "fix" problematic aspects of Barth's theology. Then, second, we must engage in a deeper reading of Barth's understanding of the relationship between dogmatics and ethics in order to see if Hauerwas strays too far from Barth to warrant his claims to be Barthian. To this end, I devote chapters two and three to exploring in greater depth what Hauerwas learns from Barth and whether it is sufficient to call Hauerwas a Barthian. In chapters four and five I will then explore specifically Hauerwas's postliberalism and the various influences that press him beyond Barth.

2

With and Beyond Barth

WHAT STANLEY HAUERWAS MEANS when he claims to be a Barthian is somewhat complicated. On the one hand, he has written, "While we have taken clues from Barth, we do not share his epistemological presuppositions that revelation is self-authenticating,"[1] and, "I fully agree with Barth, so long as the eternity/time relation is not understood in neo-Kantian fashion"[2]—comments that suggest Hauerwas rejects key philosophical presuppositions in Barth's work. On the other hand, he claims, "I am a Barthian. I've always one way or the other been within the Barthian framework."[3] Determining the parameters of what Hauerwas takes to be "the Barthian framework" is essential for determining the extent to which his work depends on Barth's theology.

In one instance, Hauerwas suggests, "My Barthianism . . . is just another way of saying my Christology."[4] Thus Hauerwas is a Barthian in the sense that from his perspective the two theologians share similar christocentric tendencies. At other points, Hauerwas cites Barth's insistence on the otherness of God,[5] the eschatological character of the gospel,[6] the humanity

---

[1]Stanley Hauerwas and William H. Willimon, "Embarrassed by God's Presence," *Christian Century*, January 30, 1985, 99.

[2]*DT*, 5 n. 2.

[3]Stanley Hauerwas, "Faculty Forum with Stanley Hauerwas: Conrad Grebel University College," *Conrad Grebel Review* 20, no. 3 (2002): 70.

[4]*DT*, 237.

[5]*BH*, 120; Stanley Hauerwas, "Karl Barth: *Dogmatics in Outline* (1947)," *First Things*, March 2000, 46.

[6]*HC*, 136.

of God,[7] rejecting natural theology,[8] and a commitment to keep dog-matics and ethics together.[9] These themes, wide-ranging as they appear, are interrelated in Barth's thought when they are understood as the implications of a basic theological move that Hauerwas thinks he learns from Barth: the rejection of Protestant liberalism. For Hauerwas, Barth's theology develops as a powerful alternative to the liberal Protestant tradition. Thus, when Hauerwas claims that he is Barthian and working in a "Barthian framework," what he really means is that he learned from Barth to reject Protestant liberalism, and he continues to work out the implications of that basic theological move in his own context.

To say Hauerwas is an American Barthian is not to say, however, that Hauerwas simply repristinates Barth's theology. I think that Halden Doerge is basically correct when he writes, "Hauerwas understands his own work to exist along the trajectory of Barth's own work in some significant sense, carrying it *forward* in a way that exceeds Barth's own limitations."[10] Hauerwas himself suggests as much. In a critical reflection on the limits of Barth's ecclesiology, Hauerwas and Will Willimon write, "Part of our task is to hold up exemplification of Barth's theology better than Barth could himself."[11]

In the process of working out Barth's rejection of liberalism in his own context, Hauerwas decides that Barth's ecclesiology is insufficient to the task. In this regard, Hauerwas sees himself as "fixing" Barth's theology in order to effectively achieve its goal in his own American context. In this chapter, I will lay out the basic argument that Hauerwas is a Barthian in the sense that he learns from Barth to reject Protestant liberalism, and then he attempts to go beyond Barth in order to demonstrate what that looks like in his own American theological context—a context that is best described as determined by the modern nation-state, free-market capitalism, materialism, and individualism. In this regard, I will present the case that Hauerwas is what Stephen Webb called "an American version of Barth's thundering voice."[12]

---

[7]*M*, 34-35, 100.

[8]*DT*, 208

[9]*CCL*, 137; *PK*, 55; *STT*, 20-39.

[10]Halden Doerge, "Dueling Ecclesiologies: Barth and Hauerwas in Con-verse," in *Karl Barth in Conversation*, ed. W. Travis McMaken and David W. Congdon (Eugene, OR: Pickwick, 2014), 116.

[11]*WRAL*, 21.

[12]Stephen H. Webb, "The Very American Stanley Hauerwas," *First Things*, June 2002, 15.

THINKING WITH AND AFTER BARTH

Karl Barth famously broke onto the theological scene with his bombshell commentary on Romans. Worried that historical-critical exegesis "empties theology's task,"[13] Barth described his own theological exegesis as an attempt to "think with" (*mitdenken*) and "think after" (*nachdenken*) the apostle Paul.[14] In the preface to the third edition of *The Epistle to the Romans*, he made this point plain. First, one must devote "utter loyalty" to Paul by writing "with" him instead of "about" him. Only then, from this position of utter loyalty, can one learn to "see beyond Paul," or extend Paul's logic in new circumstances.[15] Barth would later go on to discuss his engagement with other theological and philosophical texts in a similar manner.

For example, when Barth penned his preface to the third edition of his Romans commentary in the summer of 1922, he was also in the midst of a lecture cycle on Calvin at Göttingen. Barth took great comfort in Calvin's suggestion that we should make ourselves contemporaries with Paul by counting ourselves among those addressed when Paul writes, "To the holy ones who are in Ephesus." Not only did Calvin's comment align with Barth's own intuitions about how to read Paul, but it gave Barth occasion to suggest that Calvin should be read the same way: "We shall not do violence to [Calvin] if we look at him from the same standpoint as he did at Paul, or, I might add, as Paul did at Abraham."[16]

For Barth, this meant three things. First, Calvin cannot be relegated to the past: "The historical Calvin is the living Calvin" who still speaks today.[17] Second, a good Calvinist will not simply repeat what Calvin said; a good Calvinist will allow Calvin to teach them as they enter into "a dialogue that may end with the taught saying something very different from what Calvin said but that they learned from, or better, through him."[18] Barth used his

---

[13]Karl Barth, "An Answer to Professor von Harnack's Open Letter," in *The Beginnings of Dialectic Theology*, ed. James M. Robinson (Richmond: John Knox, 1968), 1:177.

[14]For a more detailed analysis of Barth's exegetical method and his use of the terms *mitdenken* and *nachdenken*, see Richard E. Burnett, *Karl Barth's Theological Exegesis: The Hermeneutical Principles of the Römerbrief Period* (Grand Rapids: Eerdmans, 2004), 125-28.

[15]Karl Barth, *The Epistle to the Romans*, trans. Edwyn C. Hoskyns (Oxford: Oxford University Press, 1933), 17-19.

[16]Karl Barth, *The Theology of John Calvin*, trans. Geoffrey W. Bromiley (Grand Rapids: Eerdmans, 1995), 3.

[17]Barth, *Theology of John Calvin*, 4.

[18]Barth, *Theology of John Calvin*, 4.

own theological education as an example: "If as students they have really found a good theological teacher, as I once did in Wilhelm Herrmann, then they will surely know what I mean. We listen, we learn, and then we go our own way and in so doing we give evidence of respect, of doing the teacher justice."[19] Third, and finally, our attempts to make Calvin contemporary with us must be limited by the rule that "we cannot make Calvin say something other than what he said."[20]

Late in life, Barth had occasion to reflect on the influence that Kierkegaard had on his theology. He returned to the metaphor of tutelage, reflecting on Kierkegaard's work as a school. Some theologians never pass through Kierkegaard's school; as a result, they suffer from an overly positive and naive assessment of Christianity. Others "worked themselves deeper and deeper into Kierkegaard" so that they "failed to graduate" from his school and made his work into a system of thought. These poor souls suffer from an ever-present awareness of the many different problematic forms of Christianity. Finally, there are those who pass through Kierkegaard's school and graduate on to other schools of learning. They learn to see the crisis that Kierkegaard saw such that they cannot return to their naiveté and yet they are not paralyzed by it. They learn how to go on to further studies with other masters who might provide a confident theology this side of Kierkegaard.[21]

Barth counted himself among the last group of students. For Barth, thinking through the crisis of Protestant liberalism's tendency to collapse theology into anthropology with Kierkegaard's insistence on the radical otherness of God was an important first step. He had to learn, with Kierkegaard, to reject some of the worst effects of Protestant liberalism and pietism; then he had to take the next step and relearn, after Kierkegaard, how to talk about God.

The influence that Barth has on the theological ethics of Hauerwas is not unlike the manner in which Barth came to think of his own relationship with Paul, Calvin, or Kierkegaard. For Hauerwas, this means that in the first instance he learns from Barth how to reject the Protestant liberalism of his predecessors. In the second instance, however, working within this basic

---

[19]Barth, *Theology of John Calvin*, 4-5.
[20]Barth, *Theology of John Calvin*, 5.
[21]Karl Barth, *Fragments Grave and Gay*, ed. Martin Rumscheidt, trans. Eric Mosbacher (1971; repr., Eugene, OR: Wipf and Stock, 2011), 102-4.

Barthian trajectory, Hauerwas discovers that he must go beyond Barth. For Hauerwas, this "beyond" means returning to the third article of the creed, specifically ecclesiology, after learning from Barth's insistence on the centrality of the second article on Jesus Christ.[22]

That Hauerwas's "Barthianism" works this way is perhaps something that would have pleased Barth himself. Barth, after all, had no interest in founding his own Barthian school.[23] That there is one means that Barth would at least expect his students to graduate. The story of "Hauerwas, the Barthian" is the story of a young theologian who learns some key theological intuitions from Barth—not unlike those that Barth learned from Kierkegaard—and then goes on to address concerns that Barth, in his own time and place, did not. The "with" Barth and the "after" Barth are not identical, but there is a real continuity, a continuity forged by Hauerwas's determination to mirror Barth's rejection of liberalism in his own American context.

REJECTING LIBERALISM

Some of Hauerwas's earliest theological impulses can be traced back to his studies at Yale Divinity School. There he resonated deeply with Barth's rejection of liberalism. Particularly, Hauerwas associates Barth's rejection of liberalism with three aspects of his work: his opposition to Nazism, his theological method, and his formal decision to treat dogmatics and ethics together. Here, I will give accounts of each of these aspects of Barth's theology and how they manifest in Hauerwas's own work.

When Hauerwas first arrived at Yale, he was certain he would be a Protestant liberal. Schubert Ogden—an early interpreter of Rudolf Bultmann—forewarned him that Yale would turn him into a Barthian. Hauerwas's interest in the work of H. Richard Niebuhr prevailed, however, and he matriculated in autumn of 1962.[24] Ogden was right. Between Old Testament classes with Walther Zimmerli and Brevard Childs and his systematic theology class with Julian Hartt, Hauerwas received a healthy dose of Barthian theology.[25]

---

[22]For more on what I mean by the third article, and specifically my inclusion of ecclesiology, see above.

[23]Barth, *Romans*, 21-22; Karl Barth, *Letters: 1961–1968*, trans. Geoffrey Bromiley (Grand Rapids: Eerdmans, 1981), 321.

[24]*HC*, 14.

[25]*HC*, 49-52.

Hauerwas arrived at Yale with a handful of theological problems; chief among them perhaps was the Christian failure to stand up to Nazism. In Hartt's class, Hauerwas first learned that it was Barth, and not the Protestant liberals, who mounted the strongest theological rejection of the German Christian churches.[26] From this point forward, Hauerwas considered himself a Barthian. Writing with Will Willimon, Hauerwas claims, "For Barth, and for us, Nazi Germany was the supreme test for modern theology."[27]

The reason Barth passes the test while his peers fail is rooted in Barth's earlier rejection of Protestant liberalism. On the eve of World War I, Barth was horrified when most of his theology professors supported the Kaiser's war policy, affirming Germany's cultural superiority. He decided then and there that the theological, exegetical, and ethical presuppositions that allowed his teachers to make such a mistake must be given up altogether.[28] The result was a deeply theological rejection of Protestant liberalism.

The main problem Barth has with Protestant liberalism is one he learns from the atheist philosopher Feuerbach: God is the outward projection of humanity's inward need. Protestant liberalism displaces God with human nature and then projects a god that is entirely dependent on human experience.[29] Hauerwas writes, "Barth characterized the theology he thought must be left behind, a theology identified with figures such as Schleiermacher and Troeltsch, as the attempt to respond to the modern age by underwriting the assumption that Christianity is but an expression of the alleged innate human capacity for the infinite."[30]

Barth's solution was to turn to the radical otherness of God. "God is God and we are not" is the way Hauerwas describes the diastasis that Barth emphasizes between God and humanity.[31] For Hauerwas, the sentence "God is God" is shorthand for a cluster of key theological convictions that he learns from Barth. The first such conviction is that God is "wholly other" and cannot be found in creation, experience, or culture.[32] Protestant liberalism's

---

[26]*AN*, 65; *CDRO*, 94; *DF*, 19; and Hauerwas, "Faculty Forum," 70.
[27]*RA*, 24.
[28]*AE*, 78.
[29]*WGU*, 152.
[30]*AE*, 75-76.
[31]Hauerwas, "Karl Barth," 46.
[32]*WT*, 134.

attempt to treat "God-consciousness" as an expression of human experience fails to appreciate the "infinite qualitative distinction" that exists between God the creator and the contingent created order.[33]

A second and related conviction is that this radically other God "breaks in upon us 'perpendicularly from above'" in the incarnation.[34] God apocalyptically enters into his creation in the person and work of Jesus Christ, the second person of the Trinity, in order to overcome the diastasis and reveal himself to his creation. Protestant liberalism compromises traditional Christian convictions about the Trinity and Christ's divinity by emphasizing instead an immanent God who is immediately present in creation itself and, therefore, empirically knowable to the human subject.[35] The result is the human mastery of the divine, or, what William Placher calls "the domestication of transcendence."[36] For Hauerwas, this is "an attenuated gospel."[37]

Barth, instead, proposes that Jesus Christ is the basis for all true knowledge of God. Natural theology—knowledge of God naturally accessible to humans in creation—is the liberal Protestant attempt to possess God on terms other than those determined by Jesus Christ. In this regard, Barth is "engaged in a massive attempt to overturn the epistemological prejudices of modernity."[38] This means a rejection of German culture, human reason, and the natural sciences as a source and norm for theology equal to and alongside of Jesus.[39]

The reason Barth is able to mount a theological resistance to Nazism depends entirely on his theological break with liberalism: "The heart of Barth's theology is the presumption that if we get God wrong, we get everything wrong—our politics, our science, our very lives."[40] Barth gets his doctrine of God right because he begins with Jesus Christ. In turn, Barth's christocentrism funds the Confessing Church's recognition in the Barmen

---

[33]Karl Barth, "Preface to the Second Edition," in *Romans*, 10.

[34]*AE*, 77.

[35]*WWW*, 261.

[36]William Placher, *The Domestication of Transcendence: How Modern Thinking About God Went Wrong* (Louisville, KY: Westminster John Knox, 1996).

[37]*WT*, 37.

[38]*WGU*, 190.

[39]*WWW*, 261.

[40]Hauerwas, "Karl Barth," 46.

Declaration that Jesus Christ is the one true *führer* and that Hitler's claims to lordship must be rejected.[41] For Hauerwas, Barth's rejection of natural theology is not simply a contextual move that makes sense in the face of totalitarian fascism; it is the beginning of true theology.[42] This "true theology" has its own methodological sensibility.

Part and parcel of Barth's break with liberalism is a break with a number of methodological assumptions about how to do theology. For one thing, Barth refuses the modern habit of writing theological prolegomena. These sorts of preliminary theological discussions are often attempts to determine the philosophical and anthropological grounds on which theology might be made intelligible.[43] They are, in short, a return to the problems that plague natural theology.

Related to Barth's refusal to do prolegomena is his rejection of apologetics and theologies of mediation, or translation. For Hauerwas, the liberal Protestant project repeats the habits of modernity by assuming that theology must translate the language of the Christian faith into a universal language or begin with the external questions and concerns of other disciplines in order to make itself relevant.[44] Barth, in contrast, mobilizes the uniquely Christian language of Scripture in order to demonstrate how the Christian narrative engages the world without ceasing to be Christian. Hauerwas and Willimon write, "The theologian's job is not to make the gospel credible to the modern world, but *to make the world credible to the gospel.*"[45]

For another thing, Barth's theology is always provisional and unfinished. As Hauerwas puts it, Barth knew that "Christian theology always finds itself *in medias res*";[46] it is always a theology *on the way*. Barth knew that theology must take a form that is adequate to its own subject matter. Since God is infinite, theology is necessarily repetitive and incomplete.[47] Thus Hans Frei's suggestion that Barth engages in "conceptual re-description"—a process whereby Barth constantly repeats himself—is apt.[48]

---

[41]*HC*, 51.
[42]*PF*, 19.
[43]*PK*, 55.
[44]Hauerwas, "Faculty Forum," 77; *WRAL*, 20.
[45]*RA*, 24 (emphasis original).
[46]*STT*, 3.
[47]*WGU*, 173-74; *DT*, 231.
[48]*DF*, 59; *CET*, 57; *WGU*, 182.

With this aspect of Barth's work in mind, Hauerwas refuses to do systematic theology: "I have disavowed being systematic on what I assume are Barthian grounds."[49] Often a systematic approach distorts one or more aspects of the Christian faith in the name of superimposing coherence. When this happens, the systematic "explanation" of Christian faith becomes more basic than the Christian narrative of the God who reveals himself in Jesus. This is why Barth's work is better understood as description. Description bears witness to the thing described, allowing it to present itself on its own terms; explanation purports to know what the thing is on terms that are extrinsic and prior to the thing itself.[50] With regard to God, this is, again, an attempt to have God on anthropocentric terms.

Barth's theology is not systematic in nature because Barth knew it could never be complete. That does not mean, however, that Barth's theology does not offer a holistic account of reality. To the contrary, Barth's theology is an "unending and confident display of Christian speech" meant to train us in how to think about and speak about God and the world around us.[51] It is a training manual for Christian theology that requires its readers to become apprenticed in the language and practices of the Christian faith.[52] In this regard, Hauerwas considers Barth's work to be similar to Thomas Aquinas's. Each places an "uncompromising demand" on his readers to submit to a master as an apprentice in the faith.[53] Further, each teaches his readers "the skills necessary to sustain [Christian] speech in a world that thinks what we say is unintelligible."[54]

One of the ways Hauerwas thinks Christianity abandons its own particularity in order to make itself relevant to the modern world is by artificially divorcing dogmatics from ethics.[55] According to Hauerwas, "Once there was no Christian ethics simply because Christians could not distinguish between their beliefs and their behavior."[56] This changed, however, with the

---

[49] *WT*, 270.

[50] *WGU*, 146; *DT*, 229.

[51] *WGU*, 176.

[52] Stanley Hauerwas, "Hooks: Random Thoughts by Way of a Response to Griffiths and Ochs," *Modern Theology* 12, no. 1 (2003): 93.

[53] *HC*, 37.

[54] *WT*, 66.

[55] *PK*, 55.

[56] *STT*, 20.

Enlightenment. In an attempt to create stability and consensus in the midst of deep theological disagreement, dogmatics and ethics were severed. Ethics was the name given to the pursuit of morality grounded in universal reason, and Protestant theology became the attempt to prove that Christianity was still relevant to society as an ethos. Dogmatic assertions, like the doctrine of the Trinity and the divinity of Jesus, took a backseat to an attempt "to secure the ongoing meaningfulness of Christian convictions by anchoring them in anthropological generalization and/or turning them into ethics."[57]

When Barth rejected Protestant liberalism, he was rejecting a history of separating dogmatics from ethics that ran from Kant through Schleiermacher to Ritschl and his students. For Barth, "Dogmatics and ethics are not only inseparable; they are indistinguishable."[58] His *Church Dogmatics* is a sustained attempt to demonstrate that a robust theological metaphysic (a description of reality) necessarily includes an account of how to live in the world that is so described.[59] At least that is how Hauerwas reads the *Church Dogmatics*.

Barth's rejection of Protestant liberalism, in the end, becomes the jumping-off point for Hauerwas's own project: a criticism of the liberal Protestant tendencies of North American Christianity. Concerned that Christian ethics in America has become more about the liberal project of producing good citizens to sustain the nation-state, Hauerwas intentionally tries to reconnect Christian ethics to distinctive Christian convictions.[60] In short, he learned from Barth to "keep theological ethics theological," and he develops that line of thinking into a polemic to "keep American Christianity Christian" (as opposed to American).

In summary, Barth's rejection of Protestant liberalism is a rejection of a form of theology that is anthropocentric in content and method. He turns instead to the wholly other God who reveals himself in Jesus Christ as the source and norm for all theology. This move helps him to reject Nazism and any other attempt to ground theology in something other than Jesus Christ. As a result, his theological method takes the form of repetitive and

---

[57]*STT*, 30.
[58]*AE*, 210.
[59]*WGU*, 39, 168, and 184.
[60]*WT*, 57.

incomplete witness to Jesus Christ. As such, his theology requires its readers to undergo the hard work of training themselves to learn how to speak about God truthfully. But this speaking about God cannot be separated from the way one lives in the world. So, this training is not merely language training; it is moral formation. The *Church Dogmatics* teaches us how to see the world as it really is and how to live in that world in such a way that we bear witness to the God who created it. Dogmatics is ethics all the way down.

American Christianity, seeking to prove its continued relevance after Christendom, often abandons core Christian convictions about reality for the sake of describing human moral action on universal terms. The result is that American Christianity ceases to be Christian even as it becomes more American. Thus, from Hauerwas's perspective, the overall trajectory of his theological project is an extension of a line of thinking that he finds in Barth's theology: dogmatics and ethics are inseparable. Hauerwas inherits this claim and works through the implications of it in his own late modern, American context.

If Hauerwas is a Barthian in the sense that he extends a line of thinking he learns from Barth, then the proof will be found in Barth's rejection of liberalism, with its corresponding affirmation of the radical otherness of God and the centrality of Jesus and in Hauerwas's intentional extension of this trajectory in his own work. Therefore, any attempt to argue that Hauerwas is or is not Barthian will necessarily have to take stock of this inheritance in order to determine if and how Hauerwas follows Barth here and whether that is sufficient to be considered a Barthian. Crucial to such an investigation is an understanding of how Hauerwas sees himself going beyond Barth.

"FIXING" BARTH'S ECCLESIOLOGY

It may be true that Hauerwas developed an allegiance to Barth's theology at Yale. It is also true, however, that Hauerwas develops a line of thinking that leads to a career of critical engagement with Barth's theology. He does not merely inherit Barth's theology; he critically appropriates aspects he finds helpful even as he "fixes" aspects of Barth's theology that bother him. Particularly, Hauerwas criticizes Barth from two different lines of thinking. The first, dependent on his doctoral advisor, James Gustafson, eventually disappears from his thought; while the second, dependent on postliberalism, becomes more pronounced. The result is that Hauerwas develops a unique reading of Barth. Attention to what Hauerwas thinks needs fixing in Barth and how he proposes to fix it reveals the pressure points in Hauerwas's theology where his claim to be Barthian will ultimately stand or fall.

Hauerwas's first critical engagement with Barth's theology comes at the beginning of his career. In his dissertation, published as *Character and the Christian Life*, Hauerwas argues that Barth's theological ethics—indicative of Protestant ethics as a whole—are deontological in nature and controlled by the metaphor of command. For this reason, Barth risks giving short shrift to human agency. As a correction to this tendency, Hauerwas proposes a recovery of classical teleological notions like character and virtue as a means to account for the progress of the ethical agent over time.[61] Hauerwas is particularly concerned with how deontological ethics reduce to situation ethics in some cases, suggesting that the agent is entirely accidental while the decision is primary.

For the young Hauerwas, Barth's theological ethics do not reduce to situation ethics; they are far too robust for that. Nevertheless, Barth's description of ethics as hearing and responding to the command of God in each new circumstance "has affinities with a Kantian moral philosophy with its concentration on the individual act."[62] Each ethical event presents the hearer with the decision to obey or disobey. Previous obedience or disobedience offers little guidance to future decision. This has the effect of making the continuity of the human agent tangential to Barth's ethics. As a result, "Barth cannot fully account for the kind of growth and deepening that he thinks is essential to the Christian's existence."[63]

At the heart of Hauerwas's early criticism of Barth's ethics is a basic assumption (an assumption, I might add, that was shared by Emil Brunner): Barth's ethics, rightly concerned to emphasize the priority of divine action, often risks obscuring the real and meaningful way in which God invites human action. The dialectical tension between divine and human agency is relieved by a one-sidedness on Barth's part. The result is that ethics is often

---

[61]*CCL*, 2.
[62]*CCL*, 146.
[63]*CCL*, 176.

considered in an "occasional" fashion, leading to an atomized, moment-by-moment view of human ethical agents.

Hauerwas's early criticism of Barth is largely consistent with the best contemporary scholarship of the day. John Cullberg, for instance, criticizes the treatment of ethics in Barth's second commentary on Romans as follows: "Predestination . . . allows, or in fact implies, that the ethical question 'What should I do' is exchanged for another: 'What will I do?': or, better, "What will happen to me?' With this change to the future tense, every ethos is killed. Responsible human action in the real sense is completely out of the question."[64] Particularly, Hauerwas's concern that Barth's ethics are atomistic is dependent on Robert Willis, James Gustafson, and H. Richard Niebuhr, all of whom read Barth's command ethics as a type of deontology that cannot avoid intuitionism or occasionalism.[65] In recent years, however, a number of proficient Barth interpreters have demonstrated the inadequacy of these early readings.

According to John Webster, this larger trend in early studies of Barth's ethics is the result of the limited availability of Barth's *Gesamtausgabe*. These studies depend largely on Barth's *Römerbrief* and the ethics sections of *Church Dogmatics* in the doctrines of God (II/2) and creation (III/4). The effect of reading Barth this way is "to minimize the significance of human action and to maximize the sense of divine transcendence in the earlier writings, thereby promoting the picture that it is only with [*Church Dogmatics*] that Barth attains to a proper sense of the value of contingent history."[66]

Since the publication of *Character and the Christian Life*, the body of material that we have on Barth's ethics has grown in at least three significant areas: (1) Barth's 1919 Tambach lecture and early lectures on Calvin, (2) Barth's lectures on ethics from Münster and Bonn, and (3) Barth's unfinished ethics

---

[64]John Cullberg, *Das Problem der Ethik in der Dialektischen Theologie* (Uppsala: A.-B. Lundequistska Bokhandeln, 1938), 1:45, quoted in David Clough, *Ethics in Crisis: Interpreting Barth's Ethics* (Burlington, VT: Ashgate, 2005), 33.

[65]Robert E. Willis, *The Ethics of Karl Barth* (Leiden: Brill, 1971), 171; James M. Gustafson, *Christ and the Moral Life* (New York: Harper & Row, 1968), 93-94; and H. Richard Niebuhr, *The Responsible Self: An Essay in Christian Moral Philosophy*, with an Introduction by James M. Gustafson (New York: Harper & Row, 1963), 66. This is a point that Nigel Biggar has made especially with regard to Hauerwas's dependence on Gustafson and Willis (Biggar, *The Hastening That Waits: Karl Barth's Ethics* [Oxford: Clarendon, 1993], 20 n. 67).

[66]John Webster, *Barth's Moral Theology: Human Action in Barth's Thought* (Grand Rapids: Eerdmans, 1998), 14.

of reconciliation. All of these works give scholars a fuller account of Barth's ethics from his earliest to his last writings. The picture that emerges with these texts is a Barth who from beginning to end consistently concerns himself with human moral action.[67]

Working within this newer stream of Barthian moral theology, William Werpehowski takes up Hauerwas's basic theological concerns while defending Barth from the charges of "intuitionism" and "occasionalism."[68] Werpehowski argues that both criticisms share the mistaken assumption that Barth's self "is unable to express itself as shaped through a *history*."[69] These accounts fail to understand the manner in which Barth reforms terms like "command," "history," and "continuity."

First, Barth uses the terms "command" and "obedience" in a manner that "is bound to the history of God's dealings with humanity in Jesus Christ as depicted in Scripture."[70] Thus the corresponding notions of command and obedience are reformed as they are tied directly to a likewise reformed notion of history that centers on the personal history of Jesus Christ. This opens the door for an account of continuity in Barth's ethics, whereby "continuity" is also reformed to be understood as "repetition and renewal" instead of moral progress.

Central to Werpehowski's reading of Barth is his emphasis on Barth's "formed reference." Paul Nimmo succinctly explains the formed reference:

> The significant move which Barth makes to allow greater material specification of the discipline of theological ethics is to posit that alongside the vertical dimension of the command of God as a unique, concrete, particular event, there exists a corresponding horizontal dimension. As the command of God encounters the ethical agent vertically, in all its varied particularity, it also does so in a horizontal context, as part of a history of encounter in the covenant of grace. And thus each individual encounter in this history is always part of something larger: "the history of God's own action, work and revelation," or, from the opposite perspective, the history at the heart of which

---

[67]Webster, *Barth's Moral Theology*, 1-9.
[68]William Werpehowski, "Command and History in the Ethics of Karl Barth," *Journal of Religious Ethics* 9, no. 2 (1981): 298-320; republished in William Werpehowski, *Karl Barth and Christian Ethics: Living in Truth* (Burlington, VT: Ashgate, 2014), 15-35.
[69]Werpehowski, *Karl Barth and Christian Ethics*, 16.
[70]Werpehowski, *Karl Barth and Christian Ethics*, 19.

there is always "the action of the same subject, of man, this man." . . . This horizontal dimension of the ethical event encapsulates "the constancy and continuity both of the divine command and human action," and recognizes that the ethical event "takes place in the history of God with this man but also with all other men."[71]

Crucial, then, to Barth's ethics of command is the description he gives to the horizontal dimension of the ethical event. What we know about the everyday world in which we hear God's command—this horizontal dimension—is determined by the witness of Holy Scripture, which speaks concretely about the lives of people who are constituted by God's historical relationship with Israel and by Jesus Christ, whose life *is* the history of encounter between God and humanity. Theological ethics always begins with this formed reference as its guide in seeking to understand God's command in each new ethical encounter.[72] Werpehowski notes, "The individual's life-story is to be seen as overlapping with those of Jesus' disciples, and, accordingly, with that of Jesus Christ himself."[73]

Thus Werpehowski demonstrates that the formed reference means that Barth in fact does account for the sort of growth-in-continuity that Hauerwas wants. Continuity occurs primarily in God's action on behalf of humanity in the election of Jesus Christ. Responding to God's command requires people to deny their sinful existence and to reorient their lives in accordance with the obedience that is demonstrated by Jesus Christ. For Barth, influenced here by Luther, the new life of the ethical agent is one that is *simul justus et peccator*, meaning that the possibility of growth in the Christian life is always a matter of repetition and renewal: "a repetition of conversion and a renewal of commitment in new circumstances."[74]

Hauerwas had occasion to respond to Werpehowski in 1986, when he was invited to speak in Oxford, England, at a centenary celebration of Barth's birth.[75] Zeroing in on Werpehowski's description of Barth's method

---

[71]Paul T. Nimmo, *Being in Action: The Theological Shape of Barth's Ethical Vision* (London: T&T Clark, 2007), 44-45. Here Nimmo is predominantly drawing on Barth's account in *CD* III/4:16-28.

[72]Nimmo, *Being in Action*, 46-47.

[73]Werpehowski, *Karl Barth and Christian Ethics*, 26.

[74]Werpehowski, *Karl Barth and Christian Ethics*, 34.

[75]According to Werpehowski, the two had previously spoken in congenial personal conversations. See William Werpehowski, "Talking the Walk and Walking the Talk: Stanley Hauerwas's Contribution to Theological Ethics," *Journal of Religious Ethics* 40, no. 2 (2012): 229.

as conceptual redescription instantiated particularly in Barth's work on vocation, Hauerwas reasserts that Barth's ethics are too "abstract" and that his account of the moral life continues to feel "unreal."[76] In an exposition on Barth's account of honor, Hauerwas observes that although Barth claims that any discussion of honor must have "the concrete and therefore always the individual man" in mind,[77] his actual discussion of honor never moves beyond a general conception. As such, he offers a formal account of honor that lacks material substance.[78]

Using the fiction of Anthony Trollope as a counterexample, Hauerwas demonstrates that a concrete account of honor, or any aspect of character, requires (1) a description of the sort of community that forms an honorable person and (2) a narrative of the development of moral formation over time that can account for why a particular action is consistent with the character of the agent. Barth's problem is that the possibility of constancy, or what Werpehowski calls growth-in-continuity, is undercut by his dogged insistence that the command of God can call people to act "out of character."[79]

Hauerwas's response to Werpehowski clarifies the main thrust of his earlier criticism as focusing primarily on the concern that Barth's ethics remain abstract. Thus, while Barth *can* account for something like character, the problem remains that he rarely *does*. Hauerwas furthers this line of criticism by expanding it from the moral character of ethical agents to Barth's inattention to the community as the place where character formation takes place. This is an intermediate step toward a more significant criticism that Barth's ecclesiology is too abstract.

Over time, Hauerwas's early concerns regarding occasionalism recede, and he focuses most of his energy on arguing that Barth's theological ethics lack concreteness and therefore betray similar ecclesiological concerns.[80] With this shift, Hauerwas goes from arguing that Barth does not account for human agency to admitting that he does, while arguing that he does not provide the material conditions for what that actually looks like in the lives of individual Christians and the communities that sustain them. At this

---

[76]*DF*, 61.

[77]*CD* III/4:654, quoted in *DF*, 63.

[78]*DF*, 67.

[79]*DF*, 77-78.

[80]He last mentions it in *STT* (34), and even there he forgoes suggesting it is his own position.

crucial point, Hauerwas turns away from the concerns of a line of American liberal Protestant interlocutors that includes Gustafson and H. Richard Niebuhr and toward a new set of "postliberal" concerns that focus on the performative nature of the Christian faith.

This shift to a new postliberal line of criticism is important for two reasons. First, it demonstrates Hauerwas's increasing discomfort with his own liberal Protestant heritage. Second, it demonstrates a willingness on Hauerwas's part to reconfigure his own understanding of his relationship to Barth's work as Barth scholarship develops. In other words, Hauerwas cares enough about "understanding Barth" that he is willing to adapt his evaluation of Barth as his understanding of Barth grows. This suggests that Hauerwas may in fact be a serious candidate for being a Barthian in McCormack's sense of direct influence.

Understanding where this new postliberal line of criticism comes from depends on understanding Hauerwas's intellectual biography. I will tell the story of Hauerwas's postliberalism in chapter four. In the meantime, however, a few remarks are necessary in order to further my story about Hauerwas's Barthianism.

In a way, Hauerwas's earliest engagement with Barth's theological ethics is a push toward pragmatism. His appeal to Aristotle and Aquinas in order to recover the significance of virtue and character required him to account for how virtues are habituated through practice (*phronesis*). He only begins to understand the necessity of community for this type of moral formation after he reads Alasdair MacIntyre's *After Virtue*. Simultaneously, John Howard Yoder's work convinces him that the church is the community of character where Christian moral lives are formed. This happens as Christians learn the narrative of the gospel and perform it liturgically in communal worship.[81]

Most of this occurs while Hauerwas is teaching at the University of Notre Dame (1970–1984). During this period of intellectual formation, Hauerwas rarely engages Barth's thought. We know he still reads Barth because he teaches Barth to students at Notre Dame, demanding that his doctoral students be able

---

[81]Wells elaborates on the timing and nature of MacIntyre and Yoder's influence on Hauerwas's work in *Transforming Fate*, chaps. 2-4.

to account for Barth's ethics in their comprehensive exams.[82] Nevertheless, Barth is strangely absent from Hauerwas's coterie of dialogue partners in virtually all of his publications from this time period.

At the outset of Hauerwas's academic career, he engages Barth's work in his dissertation and vis-à-vis his growing appreciation for Yoder's work.[83] Two collections of essays from Hauerwas's early years at Notre Dame suggest the extent to which Barth falls into the background of Hauerwas's thought. *Truthfulness and Tragedy* (1977) is completely absent of reference to Barth,[84] while *A Community of Character* (1981) reduces Barth to a series of footnotes, most of which are used to support points made on other grounds.[85]

Even Hauerwas's magisterial *The Peaceable Kingdom* (1983) is sparse with regard to its references to Barth. For instance, in the introduction, he acknowledges a debt to Barth for his rejection of liberal methodology while also expressing concern for the limitations of Barth's high Christology.[86] In the body of the text itself, he appeals to Barth on one occasion as a theologian who understood the danger that liberal theology poses to the development of Christian ethics.[87] From that point forward, however, Barth is again reduced to a series of footnotes.

Two other works published in the midst of Hauerwas's transition from Notre Dame to Duke Divinity School mark a shift in Hauerwas's engagement with Barth. On the one hand, *Against the Nations* (1985) marks the reemergence of Barth in Hauerwas's thought. In this work, Hauerwas turns to Barth's rejection of Nazism as an influential example of how theological convictions entail ethical performance. For Hauerwas, Barth's rejection of liberalism allows him to name the theological problem of Nazism and to reject it.[88] On the other hand, *Suffering Presence* (1986)—a work published after Hauerwas arrived at Duke but based on material largely developed at Notre Dame—is again written without a single reference to Barth.

---

[82]*HC*, 108; Hauerwas, "Between Christian Ethics and Religious Ethics," 407.
[83]*CCL*, 136-46; *VV*, 197-221.
[84]Save for a footnote reference to Bob Krieg's dissertation, "The Theologian as Narrator: Karl Barth on the Perfections of God" (*TT*, 225 n. 30).
[85]The one material reference to Barth is in an essay on abortion, where Barth is quoted without any sustained engagement with Barth's treatment of the topic in *CD* III/4 (*CC*, 225). I will return to this citation in my exploration of Hauerwas's ethics of abortion in chap. 3.
[86]*PK*, xx-xxi.
[87]*PK*, 55.
[88]*AN*, 65.

Thus it is only with Hauerwas's move to Duke Divinity School (1985–2013) that Barth reemerges as a substantial dialogue partner.[89] *Christian Existence Today*, the first book written and published after Hauerwas moves to Duke, marks Barth's full-fledged reemergence in Hauerwas's writing. The title, an echo of Barth's memorable tract *Theological Existence Today*, indicates Hauerwas's own belief that his work assumes the spirit of Barth's rejection of Protestant liberalism.[90] Now reengaging Barth's work with a more developed account of the inherently communal and performative aspects of Christianity, Hauerwas hones his concerns regarding Barth's abstract ethics. For the first time, Hauerwas suggests that Barth's problem might be an underdeveloped ecclesiology.[91]

Working forward from this point, Hauerwas develops an argument that Barth has an "insufficient ecclesiology" because he does not pay enough attention to the church practices that are capable of developing ethical agents into witnesses.[92] This line of criticism reaches its fullest expression in Hauerwas's Gifford lectures, *With the Grain of the Universe*. Central to Hauerwas's criticism are concerns that Barth ignores first, the Holy Spirit's work in the concrete community of faith and, second, how the church becomes the means by which God cares for the world.[93]

Hauerwas learns both lines of criticism—that Barth's theology has a "pneumatological worry" and that the church becomes incidental to God's engagement with the world—from Joseph Mangina and Reinhard Hütter. In the first instance, Mangina argues that "since Barth treats the cross as bringing history to a close, the Spirit's work is 'short-circuited.' The Spirit can only appear as a predicate of Christ's reconciling work, a *manifestation* of the latter rather than an *agency* of its own." The effect of Barth's "pneumatological worry" is that there is "an odd hiatus between the

---

[89]Marking the end of Hauerwas's time at Duke Divinity School is somewhat arbitrary. I have chosen 2013 in coincidence with the daylong celebration of Hauerwas's "retirement" at Duke on November 1, 2013 (see *The Difference Christ Makes: Celebrating the Life, Work, and Friendship of Stanley Hauerwas*, ed. Charles M. Collier [Eugene, OR: Cascade: 2015]). Since that time, however, Hauerwas has been a fairly active "emeritus" member of the faculty even as he assumed a faculty post at the University of Aberdeen in Scotland for a handful of years.

[90]*CET*, 18.

[91]*CET*, 63 n. 4.

[92]*WGU*, 192-93; *WRAL*, 20-21.

[93]*WGU*, 144-45.

church . . . and the ordinary, empirical practices of the Christian community across time."[94]

Drawing on Hütter's work, Hauerwas argues that Barth's pneumatological deficiencies call into question whether "Barth is sufficiently catholic." For Hauerwas, "Barth is not sufficiently catholic just to the extent that his critique and rejection of Protestant liberalism make it difficult for him to acknowledge that, through the work of the Holy Spirit, we are made part of God's care of the world through the church."[95] Barth conflates the similarities between Protestant liberalism and Catholicism, leading him to reject any sense that the Holy Spirit is present and active in the church's liturgical practices. The result is that the church becomes accidental to the economy of salvation. Thus we arrive at the second concern Hauerwas has with Barth's ecclesiology.

In the second instance, Hütter suggests that Barth is right to worry about accounts of church practices that make the Holy Spirit a captive to the institutional structure of the church. Nevertheless, Hütter worries that Barth's actualism (i.e., Barth's insistence that God's presence always occurs in a God-determined event that cannot be domesticated) prevents him from recognizing the sacramental nature of church practices. For Barth, "God is who He is in the act of His revelation"; or, God's being is always known in relation to God's action, independent of any creaturely agency.[96] In contrast, Hütter argues that the church is "the soteriological locus of God's actions, as a space constituted by specific core practices and church doctrine. These practices are understood pneumatologically as acts to be interpreted enhypostatically as 'works' of the Spirit."[97] In other words, the church's liturgical action is sacramentally construed as both the work of the Spirit and the work of human agents. The relationship between divine and human agency here is one patterned after the hypostatic union, such that divine and human agency is neither conflated nor separated. The divine agent saves and the

---

[94]Joseph Mangina, "Bearing the Marks of Jesus: The Church in the Economy of Salvation in Barth and Hauerwas," *Scottish Journal of Theology* 52, no. 3 (1999): 270 (emphasis original). On "pneumatological worry," see 282.

[95]*WGU*, 145.

[96]*CD* II/1:257.

[97]Reinhard Hütter, *Suffering Divine Things: Theology as Church Practice*, trans. Doug Stott (Grand Rapids: Eerdmans, 2000), 27.

human agent becomes a participant in God's salvation of the world without any synergism. As Mangina writes, "in baptism, eucharist, and the like, human beings 'do,' but it is the Holy Spirit who saves."[98]

These problems with Barth's theology are not fatal for Hauerwas. Barth's theology "has the resources that provide for the development of a more adequate ethic," provided that you refocus those resources toward an account of ecclesial practices.[99] In order to show the way forward through the problem, Hauerwas develops a truly creative reading of Barth. Hauerwas explains, "I read Barth my way"—a way that he variously describes as "Aristotelianizing Barth," or giving him a Jamesian and Wittgensteinian reading.[100]

Hauerwas's "Aristotelianizing," "Jamesian," "Wittgensteinian" reading of Barth is a reading that emphasizes *how* Barth's theology performs its theological task. I will explore what Hauerwas means by this in greater detail in chapter seven. In the meantime, it is worth noting that this approach pushes Hauerwas back toward Barth's rejection of Protestant liberalism and the idea that his *Church Dogmatics* is a training manual for how to speak about God without merely projecting human desires onto the divine. At the same time, however, it opens space for Hauerwas's own theological project—a postliberal ecclesial ethic based on the liturgical formation of disciples—to be a genuine extension to and correction of Barth's theological program. Barth's ecclesiology cannot provide the material conditions for the formation of people who are able to continue his rejection of Protestant liberalism in an American Constantinianism that allies the church with nationalism and late modern capitalism. Therefore, Hauerwas's argument that he "fixes" Barth depends on the idea that he develops a particular plan for the church to be the school of moral formation that is needed to create morally responsible Christians capable of continuing Barth's rejection of Protestant liberalism in contemporary America.

In order to grasp the manner in which Hauerwas sees his own theological ethics as working "with Barth" to reject Protestant liberalism and then going "beyond Barth" to ensure that the American church is capable

---

[98]Joseph Mangina, "After Dogma: Reinhard Hütter's Challenge to Contemporary Theology: A Review Essay," *International Journal of Systematic Theology* 2, no. 3 (2000): 339.

[99]*WGU*, 20–21 n. 11.

[100]Hauerwas, "Hooks," 93; Hauerwas, "Faculty Forum," 70; Hauerwas, "A Place for God? Science and Religion in the Gifford Lectures," *Christian Century*, February 21, 2006, 44.

of continuing to reject the liberalisms that threaten it, we must pay further attention to Hauerwas's understanding of how Barth's theology works. In the next chapter, I will do just this, namely, explore how Barth and Hauerwas each treat the issue of abortion. From Barth, Hauerwas learns to refocus the question christologically. Then he pushes beyond Barth in order to think through the implications of Barth's Christology for the church's witness today.

3

Abortion,
Theologically
Understood

HAUERWAS'S THEOLOGICAL ETHICS tend to shift emphasis away from moral quandaries and toward thick description of moral communities and moral agents. Even so, Hauerwas continually returns to key ethical discussions throughout the course of his career. Pacifism, disability, and abortion are perhaps the three that receive the greatest emphasis. In order to offer a more concrete account of how Hauerwas's theological ethics depend on Barth's rejection of liberalism and then go beyond Barth's ecclesiology, I will attend here to Hauerwas's work on abortion. In the first and second sections, I will show how Barth's rejection of natural theology becomes the pattern for Hauerwas's rejection of natural law ethics. Then, in the third section, I will show how Hauerwas's ecclesial ethics transpose the debate over abortion into a specifically Christian idiom. This has the effect of considering the matter theologically, not from the first article of the creed as Barth did, but from the third article.

KARL BARTH: THE MOST "NATURAL" NATURAL THEOLOGIAN

Karl Barth's famous *Nein!* in 1934 continues to epitomize his radical rejection of natural theology and his break with his friend the Swiss, Calvinist, dialectical theologian Emil Brunner. Truthfully, the differences between the two theologians were always there: Barth gravitated toward the radical otherness of God, while Brunner—worried that this suggested a "one-sidedness" toward divine agency—gravitated toward the Christian life and moral progress.[1] Given that the early Hauerwas expressed similar concerns with Barth's theological ethics,[2] it would seem natural for Hauerwas to side with Brunner in this regard. That he sides, instead, with Barth is instructive for the manner in which Hauerwas sees himself as both continuing a line of theological ethics initiated with Barth's rejection of natural theology and returning to the question of the moral life after Barth.

In the pamphlet that provoked Barth's ire, *Nature and Grace*, Brunner attempted to defend the Reformed basis of his theology in six theses. The six theses are summarized as follows:

1. A distinction can be made between the formal *imago Dei* and the material *imago Dei*. In the fall, the material *imago* is destroyed while the formal *imago*—the human capacity for rationality and responsibility—remains intact.[3]

2. Knowledge of the Creator is revealed through the creation. This means that there is a double revelation: creation and Christ. The former, however, is not sufficient in and of itself to effect a saving knowledge of God.[4]

3. God establishes a preserving grace so that the worst effects of sin do not overcome human nature. In this regard, God graces all human life and activity.[5]

4. Within the sphere of God's preserving grace there are ordinances of creation and ordinances of preservation. On the one hand, marriage is an ordinance of creation, ordained by God prior to the fall. On the other hand, the state is an ordinance of preservation, ordained by God to preserve human flourishing in the face of sin and evil. Although the true meaning of these ordinances can be known only by faith, all humans naturally recognize their mere existence and necessity.[6]

---

[1] John W. Hart, *Karl Barth vs. Emil Brunner: The Formation and Dissolution of a Theological Alliance, 1916–1936* (New York: Peter Lang, 2001), 16.
[2] *CCL*, 171-72.
[3] Brunner, "Nature and Grace," 23-24.
[4] Brunner, "Nature and Grace," 25-27.
[5] Brunner, "Nature and Grace," 28-29.
[6] Brunner, "Nature and Grace," 29-30.

5. The formal *imago Dei* is a "point of contact" between God and humanity. After the fall, humans retain a natural capacity to receive divine revelation and are therefore responsible for sin. Humans know enough about God to know they are sinners, but not enough to know the extent of their sin and rebellion against God. This epistemic ability becomes the point of contact for faith as the knowledge of God's grace.[7]

6. The death of the old self that occurs in faith does not mean the end of the personal identity of the believing subject. Indeed, new life in Christ is a *reparatio* of human nature to its original created state. Thus there can be no talk of the destruction of original human nature and the *imago*.[8]

At the heart of Brunner's six theses is a concern that Barth's theology is "one-sided" regarding the doctrine of revelation. Barth's one-sided allegiance to an actualistic ontology prevents him from admitting "that where revelation and faith are concerned, there can be anything permanent, fixed, and, as it were, natural."[9] For Brunner, revelation is not just that God speaks (an act or event), but that God *has spoken* and this past speaking has become permanent in Scripture. There is a record of God's speaking that is now "at anyone's disposal."[10] Similar to the book of Scripture, the book of nature is a record of God's past revelation; creation is a record of God's actions. To deny that it is revelation is to deny that Scripture is revelation.

At stake for Brunner is a certain understanding of ethics and ecclesiology. First, with regard to ethics, Brunner states, "The theologian's attitude to *theologia naturalis* decides the character of his ethics."[11] A proper Christian social ethic will appeal to the double revelation of both the orders of creation and preservation as well as to God's self-revelation in Jesus Christ. Second, with regard to ecclesiology, Brunner is convinced that there are missiological and apologetic reasons for maintaining the idea of a point of contact, or a natural human capacity to receive revelation. The church's mission to proclaim the gospel depends on the idea that the Word of God might be received because it bears a resemblance to human words. Indeed, the church

---

[7]Brunner, "Nature and Grace," 31-32.
[8]Brunner, "Nature and Grace," 33-34.
[9]Brunner, "Nature and Grace," 48-49.
[10]Brunner, "Nature and Grace," 49.
[11]Brunner, "Nature and Grace," 51.

is responsible to make God's Word "comprehensible" through human words.[12] Brunner uses the example of children's and youth ministry in order to suggest that the church has the responsibility to prepare the message to overcome obstacles to its reception. Presumably this means translating the Word of God into an idiom that fits the audience.

Brunner ends his tract with the suggestion that "it is the task of our theological generation to find the way back to a true *theologia naturalis*."[13] This claim becomes the entry point into the discussion for Barth. It reminds Barth of the liberal Protestant tendencies of his teachers—tendencies that horrified him. Barth writes,

> Ever since about 1916, when I began to recover noticeably from the effects of my theological studies and the influences of the liberal-political pre-war theology, my opinion concerning the task of our theological generation has been this: we must learn again to understand revelation as *grace* and grace as *revelation* and therefore turn away from all "true" or "false" *theologia naturalis* by ever making new decisions and being ever controverted anew.[14]

To devote any time to the consideration of natural theology is to divert time from inquiry into the one true subject matter of theology: Jesus Christ. Barth calls natural theology a snake: "If you really reject natural theology you do not stare at the serpent, with the result that it stares back at you, hypnotises you, and is ultimately certain to bite you, but you hit it and kill it as soon as you see it!"[15]

Talk of a "point of contact," a "double revelation," and a preserving grace that is independent of God's redeeming grace all suggest to Barth that Brunner is snakebit. Each of these claims shifts focus from God's saving action in Jesus Christ to the innate human capacities of receptivity and responsibility. For Barth, this is a rejection of the Reformed hallmarks of *sola gratia* and *sola Scriptura*. First, Brunner's claims that humans retain a capacity to receive revelation after the fall and that creation is a source for knowledge of God independent of Christ both suggest that he has forsaken the hallmark of *sola gratia*. In the first case, if knowledge of God is dependent on a natural

---

[12]Brunner, "Nature and Grace," 56.
[13]Brunner, "Nature and Grace," 59.
[14]Barth, "No!," 71.
[15]Barth, "No!," 76.

human capacity, then humans contribute to their own salvation. In the second case, if creation gives certain and true knowledge of God, then that knowledge must necessarily be salvific. Second, when Brunner posits that there is a natural knowledge of God and natural laws in creation, he undermines *sola Scriptura*. Barth writes, "It is now purely arbitrary to continue to say that only Holy Scripture may be the standard of the Church's message . . . that the Church must be free from all natural and political restrictions!"[16]

With this claim, Barth already hints at the ethical concerns he has with Brunner's natural theology. Brunner's natural theology depends largely on the suggestion that the formal *imago Dei* is the natural human capacity to receive revelation and to respond. In other words, Brunner's theological anthropology has the ethically problematic force of defining human nature in terms of capacities that risk excluding infants, the mentally incapacitated, or anyone else who is incapable of making decisions.[17] Barth's christological anthropology, in contrast, functions eccentrically, determining what it means to be human in terms of the relationship that exists between God and each person.[18] As Joan O'Donovan points out, the strength of Barth's position is particularly striking against the historical background of the gas chambers. Barth's christological anthropology championed "those individual beings at the borders of human life: the unborn child, the severely defective infant, the very old and senile, the comatose patient."[19]

The Word of God, for Barth, creates its own capacity for reception in the person it addresses. Barth will have no talk of building hermeneutical bridges between the Word of God and human words. Rebutting Brunner's appeal to youth ministry, Barth writes:

> In my experience the best way of dealing with "unbelievers" and modern youth is not to try to bring out their "capacity for revelation," but to treat them

---

[16]Barth, "No!," 87.

[17]Barth, "No!," 88-89.

[18]I am, of course, borrowing the term "eccentric" from David Kelsey, whose two-volume theological anthropology *Eccentric Existence* is an exploration of what it means to be human from the perspective that humans receive their personal identity from without as both a gift from the triune God and a vocation (David H. Kelsey, *Eccentric Existence: A Theological Anthropology*, 2 vols. [Louisville, KY: Westminster John Knox, 2009]).

[19]Joan E. O'Donovan, "Man in the Image of God: The Disagreement Between Barth and Brunner Reconsidered," *Scottish Journal of Theology* 39, no. 4 (1986): 456.

quietly, simply (remembering that Christ has died and risen also for them), as if their rejection of "Christianity" was not to be taken seriously. It is only then that they can understand you, since they really see you where you maintain that you are standing as an evangelical theologian: on the ground of justification by faith alone.

I have the impression that my sermons reach and "interest" my audience most when I least rely on anything to "correspond" to the Word of God already "being there," when I least rely on the "possibility" of proclaiming this Word, when I least rely on my ability to "reach" people by my rhetoric, when on the contrary I *allow* my language to be formed and shaped and adapted as much as possible by what the text seems to be saying.[20]

For Barth, the theologian is confronted with two questions: "*What* has to be done? and: *how* is it to be done?"[21] Brunner's mistake is that he treats them as two separate and equal questions. Barth, in contrast, refuses to "seek the How outside the What."[22]

The question of the *what* and the *how* becomes, for Hauerwas, the question of the relationship between dogmatics and ethics. Brunner continues a line of Protestant liberalism that treats ethics as a second and equal subject matter alongside of dogmatics. Barth, in contrast, refuses to separate the two, addressing ethics within his doctrinal loci. Thus, while Brunner expresses similar concerns with Hauerwas regarding Barth's theology (i.e., a one-sidedness regarding divine agency), Hauerwas sides with Barth over and against Brunner because the manner in which the concern is expressed reflects liberal Protestant presumptions about the relationship between divine and human agency, dogmatics and ethics, and so on.

Hauerwas's treatment of Barth in *With the Grain of the Universe* amounts to an argument that Barth is "the most 'natural' natural theolog[ian]" because he properly understood that to devote time to the *how* without subsuming it within the *what* is "unnatural."[23] The story of how Barth rejects

[20]Barth, "No!," 127.
[21]Barth, "No!," 122.
[22]Barth, "No!," 126.
[23]*WGU*, 26; I borrow the expression "most 'natural' natural theologian" from Stanley Grenz, "Stanley Hauerwas, the Grain of the Universe, and the Most 'Natural' Natural Theology," *Scottish Journal of Theology* 56, no. 3 (2003): 381-86.

the unnatural theology of Protestant liberalism becomes, for Hauerwas, the story of how to reproduce a similar move in his own North American context. In short, the story of how Barth refuses to separate dogmatics and ethics becomes the inspiration for Hauerwas's own attempt to maintain the explicitly Christian character of Christian ethics. Thus, for Hauerwas, when it comes to attending to issues like abortion from a theological perspective, what Barth said about abortion is less important than how he frames the discussion, namely, making sure the *how* is always subsequent to and within the context of the *what*.

STANLEY HAUERWAS: THE CHRISTIAN DIFFERENCE

Hauerwas expresses discomfort with the idea of natural law. Particularly, he worries that after the Enlightenment, natural law theory reflects the divorce of theology from ethics by severing the relationship between nature and grace, law and gospel. In other words, Hauerwas expresses the same concerns that Barth expressed with natural theology: that the *how* question is treated as separate and equal to the *what* question.

Historically, natural law was always understood to be that set of moral convictions that a community presupposed to be basic.[24] In this regard, "natural" really meant something like "second nature," or convictions and practices that became so habituated in the life of the community that they felt "natural." In other words, "appeals to natural law, 'human nature' or 'reason' are best understood not as metaphysical descriptions necessary to ground ethical judgments, but rather value-laden notions that remind us of how we should best score and order our roles in the world."[25] Indeed, many classical theological treatments of natural law attend to the Decalogue, suggesting that natural law reflects a particular way of ordering the moral world that depends on the narrative of God's historical relationship with his people.[26]

With the Enlightenment, the attempt to secure morality on grounds that were common to people who had deep theological disagreements required that natural law be jettisoned from the particularity of the communities that

---

[24]*PK*, 51, 120.
[25]*TT*, 64.
[26]*STT*, 45.

made it "natural." Natural law was reimagined as a universal set of laws that governed the moral universe. Anthropologically, the human was also reimagined as primarily a thinking being. Rationality became the mark of what makes a human "human."[27] Thus natural law was naturally accessible to all humans by virtue of their natural reasonableness.

On these terms, Catholics and Protestants, Christians and non-Christians could all appeal to something more basic than their particular theological beliefs: a universal moral order. For many theologians, this meant that one of the tasks of theology should be to establish "the existence of an independent and objective realm of morality."[28] For Hauerwas, however, to consider such a project is to give weight to the "other task" of theology that Brunner spoke of when he spoke of natural theology. With Barth, Hauerwas worries that when theologians and Christian ethicists pursue natural law theory, they tend to give too much prominence and independence to the *how* question. As Hauerwas points out, "on this presumption, the theological task seems to entail trying to locate what all men . . . morally share in common."[29] The subject of natural law is not God, but humanity, and any theology that considers the pursuit of natural law independent of the God who gives the law to his people will necessarily become distracted from its primary task: to speak about God.

Hauerwas's rejection of natural law theory as a post-Enlightenment attempt to secure universal moral foundations is an extension of Barth's rejection of natural theology. In this regard, much of Hauerwas's theological ethics are a self-conscious attempt to beat back the "false universalism of liberalism."[30] This includes calling into question the presumptions that remain tacit in much of our modern moral discourse. One clear example of this is Hauerwas's treatment of the moral questions surrounding abortion. A comparison of Barth and Hauerwas on the topic demonstrates how Hauerwas learns from Barth to ground the question christologically and, then, how he breaks with Barth by pressing the question forward into the third article of the creed instead of backward into the first article.

---

[27]*TT*, 63.
[28]*TT*, 57.
[29]*TT*, 57.
[30]*AC*, 16.

ABORTION, THEOLOGICALLY CONSIDERED

Barth's treatment of abortion falls, unsurprisingly, in his ethics of creation in *Church Dogmatics* III/4.[31] I will elaborate on the theological ethics of the *Church Dogmatics* in chapter six. Briefly, however, let me summarize key aspects of Barth's *Church Dogmatics* in order to situate his account of abortion.

In *Church Dogmatics* II/2, Barth establishes that ethics inquires after the question of human action from the perspective of the human as the one who hears and responds to the command of God. Thus ethics is always entertained within the context of the God who commands. Inquiry into God's command begins with Jesus Christ because Jesus is both the God who commands and the human who obeys God's command. This insight carries forward into Barth's doctrine of creation in *Church Dogmatics* III. There, Barth treats creation christologically, arguing first that faith in God the Creator is grounded in Jesus Christ, who is both Creator and creature and, therefore, is capable of mediating knowledge of the Creator to the creation (§40). Jesus is also the fullest expression of human nature; therefore, he is the source for all true knowledge of human nature (§43).

Barth's ethics of creation in *Church Dogmatics* III/4 presuppose a christological determination for the relationship between God and humanity. What it means to be a creature of God is determined by the incarnation. From Christ's humanity, Barth discerns four lines of inquiry into human agency as it pertains particularly to humanity's creaturely existence: (1) the responsibility a creature has to her Creator; (2) the fellowship that creatures share with each other; (3) creaturely life, specifically human life as a union of body and soul; and (4) the limitation of creaturely life by time and space. For Barth all of these things follow from the fact that in the incarnation, Jesus becomes (1) a creature, "elected and summoned by God . . . to be responsible before Him"; (2) a human who encounters other humans, and therefore, his "fellow-humanity" as the image of God; (3) the subject of a material body that is indivisibly united to a soul; and (4) "a being which is allotted a fixed span" of life.[32]

Within Barth's treatment of human life, he identifies three broad lines along which the command of God usually occurs: the respect for life, the

---

[31]"Abortion, Theologically Considered" is the name of a lecture Hauerwas gave to a group of Methodist pastors from North Carolina in 1990 (*HR*, 603-22).

[32]*CD* III/4:43-44.

protection of life, and the active life. Abortion particularly falls within Barth's larger discussion of the command to protect life (§55.2). There, Barth first articulates that we must acknowledge the humanity of the unborn as a child, not a fetus, and therefore admit that abortion is a life-taking act. This is sinful to the extent that humans give themselves the last words with regard to the temporal life of another human; they take on themselves a decision that belongs to the divine office alone. The child in question is not merely a child who has a right to life:

> This child is a [human] for whose life the Son of God has died, for whose unavoidable part in the guilt of all humanity and future guilt He has already paid the price. The true light of the world shines already in the darkness of the mother's womb.[33]

For Barth, the chief problem in most accounts of abortion is the mistaken assumption that life is a necessity. Christians, instead, must cling to the doctrine of grace. Only then will the truly awe-inspiring nature of human life be appreciated for the gift that it is. Reconciled sinners will recognize the unborn child as a reconciled sinner as well and will receive the command to protect life: "Those who live by mercy will always be disposed to practise mercy, especially to a human being which is so dependent on the mercy of others as the unborn child."[34]

Thus Barth's treatment of abortion is conditioned by key theological and christological claims: God is the creator and giver of life, life is a gift that is received with gratitude; all human life is reconciled by Christ and, therefore, in covenant relationship with God; and finally, God's command generally comes in the mandate to protect life. This does not mean, however, that life becomes an absolute law. For Barth, there is always the *Grenzfall*, the borderline case.

One example that Barth anticipates is when the life of the mother is in conflict with the life of the unborn. Barth writes, "These situations may always be known by the concrete fact that in them a choice must be made for the protection of life, one life being balanced against another, i.e., the life of the unborn child against the health of the mother, the sacrifice of either

---

[33]*CD* III/4:416.
[34]*CD* III/4:418.

the one or the other being unavoidable."[35] In the case of life versus life, a decision must be ventured after a deliberate discernment of the question of the command of God. The one who is commanded can never know with certainty whether he has truly heard and obeyed God's command. He can only trust that he has heard it correctly, taking comfort in God's forgiveness should he have misheard the command and become disobedient. In this way, Barth ensures that neither the general prohibition against taking life nor the exceptional case of taking one life for another becomes an absolute or fixed ethical principle. In all cases, the command of God must be discerned anew and a decision must be made as a leap of faith.

Hauerwas sympathizes deeply with Barth's attempt to keep a christological focus on questions of creation and human life. His own treatments of abortion, however, focus not on the theme of discerning God's command but on the question of the church's vocation to welcome children. Thus Hauerwas seems focused not on abortion as a command pertaining to human life, but as a calling pertaining to ecclesial identity.[36] In short, Hauerwas seems to push the issue from the first article of the creed to the third article.

On the surface, this seems to undermine the suggestion that Hauerwas's ethics of abortion demonstrate a deep dependence on Barth. Further, it suggests that those who accuse Hauerwas's theology of reproducing the ecclesiocentric liberalism of Schleiermacher might be on the right track. Against these concerns, I want to argue that Hauerwas's ethics of abortion are deeply Barthian in the sense that they maintain a similar christological commitment.

Hauerwas begins his treatment of abortion by dismantling the liberal presuppositions that undergird the common arguments. Then he pivots toward a positive explication of how Christians should think about abortion from the perspective of the church's vocational self-understanding as a community of hospitality that bears witness to God's providence. This two-step pattern in his thinking is crucial for understanding how his theological ethics think with and beyond Barth. Insofar as he engages the matter with

---

[35]*CD* III/4:421.

[36]Hauerwas may not be far from Barth in this regard. In conversation with pietists, Barth suggests that God's command (grace) always entails a calling (apostleship). See Karl Barth, "Dialogue with Representatives of the [Evangelical] Community Movement (10/6/1959)," in *Barth in Conversation*, vol. 1, *1959–1962*, ed. Eberhard Busch, trans. Center for Barth Studies (Louisville, KY: Westminster John Knox, 2017), 21-24.

this two-step move, we see a clear example of how Hauerwas employs a Barth-like rejection of liberalism's attempt to treat the *how* without the *what*—or to address ethics outside of the scope of theology proper—and then moves beyond Barth's own theology toward an explicitly ecclesiological treatment of the matter.

In his earliest writings on the topic, Hauerwas expresses discomfort with the public discourse that surrounds the topic of abortion. Particularly, he worries that a public policy approach to the topic is fraught with problems.[37] Both sides of the debate appeal to common lines of argument that talk past each other because they depend on different moral descriptions of the act.[38] Ironically, both sides attempt to appeal to descriptions that can compel agreement from anyone (i.e., life and liberty); thus both sides are beholden to the liberal assumption that ethical questions should be considered in universal terms.[39]

For Hauerwas, when Christian ethicists attempt to join these public debates, they end up ceasing to be Christian. They capitulate to the assumption that if their moral principles depend on theological claims, their arguments will be ineffective in the public sphere.[40] In so doing, Christians actually underwrite the very liberalism that disconnects Christian morality from the narratives and traditions that make Christian claims intelligible in the first place.[41]

Hauerwas shifts the discussion of abortion from a public policy question to a question of Christian identity. The church, as the communal expression of Christianity, becomes the proper locus for a discussion of abortion. On these terms, the central question is not, When does life begin? or, Do I have a right to make decisions about my own body? but, Why do we have children? Christians are not required to get married and procreate; therefore, having children is not "natural" for Christians.[42]

For this reason, getting married and becoming a parent are reconceived as vocations. Particularly, being a parent is a vocation to which all Christians are called. Baptism reconfigures natural relationships so that the primary

---

[37]*RA*, 69-71.
[38]*VV*, 134.
[39]*CC*, 198.
[40]*BH*, 119.
[41]*IGC*, 105.
[42]*CC*, 209-10.

concept of family is no longer the biological family but the church. In baptism, the whole community makes a commitment to raise a child in the faith, thus making each member a parent.[43]

As the community continues to welcome new children, it bears witness to the rest of the world that God is in control. Amid all of the dangers of the world and fears about the future, Christians continue to demonstrate confidence in God's coming kingdom by having children. Abortion undermines the church's witness to God's providence to the extent that it is a vote of no confidence in the future.[44]

Hauerwas's rejection of the liberal presumptions that fund abortion discourse followed by his attempt to refocus the discussion in terms of the church's language and vocation demonstrates clearly the two-step pattern I described above. First, he learns from Barth to reject natural theology, in this case appeals to rationality and universal laws regarding what constitutes life or liberty. Second, he moves beyond Barth in order to explicate the church's approach to vocation. Where Barth returns to the first article of the creed to treat the ethics of abortion from the question of the doctrine of creation and questions of life as a command of God the Creator, Hauerwas moves forward to the third article of the creed in order to treat it from the question of the church's vocation to bear witness to God.

This shift to the third article certainly represents a move "beyond" Barth. What is often missed, however, is the deeply christological heart of Hauerwas's move toward ecclesiology. Going "beyond" Barth, even here, depends significantly on Barth's christological anthropology. This is a point that requires further illustration.

In "Abortion: Why the Arguments Fail," Hauerwas repeats the line of argumentation I've described above. First, he attends to the discourse on abortion in liberal societies. Drawing on Alasdair MacIntyre, Hauerwas argues that to the extent that liberalism promises to free individuals from the yoke of tradition, it creates people who argue from presuppositions that seem arbitrary and contradictory. Christians, attempting to work within a liberal framework, have neglected their own traditional accounts of morality, preferring instead to appeal to theories of behavior that appear reasonable in a

---

[43]HR, 612-13.
[44]CC, 209.

pluralist context. For this reason, Hauerwas contends, "Christian opposition to abortion on demand has failed because, by attempting to meet the moral challenge within the limits of public polity, we have failed to exhibit our deepest convictions that make our rejection of abortion intelligible."[45]

Hauerwas calls for Christians to attend to how the church thinks about abortion instead of how society should think about it. Communities are constituted by forms of life and share a common language. The mere fact that Christians use the language of "abortion" instead of "terminating a pregnancy" means that the church has a particular moral assumption about the act that is being described. Any subsequent question about permitting abortion begins with the shared presupposition that the act of abortion is not a moral good.

Christian language has its origin in the Christian narratives about God's historical relationship with Israel and the life of Jesus Christ. To be sure, Christians share an affinity with the argument from natural law that life is sacred and therefore must not be taken. But more importantly, for Hauerwas, the Christian narratives about creation tell us not only that God is the author of life but also that life itself is a gift from God. Thus the argument for respect for life is not, finally, grounded in a natural law about the inherent worth of life, but in a theological claim about the God who gives life.

Even creation, however, is not the central theological impetus for challenging abortion. Following Barth, Hauerwas turns to the doctrine of reconciliation—the second article of the creed—to ground a theological account of abortion. For Barth, remember, the unborn is a person "for whose life the Son of God has died, for whose unavoidable part in the guild of all humanity and future individual guilt He has already paid the price."[46]

In the first instance, then, the Christian prohibition of abortion bears witness to the God it worships: "The Christian respect for life is first of all a statement, not about life, but about God."[47] For Hauerwas, shifting the conversation from the public sphere to the church is a clear rejection of the liberal assumptions that divorced ethical discourse from theological commitments in the first place. It is an attempt to articulate the *how* of human life within the *what* of the God who gives life.

---

[45]*CC*, 212.
[46]*CD* III/4:416, quoted in *CC*, 225.
[47]*CC*, 226.

Hauerwas does not simply stop with Barth at this point. Second, Hauerwas goes on to positively articulate the role the church plays in reengaging society with a theologically loaded response to abortion. In this sense, he goes "beyond" Barth on this topic in order to develop an ecclesiology of witness. Hauerwas writes, "We also believe that God has created and called us to be a people whose task it is to manifest and witness to his providential care of our existence."[48] Particularly, the church is a historical community that demonstrates a historic trust in God. On these terms, "children represent our continuing commitment to live as a historic people" because we can trust that the God who is Lord over history is in control.[49]

The Christian vocation of marriage entails openness to children because the love that Christians share is a love that is always open to strangers: "Children, the weak, the ill, the dispossessed provide a particularly intense occasion for such love, as they are beings we cannot control."[50] Welcoming these strange children and parenting them is a vocation the whole church shares. Christians cannot publicly decry abortion unless they themselves demonstrate they are a community of "people who stand ready to receive and care for any child."[51] When they do so, they bear witness to their abiding trust in God.

In summary, Hauerwas's treatment of abortion works something like this: Christians are a people who do not permit abortion because the very act calls into question their deepest convictions about who God is as creator and provider. It further calls into question the lordship of Jesus Christ, suggesting that we must act to secure our own futures against the fears of our present age. By refusing to practice abortion, the church bears positive witness to God's sovereignty by accepting children and raising them. This is "a sign of the trustworthiness of God's creation and his unwillingness to abandon the world to the powers of darkness."[52] Thus, for Hauerwas, rejecting the liberal attempt to separate theology from ethics is not just grounding ethical claims in theological convictions; it also requires a prescriptive move toward ethical action grounded in the very theological convictions exemplified by that ethical action.

---

[48]*CC*, 226.
[49]*CC*, 226.
[50]*CC*, 227.
[51]*CC*, 229.
[52]*CC*, 227.

Here, Hauerwas presses beyond Barth insofar as Barth prefers to leave his ethical account of abortion within his doctrine of creation. There are, to be sure, clear implications for Barth's account of abortion. At the same time, for Barth, any prescription would undermine his insistence that ethics is a response to God's command. When Hauerwas presses toward the third article of the creed in order to explicate the church's ethical responsibility in light of its convictions regarding God's providence, he contradicts Barth's ethical sensibilities. Mainly, he risks foreclosing on the possibility that God might speak a new command. For Barth, this means to return to the problem at the heart of natural theology: anthropocentrism. The knowledge of God secured through attention to God's historical providential care of Israel becomes a truism that can now be appealed to without a fresh discernment of God's command for us today.

This is a real concern to be sure, and I will address it in the following chapters. In the meantime, however, it is worth pointing out that Hauerwas's move to the third article of the creed, his so-called ecclesiocentrism, is not anti-Barthian in this instance. In fact, his insistence on the church's vocation to parent children as a witness to God's providence is actually deeply Barthian with regard to its insistence on a christological anthropology. Not only does Hauerwas appeal to Barth's claims regarding the unborn child falling within the scope of Christ's reconciling action; his appeal to baptism as a means for understanding the church's vocation to witness grounds his ecclesial ethics in Christ's humanity. Drawing on Robert Jenson, Hauerwas reminds us that baptism is "the only available paradigm of human personhood."[53] Thus for Hauerwas to begin his ethics of abortion within the context of the church's practice of baptism means to begin with a central christological conviction: that what it means for Christians to speak of human nature begins with the human nature that we share with Jesus Christ through our baptism. The ecclesial practice is always rooted theologically in the understanding of both divine and human agency that is revealed in Jesus Christ.

This point often goes unnoticed in explorations of Hauerwas's theological ethics. Scholars are quick to notice that Hauerwas's treatment of these matters often begins in the third article while Barth's begins in the first. I

[53]Robert Jenson, *Systematic Theology*, vol. 2, *The Works of God* (New York: Oxford University Press, 1999), 289, in *BH*, 124-25.

have demonstrated here that Hauerwas's ecclesial ethics share a similar christological center in the second article with Barth before moving in different directions. In other words, I have tried to suggest that Hauerwas learns to begin with Jesus Christ as the *what* of theological ethics and then he presses toward ecclesiology in order to express his own understanding of the *how* question. Those who hold the Schleiermacher thesis, however, worry that what really happens in Hauerwas's theology is that he differs with Barth not merely about the *how* but about the *what*. This is why Nicholas Healy argues so forcefully that Hauerwas's theology takes the *what* of theology to be the church itself.[54] Before I move further in my narrative of Hauerwas's creative move beyond Barth, I must pause and address these objections head on.

SUMMARY

In this chapter, I have argued that Hauerwas learns from Barth to reject liberalism by rejecting the attempt to sever dogmatics from ethics, the *what* from the *how*. In Hauerwas's own application of this lesson, however, some tensions with Barth's theology emerge. For one thing, it is not clear that both theologians share a common definition of dogmatics. For Barth, dogmatics is talk about God and cannot be reduced, as he worries the Protestant liberals and the Catholics do, to talk about the church. At the same time, however, dogmatics is clearly a task for the church; it is the means by which the church tests its own language about God. Healy and others have suggested that for Hauerwas, dogmatics is actually about the church. Therefore, Hauerwas's theology is a return to liberal Protestant sensibilities. This question must be deferred until parts two and three, where I will be in a better position to answer this concern after I have explicated Hauerwas's postliberalism.

A more immediate problem, however, is that even if Barth and Hauerwas share a common conception of the *what* of dogmatics, Hauerwas clearly breaks with Barth regarding the *how*. Where Barth turns to the God who commands, Hauerwas turns to the church that worships God; where Barth is concerned with divine agency, Hauerwas attempts to give greater focus to human agency. In other words, Hauerwas returns to some of Brunner's most

---

[54]Nicholas Healy, *Hauerwas: A (Very) Critical Introduction* (Grand Rapids: Eerdmans, 2014).

basic theological concerns with the assumption that Barth is right to insist that these things cannot become more determinative than Jesus Christ and, yet, through Jesus Christ we can and must say something about them. Ultimately, this leads Hauerwas to embrace casuistry where Barth previously rejected it.

4

Breaking Barthian

ONE OF THE MOST SIGNIFICANT challenges to the argument that Hauerwas is a Barthian is the widespread assumption that Hauerwas's work, with its central focus on the church, bears a certain resemblance to the liberal Protestant theologians with whom Barth makes a break. Muddying the waters is Hauerwas's own admission that his work continues to repeat the habits of Protestant liberalism even as he tries to break them. More so, he readily admits that he learned many things from Protestant liberalism, not the least of which is the importance of the life of Jesus.

When Hauerwas admits that his work retains these themes, is he blind to the manner in which they contradict his claims to be a Barthian? To the contrary, I propose that Hauerwas thinks of himself as a sort of Barthian postliberal: a theologian who returns to some of the key concerns of the liberal Protestant tradition with a chastened Barthian awareness of the dangers that lie within. To that end, I have told a story about how Stanley Hauerwas found in Karl Barth a teacher who taught him to do theology in a manner that overcame the liberal divide between dogmatics and ethics. It is time to finish that story now by attending to a second stream of theological influence in Hauerwas's thought: postliberalism. For Hauerwas, postliberalism comes to represent how to speak meaningfully about human agency without giving it precedence over divine agency.

In this final narrative-driven chapter, I will locate Hauerwas within the postliberal tradition by attending, first, to the influence that H. Richard Niebuhr and John Howard Yoder have on Hauerwas and, second, to Hauerwas's own understanding of postliberalism as performance. Then, in chapter five, I will demonstrate how Hauerwas's postliberalism shapes his Barthianism. Ultimately, I will conclude by arguing that Hauerwas's way of interpreting Barth is a legitimate interpretation that includes him within the scope of Bruce McCormack's definition of "direct influence."

THE ORIGINS OF HAUERWAS'S POSTLIBERALISM

From the outset I have entertained the suggestions made by Barthian theologians that Hauerwas's theology is a revival of the liberal theologies of Schleiermacher and Ritschl. While these suggestions continue to have merit, I offer instead an alternative thesis: Hauerwas's theological ethics are the result of a fusion of Barthian and postliberal theologies. In this regard, scholars who see vestiges of Protestant liberalism in Hauerwas's thinking would probably do better to look to Troeltsch than to Schleiermacher or Ritschl.

Nathan Kerr nods in this direction when he puts Hauerwas on a spectrum between Barth and Troeltsch. For Kerr, Barth's rejection of Protestant liberalism sets the foundations for an apocalyptic Christology over and against Troeltsch's immanentist historicism. Kerr worries, however, that

> Barth's "actualism," particularly as it frames his understanding of the resurrection, makes of God's action in Christ an event of history precisely as it maps that history onto a privileged ontological framework, which is part and parcel of a privileged metaphysics of eternity. As a result, Barth identifies Jesus with God's being-in-act in such a way as to effect a twofold abstraction from the *contingent* reality of Jesus' historicity and of ours.[1]

The result of this abstraction is that "while the resurrection brings closure to Jesus' history, so also does it bring with it the very foreclosure of all history qua 'history.'"[2]

Further, Hauerwas, according to Kerr, takes Barth's apocalyptic Christology and supplements it with a narrative ecclesiology. This has the effect of "shifting the doctrinal locus of apocalyptic from Christology to ecclesiology" and, therefore, expounding "a 'community-dependent' understanding of

---

[1] Nathan R. Kerr, *Christ, History, and Apocalyptic: The Politics of Mission* (Eugene, OR: Cascade, 2009), 80.

[2] Kerr, *Christ, History and Apocalyptic*, 87.

Christ's person that is a reduction of Jesus' historicity or 'independence' as a singular event of God's apocalyptic action."[3]

Hauerwas follows Barth by rejecting liberal conceptions of history that are not "christologically disciplined"; then he goes beyond Barth to espouse an ecclesiology that posits the church as an alternative polis.[4] Thus Hauerwas seeks to overcome Barth's foreclosing of history through attention to the historical identity of the church as the community that bears witness to and lives by Christ's lordship in time and space. In so doing, however, he "insist[s] upon privileging the church itself as *subject* and *agent* of the Christ-story." The narrative becomes less about Jesus and more about the community that embodies the narrative: "the teller and the tale are one."[5]

For Kerr, this is obviously demonstrable by the fact that Hauerwas ultimately privileges the church to the Scriptures. The Christian community, with its particular cultural-linguistic identity, becomes the mediator of the Jesus narrative at the expense of the Gospel texts that bear witness to Jesus' own historical identity. In this regard, Hauerwas repeats some of the same theological mistakes Kerr sees in Troeltsch: "Hauerwas's anti-liberalism involves the church in its own *teleological*-eschatological concern to 'organize' and to 'order' the given contingencies and complexities of human historicity, precisely for the sake of 'keeping [its] story straight' in history."[6]

If Kerr is right to suggest that Hauerwas's theology reflects a vestigial Troeltschianism, then I am confident that Hauerwas owes it to his postliberal sensibilities, sensibilities that were forged in his early encounters with Niebuhr. Indeed, we might say that H. Richard Niebuhr is the father of postliberalism. Although the term *postliberal* became famous with Lindbeck's *The Nature of Doctrine*, to my knowledge the first use of the term actually occurs in Niebuhr's 1946 essay, "The Doctrine of the Trinity and the Unity of the Church." There Niebuhr used the term *post-liberal* (with a hyphen) in order to describe a group of theologies that attempt "to recover the Christian theological heritage and to renew modes of thought which the anti-traditional pathos of liberalism depreciated."[7]

---

[3] Kerr, *Christ, History and Apocalyptic*, 93.
[4] Kerr, *Christ, History and Apocalyptic*, 96.
[5] Kerr, *Christ, History and Apocalyptic*, 106-7.
[6] Kerr, *Christ, History and Apocalyptic*, 126.
[7] H. Richard Niebuhr, "The Doctrine of the Trinity and the Unity of the Church," *Theology Today* 3, no. 3 (1946): 371.

Although Hauerwas does not come to think of his theology as postliberal until after Lindbeck's *The Nature of Doctrine*, if we want to understand the origins of his postliberalism, we have to begin with Niebuhr. In order to tell this story, we must go back to the beginning; back to Pleasant Mound, Texas—the place of Hauerwas's youth.

Between Barth and Troeltsch

Stanley Hauerwas was baptized and grew up among the faithful members of Pleasant Mound Methodist Church. His father—a bricklayer—oversaw the construction of the church's sanctuary, and his mother devoted her life to its service. In a letter written to his grandchildren, Hauerwas reports, "our lives centered around the church."[8]

Pleasant Mound was a rural Methodist church. By Hauerwas's account, it was a liturgically low Methodist church and probably had more in common with local Baptists than it did with the high church Methodists of the urban centers of mid-twentieth-century America. Pleasant Mound was a rural mainline Protestant church, which means that it was neither liberal nor fundamentalist. It simply did not have the sophistication to fashion itself in either mold. Nevertheless, it demonstrated both the tendencies of Protestant liberalism and conservative American politics.

It was in Pleasant Mound where Hauerwas first became indoctrinated into the theology of Protestant liberalism. In high school, he was invited to preach before the congregation. Scared that he would not be up to the task, he borrowed a sermon from a book he found in the church library by Harry Emerson Fosdick. Reflecting on this experience, he writes, "It gives me great pleasure to remember that my first sermon was stolen from a Protestant liberal."[9]

Hauerwas, by his own account, was an avid reader and had a fondness for theological texts. During his senior year in high school, Hauerwas read two works by H. Richard Niebuhr: *The Meaning of Revelation* and *Christ and Culture*. In many ways, these two theological works frame the story of the next fifteen or so years of Hauerwas's life.

---

[8]*HC*, 24.
[9]*HC*, 5.

When Hauerwas first read *The Meaning of Revelation*, he did not understand what he was reading. He writes, "I read it when I was a senior in high school well before I had ever heard the names of Lessing, Troeltsch, or Barth. Reading it that first time did little for me, as I had no idea why there was a problem about history."[10] It was not until the end of his time as a philosophy major at Southwestern College in Georgetown, Texas, that Hauerwas came to appreciate Niebuhr's argument.

In college, Hauerwas encountered the work of philosopher R. G. Collingwood and became deeply concerned with "the problem of history." According to Collingwood, the chief innovation that Christianity made on Greco-Roman historiography was to understand human agency as derivative of divine agency. Thus human action in history is determined by divine providence instead of human wisdom or determination. For Collingwood, this is a marked improvement on the Greco-Roman conception of history because it locates human agents in particular times and places and posits that they are the product of a grander historical process.[11] Nevertheless, for Collingwood, history must be about human action as we can know it, not divine action.

Collingwood's account of historical research and his particular concern for human action left a strong impression on the collegiate Hauerwas, who "was sure any account of Jesus' life and its relation to our own involved questions of historical explanation and human activity."[12] In short, Collingwood gives Hauerwas a way to pay attention to human agency without getting his metaphysics "right" first.[13] Hauerwas's critics often take his lack of attention to articulating his metaphysical presuppositions to mean he does not have any. To the contrary, Hauerwas's career has been a sustained focus on the intelligibility of human actions in light of basic Christian convictions about the nature of reality.

Collingwood turned Hauerwas toward the importance of history and human agency, but it was Niebuhr who helped him work through some of the christological implications of this turn. Rereading *The Meaning of*

---

[10]*US*, 84.
[11]R. G. Collingwood, *The Idea of History* (Oxford: Oxford University Press, 1956), 46-50.
[12]*PK*, xx.
[13]Stanley Hauerwas, "Connecting: A Response to Sean Larsen," *Scottish Journal of Theology* 69, no. 1 (2016): 42.

Revelation after his study of Collingwood proved significant for Hauerwas. Niebuhr gave him "a way to think 'Jesus'" in a manner that respected some of the concerns with history that he learned from Collingwood.[14]

The Meaning of Revelation is an attempt to think about the relationship between faith and history in the face of relativism by combining Barth's theology of revelation with Ernst Troeltsch's historicism. Niebuhr explains, "I have tried to combine their main interests, for it appears to me that the critical thought of [Troeltsch] and the constructive work of [Barth] belong together."[15] This combination results in the birth of several themes that will become central to Niebuhr, his Yale students, and eventually Hauerwas.

We are "unable to avoid the acceptance of historical relativism," claims Niebuhr.[16] Historical relativism requires us to be aware of the fact that our point of view inescapably shapes the way we come to know anything. Like all other forms of philosophical inquiry, theology must also take note of this observation.[17] An appropriately critical historical theology is one that understands it cannot prescribe a religious form of life for all times and places. Instead, it seeks to

> state the grammar, not of a universal religious language, but of a particular language, in order that those who use it may be kept in true communication with each other and with the realities to which the language refers. It may try to develop a method applicable not to all religions but to the particular faith to which its historical point of view is relevant.[18]

Theology, with its own grammar and its own method, has its proper home in a community that maintains a historic faith—the church. This does not make theology private or subjective. Quite the opposite, in fact; because it is done historically and becomes a part of the historical tradition of a living community, theology is subject to both the test of contemporaries who hold the same point of view and the determinations of the community's past experiences.[19]

---

[14]*HC*, 14.

[15]H. Richard Niebuhr, *The Meaning of Revelation* (1941; repr., Louisville, KY: Westminster John Knox, 2006), xxxiv.

[16]Niebuhr, *Meaning of Revelation*, xxxiii.

[17]Niebuhr, *Meaning of Revelation*, 7.

[18]Niebuhr, *Meaning of Revelation*, 9.

[19]Niebuhr, *Meaning of Revelation*, 9-11.

The appropriate sort of critical historical theology that Niebuhr has in mind is a theology of revelation. Such a theology begins in and with a historical community because there is no neutral point of view. For this reason, a theology of revelation is necessarily confessional. It cannot privilege revelation as a superior form of knowledge, turning revelation itself into an idol. Instead, it can only begin with a confessional statement about "what has happened to us in our community, how we came to believe, how we reason about things and what we see from our point of view."[20]

This confession is the "story of our life," and it is the story of the God of Israel and Jesus Christ. The church is a community that is sustained not by metaphysical or moral systems, but by this story as it is told in the New Testament. The relationship between the story and the community who tells it is significant. For instance, to a nationalistic community, the New Testament can point to blood and soil; or to a democratic society it may point to the individual and political or economic notions of freedom. In neither case does the Bible fit the description of revelation. Scripture becomes revelation when it is viewed from the perspective of a historical and traditional community of people who "listen for the word of God."[21]

Revelation in this sense need not be excluded from the category "history." Instead, it holds a prominent place within the history of a particular community. This type of history is the difference, according to Niebuhr, between history as "lived" and history as "seen from the outside," or inner and outer history. In a series of comparisons, Niebuhr draws out the distinction between inner and outer. It is the difference between selves and things (Buber's Thou and It), between time as quantitative and time as duration, between humans as individual biological units and humans as people in a web of personal relationships. Finally, it is the difference between Kant's concepts of pure and practical reason.[22]

Niebuhr's *The Meaning of Revelation* holds a significant place in Hauerwas's theological education. It forms his imagination with regard to how he understands the relationship between Jesus and history. Over time, Hauerwas becomes critical of the inner/outer history distinction (a position that

---

[20]Niebuhr, *Meaning of Revelation*, 20-21.
[21]Niebuhr, *Meaning of Revelation*, 26-27.
[22]Niebuhr, *Meaning of Revelation*, 30-40.

Hans Frei attributes to Niebuhr's allegiance with Troeltsch);[23] however, his overall posture toward *The Meaning of Revelation* remains positive. He continually compares it to Niebuhr's other works in order to distinguish which aspects of Niebuhr influence him. In a particularly insightful note in the introduction to *The Peaceable Kingdom*, Hauerwas explains:

> The Niebuhr to whom I was attracted was the Niebuhr of *The Meaning of Revelation*. In that book Niebuhr wrestled hard with Christological issues. . . . Given this, it puzzled me that the Niebuhr of *The Meaning of Revelation* could write *Radical Monotheism and Western Culture*, since the God of the latter seemed to lack the characteristics necessary to be identified with a particular people and their distinct history.[24]

To this day, Hauerwas's work continues to draw on a number of themes from *The Meaning of Revelation*. Most notable, perhaps, are those that become associated with the so-called Yale school of postliberal theology: theology as grammar, the significance of narrative, the role of community in biblical interpretation, and the idea of a living tradition. I will return to these themes in the next section. In the meantime, however, I must say something of Hauerwas's break with Niebuhr.

Niebuhr's *Christ and Culture* has an opposite effect on Hauerwas's work. Hauerwas read *Christ and Culture* during his senior year of high school and recalls engaging in a discussion of the book with John Score—the man who would become his mentor—during a college visit to Southwestern.[25] After college, he went to Yale and studied under Niebuhr's protégé James Gustafson. Yale taught Hauerwas to do theology in a manner similar to Niebuhr's typological method in *Christ and Culture*. Hauerwas writes, "The conceptual tools we acquired were often imitations of Niebuhr's 'method' in *Christ and Culture*. Accordingly, as graduate students at Yale we assumed that the person with the most inclusive typology at the end won."[26] In this regard,

---

[23] *HC*, 58. Hans Frei, "The Theology of H. Richard Niebuhr," in *Faith and Ethics*, ed. Paul Ramsey (New York: Harper & Row, 1965), 89-90, cited by George Hunsinger, "Between Barth and Troeltsch: H. R. Niebuhr's *The Meaning of Revelation*," in *Conversational Theology: Essays on Ecumenical, Postliberal, and Political Themes, with Special Reference to Karl Barth* (New York: Bloomsbury, 2015), 160.

[24] *PK*, xx-xxi.

[25] *HC*, 9.

[26] *HC*, 74.

Christ and Culture initially represents a positive development in Hauerwas's theology. Eventually, however, it becomes the breaking point between Hauerwas and Gustafson, his *Doktorvater*.

Niebuhr's *Christ and Culture* is an attempt to identify the most common theological responses to the perennial problem of the relationship between Jesus Christ and human culture. Christ and culture are the two poles between which Christianity exists. According to Niebuhr there are five typical positions that Christians have occupied on the spectrum between these poles. These he calls "Christ Against Culture," "Christ of Culture," "Christ Above Culture," "Christ and Culture in Paradox," and "Christ the Transformer of Culture."[27]

The first two types represent extreme polar opposites. The *against culture* type places Christ in opposition to culture and usually occurs when Christians flee from culture into quietism or when Christians are openly hostile to culture as in some forms of sectarianism. The *of culture* type is the opposite. Here Christ is approximated with culture such that he becomes nothing more than the pinnacle of human cultural achievement.

In between these two extremes lie three mediating positions. Christ *above culture* recognizes Jesus' transcendence over human culture while also emphasizing the incarnation as the event that makes real the connection between Christ and culture. The *in paradox* position acknowledges humanity's debt to both poles of the spectrum by trying to hold the two in tension. Here, Christians are described as citizens of two kingdoms, constantly navigating between the claims that both loyalties hold on their lives. The final mediating position is the *transformer* position. In this type, Christ is intimately involved in the creation of a good world and its ultimate restoration. In this sense, human culture is in some way good and Christ will transform it in order to redeem it.[28]

---

[27]H. Richard Niebuhr, *Christ and Culture*, 50th anniversary ed. (San Francisco: HarperSanFrancisco, 2001), 1-44. In this regard, Niebuhr is heavily dependent on Ernst Troeltsch's *The Social Teachings of the Christian Churches*. Niebuhr uses a similar methodology in order to modify and build on Troeltsch's three-part typology of sect type, church type, and individual mysticism. See *RA*, 39. See also Samuel Wells, *Transforming Fate into Destiny: The Theological Ethics of Stanley Hauerwas* (Carlisle, UK: Paternoster, 1998; repr., Eugene, OR: Cascade, 2004), 7.

[28]Niebuhr summarizes these types in his first chapter (*Christ and Culture*, 39-44) and then devotes a chapter to each type. A helpful chart summary of each type, including Niebuhr's own examples, is available in Peter Gathje's "A Contested Classic: Critics Ask: Whose Christ? Which Type?," *Christian Century*, June 19-26, 2002, 29.

If *The Meaning of Revelation* has a lasting positive influence on Hauerwas's theological development, Niebuhr's *Christ and Culture* comes to represent a significant divergence between Hauerwas and Niebuhr's theological influence. Measuring Hauerwas's break with the sort of theology that *Christ and Culture* represents is probably best done by noting the break in theological agreement between Hauerwas and Gustafson.

Hauerwas eventually became so influenced by the work of Mennonite theologian John Howard Yoder that he shared Yoder's concerns regarding *Christ and Culture*. Hauerwas acknowledges as much in an essay on Niebuhr: "I believe that John Howard Yoder is right to criticize *Christ and Culture* for the assumed objective stance Niebuhr takes when in fact he uses that book to advance his theological agenda."[29] With this quote, Hauerwas alludes to Yoder's twofold critique of Niebuhr's typology in *Christ and Culture*.

Yoder argues that Niebuhr simultaneously overcriticizes the against culture position and underdevelops the transformer position. The effect is that most readers tend to adopt Niebuhr's explicit critiques of the former as sectarian and anticultural while accepting the implicit assumption that the latter is both a real option and, in fact, the best option. Yoder argues this claim by noting the discrepancies between Niebuhr's treatment of each type. Every position in the typology except the transformer position is accompanied by a list of shortcomings. Further, each type is accompanied by specific examples and an explanation for how that example is a test case that legitimates the type. Further, the examples given for the transformer type— Augustine, Calvin, and F. D. Maurice—are underdeveloped as test cases. The reader is turned back on her own previous knowledge of these historical figures to determine if their approximation to the transformer type is valid. Yoder is highly skeptical: "The reader who does not already know it would not learn from Niebuhr's account that (or why) Augustine urged for war against the Arians, that (or why) Calvin opposed religious liberty, or that (or why) F. D. Maurice was a socialist."[30]

---

[29]Stanley Hauerwas, "H. Richard Niebuhr," in *The Modern Theologians: An Introduction to Christian Theology Since 1918*, ed. David F. Ford with Rachel Muers, 3rd ed. (Malden, MA: Blackwell, 2005), 200. See also *RA*, 44-45.
[30]John Howard Yoder, "How H. Richard Niebuhr Reasoned: A Critique of *Christ and Culture*," in *Authentic Christian Transformation: A New Vision of Christ and Culture*, ed. Glen H. Stassen, D. M. Yeager, and John Howard Yoder (Nashville: Abingdon, 1996), 42.

While Niebuhr's description of the transformer position is too abstract and fails to provide the same level of critique and analysis as the other types, his description of the sectarian, against position suffers from the opposite problem. His description is hypercritical and actually attempts to undermine the position at the level of doctrine. Here Niebuhr makes an unparalleled appeal to the doctrine of the Trinity in order to suggest that those who represent the against type rely on Jesus' life and teachings as a normative vision for the Christian life to the exclusion of the Father and the Spirit. By this he means to suggest that Christians must balance their confession that Jesus Christ is Lord with their study of creation (God the Father as Creator) and the contemporary experience of the church (God the Holy Spirit).[31] Yoder notes that this sort of weighty appeal to Christian doctrine is strangely absent from Niebuhr's critiques of all other types, suggesting that Niebuhr's description of the five types becomes more than description at this point. In this instance, the critique itself is actually undermined by Niebuhr's use of the doctrine of the Trinity to undergird a modalist description of God where the work of the Father and the work of the Son are differentiated in a manner that countermands the biblical witness of the Son's intimate involvement in creation.[32]

Influenced by Yoder, Hauerwas makes a definitive break with the type of theology that *Christ and Culture* represents. This break is well documented in a series of back-and-forth essays between Hauerwas and Gustafson. For Gustafson, still using Niebuhr's typology, Hauerwas becomes a sectarian in the mold of the against type. He relies too much on Jesus to determine his ethics at the expense of the doctrine of creation.[33] For Hauerwas, Gustafson is incapable of understanding and appreciating Hauerwas's theology because he continues to operate from within Niebuhr's faulty typology, a typology that traces back ultimately to Troeltsch.[34]

---

[31]This is an idea Niebuhr develops more fully in "Doctrine of the Trinity," 371-84.

[32]Yoder, "How H. Richard Niebuhr Reasoned," 43, 61-65. George Hunsinger notes that this is not unlike the "non-trinitarian, or sub-trinitarian" position that Niebuhr presents in *Meaning of Revelation* ("Between Barth and Troeltsch," 148, 153).

[33]James F. Gustafson, "The Sectarian Temptation: Reflections on Theology, the Church and the University," *Proceedings of the Catholic Theological Society of America* 40 (1985): 88.

[34]*CET*, 7. Despite Hauerwas's insistence that the typology mischaracterizes his work, it continues to hold descriptive power over theological engagements with him. Some, like Richard J. Mouw, do so in a self-critical manner (See "Cultural Discipleship in a Time of God's Patience," *Scottish*

William Werpehowski articulates the difference between Hauerwas and Gustafson as a difference between different aspects of Niebuhr's work. In *American Protestant Ethics and the Legacy of H. Richard Niebuhr*, Werpehowski argues that Paul Ramsey's agape ethics, Hauerwas's community of character, Gustafson's theocentric ethics, and Kathryn Tanner's progressive politics can all legitimately claim to be influenced by Niebuhr.[35] This is possible because Niebuhr operates with a method of "polar analysis," developing (at least) five key polarities and then allowing his work to move dynamically between them. The polarities Werpehowski identifies are (1) divine sovereignty and transcendence versus the relative historical existence of the individual Christian, (2) radical monotheism versus the normativity of the life of Jesus Christ, (3) a confessional particularity versus universal truth, (4) specific human actions versus actions understood in a wider context, and finally, (5) "Christ transforming culture" versus periods of identification with and/or withdrawal from the world.[36]

Werpehowski contends that Niebuhr's work, taken as a whole, represents more of a "both/and" approach than an "either/or" in the case of each of these polarities. Werpehowski's reading of Niebuhr's students and their various trajectories helpfully demonstrates the extent to which Hauerwas is influenced by certain aspects of Niebuhr while he leaves behind other aspects. In the case of his disagreement with Gustafson, we see that Hauerwas moves further along certain trajectories (the historical relativity of the Christian, the normativity of the life of Jesus, the narrative dimensions of the moral life and human action, the particularity of Christian faith, and the distinctiveness of the Christian community) while Gustafson moves toward

---

Bulletin of Evangelical Theology 28, no. 1 [2010]: 80-91). Others, however, have been so shaped by Niebuhr's typology that they seem unaware of the descriptive power it holds over them. A prominent example of this is Jürgen Moltmann's *Ethics of Hope* (Minneapolis: Fortress, 2012). There, Moltmann argues that every Christian ethic is driven by a particular eschatology. Then, he describes four positions that run parallel to Niebuhr's types: an apocalyptic eschatology based on Luther's two kingdoms (think: paradox), a christological eschatology like Karl Barth's (think: above culture), a separatist eschatology like Anabaptists and contemporary postliberals like Hauerwas (think: against culture), and finally, a transformative eschatology, which Moltmann proposes (think: transforming culture).

[35]William Werpehowski, *American Protestant Ethics and the Legacy of H. Richard Niebuhr* (Washington, DC: Georgetown University Press, 2002), 1-13. To my knowledge, Werpehowski is the only person to explore the relationship between Hauerwas and Niebuhr with any depth. This is certainly an aspect of Hauerwas's work that remains underdeveloped in the literature.

[36]Werpehowski, *American Protestant Ethics*, 27-30.

others (the transcendence of God, radical monotheism, the universality of truth, and "Christ transforming culture").

In summary, Niebuhr's theology presses Hauerwas into a theological position that is somewhere between Barth and Troeltsch. On the one hand, Barth's insistence on God's self-revelation in Jesus Christ and his corresponding Chalcedonian Christology are essential. On the other hand, Troeltsch's insistence on the historical community of faith centered on the life and teachings of Jesus cannot be ignored. For Hauerwas, however, Niebuhr's social ethics tend to reflect more his preference for Troeltsch over Barth at the end of the day. This is something he ultimately cannot clearly articulate until he encounters John Howard Yoder. After Yoder, Hauerwas breaks away from the more Troeltschian Niebuhr of *Christ and Culture* and toward the more Barthian Niebuhr of *The Meaning of Revelation*. At the same time, he carries with him some of Troeltsch's concern for history as it is represented by proto-postliberal impulses in Niebuhr's *The Meaning of Revelation*: narrative, theology as grammar, the communal nature of truth claims, and so on. For Hauerwas, these themes do not originate with Frei or Lindbeck; they originate with Niebuhr. When he sees them in Frei and Lindbeck, he recognizes them for what they are and gravitates toward them. Particularly, he is drawn to Lindbeck's discussion of performance in *The Nature of Doctrine*. Before I turn to Lindbeck, however, I think it is worth saying something about Yoder's place in Hauerwas's work.

THE INFLUENCE OF JOHN HOWARD YODER

As we have seen, Yoder pushes Hauerwas toward Barth and away from Troeltsch. At the same time, however, Yoder maintains a deep concern for the earthly life of Jesus and the historicity of the church in a manner that reflects the aspect of Protestant liberalism that Hauerwas greatly admires. For this reason, Yoder becomes a midwife to Hauerwas, helping him give birth to his own break with the liberal Protestant theological education he received.

Yoder's influence on Hauerwas is one that is perhaps too great to explore in all of its significance. Hauerwas once claimed, "I oftentimes feel I learned everything from John [Howard Yoder]."[37] While many will rightfully attribute

---

[37]Stanley Hauerwas and Chris K. Huebner, "History, Theory, and Anabaptism: A Conversation on Theology After John Howard Yoder," in *The Wisdom of the Cross: Essays in Honor of John*

Hauerwas's conversion to pacifism to his engagement with Yoder, it would be unfair to stop there. More basic than Hauerwas's commitment to Christian pacifism are the christological and ecclesiological commitments that he believes make pacifism necessary. In order to understand those, we have to understand how they represent an alternative to the christological and ecclesiological commitments of Protestant liberalism.

Hauerwas, like most of his Yale colleagues, fashioned himself a sort of Niebuhrian realist. His early work at Augustana bears this out. An article he wrote for the Augustana student paper on Black Power demonstrates a particular affinity with Niebuhrian realism. Hauerwas writes that the Black Power movement "perceives with greater clarity and honesty the role of power in group relations," and it teaches us that "unless we realistically and honestly examine our value assumptions in the light of the concrete situation, our highest values may become but a way of blinding us to the injustice that we are helping to perpetuate."[38] There is clearly something here of Reinhold Niebuhr's account of human sinfulness and the requisite posture of realism. This seems to be part and parcel of what it means to be a Christian ethicist for the young Hauerwas.

At the same time, Hauerwas also thought himself a Barthian. These two commitments seemed largely congruent, if not identical, in his mind's eye. Reflecting on this period in his life, Hauerwas writes, "I assumed that Reinhold Niebuhr was largely right; and I thought that somehow Barth was congruent with all of this and more."[39] This all changed when Hauerwas encountered Yoder.

Hauerwas remembers first learning of Yoder from a Mennonite student at Yale named Leroy Walters. Shortly thereafter, he came across Yoder's *Karl Barth and Christian Pacifism* in the Yale Divinity bookstore. Hauerwas remembers thinking, "That is the best critique of Barth's ethics I have ever read, but you would have to be crazy to accept Yoder's ecclesiology."[40] This encounter registered little impact on Hauerwas. It is only after Hauerwas moves to Notre Dame, a mere fifteen miles from Elkhart, Indiana, that he begins to seriously study Yoder's work.

Howard Yoder, ed. Stanley Hauerwas, Chris K. Huebner, Harry J. Huebner, and Mark Thiessen Nation (Grand Rapids: Eerdmans, 1999), 399.

[38] Stanley Hauerwas, "The Ethics of Black Power," *The Augustana Observer*, February 5, 1969, 3.

[39] *HC*, 67.

[40] *DT*, 236-37.

Over a series of personal conversations and through reading early drafts of Yoder's *The Politics of Jesus* in 1970, Hauerwas became theologically enamored of Yoder's work. One aspect that especially attracted Hauerwas was Yoder's christocentrism. Yoder's *The Politics of Jesus* resembles the sort of Christology that Hauerwas learned from Frei. In Frei's class, Hauerwas was simultaneously exposed to the importance of the orthodox doctrinal claims about Jesus *and* liberal Protestant studies of the life of Jesus. This had the effect of instilling the importance of Jesus' own life and teachings without diminishing the doctrinal claims of Nicaea and Chalcedon.[41] The result is that when Hauerwas read Yoder's *The Politics of Jesus* he saw it as "an extraordinary Christological proposal."[42]

Hauerwas's first theological engagement with Yoder's work took place in a lecture he gave to a colloquium of faculty from Notre Dame and Valparaiso. In this lecture, we see a growing discomfort with Niebuhrian realism. Hauerwas began by pointing out that modern Christian ethicists share a common presupposition that Christians are called to better society. This presupposition usually calls for another assumption: that the Christian must discriminate between greater and lesser forms of evil and opt for the lesser forms in some circumstances. As such, "this means that Christians must be willing to employ force and violence to secure the good."[43] This presupposition and its corresponding set of responsibilities Hauerwas calls "Christian realism."

Hauerwas claims that Christian realism unwittingly normalizes violence to the extent that Christians no longer think it odd that they should use violence. He then uses Yoder in order to recover that sense of oddness. At this point, Hauerwas is not ready to make a strong argument for pacifism as a normative Christian practice; instead, he appeals to Yoder to critique an often-unnoticed transformation of violence from a lesser evil to a good in itself. Hauerwas argues that Yoder's Christian pacifism is "theologically

---

[41]*PK*, xxiv; *HC*, 62-63; *DT*, 238. Hauerwas gives further credence to the link between Frei and Yoder: "I think that what I learned from George [Lindbeck] and Hans [Frei] set me up for Yoder, no matter how much their Niebuhrian hearts may dislike that." See "'Blessed Are the Peacemakers, for They Shall See God': An Interview with Stanley Hauerwas," in *Postliberal Theology and the Church Catholic: Conversations with George Lindbeck, David Burrell, and Stanley Hauerwas*, ed. John Wright (Grand Rapids: Baker Academic, 2012), 108.

[42]*DT*, 238.

[43]*VV*, 198.

more defensible" than Christian realism because it is able to engage in a form of Christian social criticism that realism has given up in its eagerness to better society.[44]

At this point, Hauerwas is waffling. He is coming under the spell of Yoder's critique, and yet he cannot give up his Niebuhrian background. He continues to depend on Troeltsch and H. Richard Niebuhr's sociological work insofar as he continues to call Yoder's ecclesiology "sectarian," even as he acknowledges the prejudices that come with that description.[45] Hauerwas's main critiques of Yoder at this point are that his account of the state as inherently violent is too simplistic, failing to note the positive aspects of political community, and that he draws too sharp a division between faith and unbelief (or church and world).

Sometime between 1970 and 1975 Hauerwas became a pacifist. In an essay published in *The Christian Century* in April of 1975, Hauerwas admitted, "I have been convinced by Yoder that violence is not an option for Christians. . . . The use of violence, even by 'legitimate' authority, cannot be a Christian choice if we are to be obedient to the way Christ chooses to have us deal with the powers—i.e., by nonresistant love."[46] Having already bought Yoder's Christology, Hauerwas started to see that he could not help but have an ecclesiology that calls for the church to imitate Christ. This forever shuts the door on Niebuhr's realism, which was determined more by a strong account of sin than it was by an account of the God who reveals himself in the life, death, and resurrection of Jesus Christ. Hauerwas writes, "The social-ethical task of the church would not be simply to develop strategies within the current political options . . . but rather to stand as an alternative society that manifests in its own social and political life the way in which a people form themselves when truth and charity rather than survival are their first order of business."[47]

Now that Hauerwas accepted Yoder's christological and ecclesiological claims, he began simultaneously to critique the Niebuhrian position and to extrapolate positively the way forward. Hauerwas's next major publications

[44]*VV*, 198.
[45]*VV*, 214.
[46]Stanley Hauerwas, "The Ethicist as Theologian," *Christian Century*, April 23, 1975, 411.
[47]Hauerwas, "Ethicist as Theologian," 411.

bear out the development of these lines of thinking in his work. With the publication of *A Community of Character* in 1981, Hauerwas self-consciously set Yoder over and against a tradition of social ethics, established by Troeltsch, that marginalizes Jesus' importance.[48] As suggested in chapter one, this tradition of scholarship stretches from Troeltsch to H. Richard and Reinhold Niebuhr, and finally to James Gustafson and Paul Ramsey.[49] This is the tradition into which Hauerwas was initiated when he studied at Yale, and it is this tradition that became increasingly uncomfortable for him in light of Yoder's work.

A few years later, with the publication of *The Peaceable Kingdom*, Hauerwas gave a more positive account of what Christian ethics should look like, acknowledging his debt to Yoder's Christology and ecclesiology. Yoder emphasized Jesus' whole life in a manner that made the work Hauerwas was doing on character and virtue more concrete. Further, Yoder's ecclesiology seemed to be the answer to the concern that Hauerwas's work in *Character and the Christian Life* did not have a strong enough account of the communal nature of character and virtue, a concern made poignant by Alasdair MacIntyre's *After Virtue*.[50] That this move required Hauerwas to accept an "ethic of nonviolence" was unexpected—although not illogical—and required him to radically rethink his theological education and convictions.[51] Thus Samuel Wells is right to suggest that Hauerwas's encounter with Yoder's work "is the fundamental watershed in his relationship with Niebuhrianism."[52] After Yoder, Reinhold Niebuhr's work (as well as the more Troeltschian parts of H. Richard Niebuhr's work) came to represent the sort of liberal Protestant social ethics that Hauerwas defines himself over and against. At the same time, Barth and Yoder came to represent similar christological positions in Hauerwas's theological imagination.[53] In this regard, Yoder shows Hauerwas what his own break with liberalism should look like in his American context.

Central to the story of how Yoder convinces Hauerwas to become a Christian pacifist is Hauerwas's determination that Yoder's Christology is

---

[48]*CC*, 37-38.
[49]Wells, *Transforming Fate*, 3-12.
[50]*PK*, xxv.
[51]*PK*, xxiv.
[52]Wells, *Transforming Fate*, 10.
[53]*DT*, 237.

basically right and that the ecclesiological implications that are drawn from that Christology—including pacifism—are necessary. For this reason, it is worth giving a little more texture to the content of Yoder's christological and ecclesiological commitments.

Most people interpret the influence of Yoder on Hauerwas to be one that emphasizes predominantly the life and teachings of Jesus, and therefore the humanity of Christ. Nigel Biggar, for instance, distinguishes Barth's Christology from Hauerwas's by arguing that "Barth's [Christology] in the first place is Nicaean and Chalcedonian, whereas Hauerwas's is predominantly Anabaptist."[54] The suggestion here is that Hauerwas, dependent as he is on Yoder, focuses on Jesus' humanity at the expense of his divinity. To the contrary, the effect of Yoder's theology on Hauerwas is to press Hauerwas toward a greater commitment to Christ's kingly office, not merely his prophetic one. Central to Hauerwas's understanding of Christ's kingship is a strong christological commitment to divine sovereignty.

Hauerwas, tying Yoder's Christology to eschatology, argues that "Christians are a people who believe that we have in fact seen the end; that the world has for all time experienced its decisive crisis in the life and death of Jesus of Nazareth. . . . Through Jesus' cross and resurrection the end has come; the kingdom has been established."[55] For this reason, the Christian response of pacifism is one that is grounded, not in political effectiveness, but in hope. Pacifism is "not first of all an 'ethic' but a declaration of the reality of the new age." It is the fruit of a particular eschatological claim that God's kingdom is already here.[56]

Yoder's eschatological commitment to the ontological claim that Jesus Christ is Lord over heaven and earth is the culmination of his Christology. Any Christology that stops short of the resurrection and the eschatological convictions that it entails fails to take seriously the full biblical narrative and Christ's two natures. Wells is right to point out that for Yoder, and subsequently for Hauerwas, this is a strong statement about divine sovereignty:

---

[54]Nigel Biggar, *The Hastening That Waits: Karl Barth's Ethics* (Oxford: Clarendon, 1993), 143.

[55]*AN*, 165. Hauerwas previously described eschatology using Yoder's own definition: "This is what we mean by eschatology: a hope which, defying present frustration, defines a present position in terms of the yet unseen goal which gives it meaning" (John Howard Yoder, *The Original Revolution* [Scottsdale, PA: Herald, 1971], 56, quoted in *AN*, 160).

[56]*AN*, 194.

"The issue is one of sovereignty. If Jesus is Lord, then it is his activity, not that of these competing powers that determines the meaning of history. Jesus' lordship relativizes the sovereignty of all other powers."[57] In this regard, Yoder and Barth became allies in asserting the lordship of Christ as ethically significant, to the dismay of Niebuhrians, who chide such a position as an "overly-realized eschatology."[58]

Yoder's eschatology and its complementary claims regarding God's sovereignty underwrite the move from Christology to ecclesiology, from Christ's nonviolent life to a nonviolent church. The church's existence in the world is one that proclaims Christ's lordship through faithful, peaceful witness. That the church no longer resembles such a witness is the result of something Yoder calls Constantinianism, a term he uses to describe a historical shift that occurs in the church's mission and witness when it goes from being a minority church of martyrs to a culturally dominant church of kings and Caesars.[59]

Hauerwas pays close attention to this aspect of Yoder's argument, noting, "Prior to the time of Constantine, Christian belief in God's rule of the world was a matter of faith. However, with Constantine the idea that providence is no longer an object of faith for God's governance of the world was now thought to be empirically evident in the person of the Christian ruler."[60] In other words, Christian trust in God's sovereignty over the world gave way to the idea that God's sovereignty was tangibly demonstrated in the sovereignty of human authorities. Trust was transferred from God himself to those who

---

[57] Wells, *Transforming Fate*, 91.

[58] See again Brandon L. Morgan, "The Lordship of Christ and the Gathering of the Church: Hauerwas's Debt to the 1948 Barth-Niebuhr Exchange," *Conrad Grebel Review* 33, no. 1 (2015): 49-71. Interestingly, this has the ironic effect of placing Yoder and Hauerwas's so-called Anabaptist theology on the side of divine transcendence and providence over and against the "Reformed" theology of someone like Jürgen Moltmann, who emphasizes the Spirit's immanent work in the human struggle for liberation (Arne Rasmusson, *The Church as Polis: From Political Theology to Theological Politics as Exemplified by Jürgen Moltmann and Stanley Hauerwas* [Notre Dame, IN: University of Notre Dame Press, 1995], 83-88). In particular, Hauerwas's emphasis on pacifism reflects trust in God's providence and a priority on divine agency while Moltmann's suggestion that Christians participate in violent revolution in the name of liberation (Rasmusson, *Church as Polis*, 136-48) reflects an optimism regarding human knowledge of God's will and a conflation of divine and human agency.

[59] For an excellent treatment of what Yoder means by Constantinianism, see Chris K. Huebner, *A Precarious Peace: Yoderian Explorations on Theology, Knowledge, and Identity* (Scottdale, PA: Herald, 2006), 57-58.

[60] *CET*, 181.

claimed to act in God's name. Concomitantly, the idea that God's people are nonviolent gave way to violence for the sake of preserving God's people.

Thus, for Hauerwas, Barth and Yoder represent similar christological commitments that force a break with Protestant liberalism. Yoder shows Hauerwas the way forward because he shows Hauerwas how to take his Barth-like christological commitments absolutely seriously when thinking through his ecclesiology. Through a particular type of *imitatio Christi*, Yoder and Hauerwas come to believe that the church's call to bear witness to Jesus Christ means an absolute commitment to Christian pacifism. In short, Yoder teaches Hauerwas how to take seriously the church's historicity without collapsing theology into sociology, as he feared the Protestant liberalism of Troeltsch inevitably did.

SUMMARY

In summary, Hauerwas's earliest theological impulses were shaped by his encounter with the theology of H. Richard Niebuhr. Niebuhr pressed on Hauerwas a deep concern to balance Barth's theology with a concern for the historical embodiment of the Christian faith. Eventually, however, when pressed by Yoder to choose between Gustafson's more Troeltschian Niebuhr or a more Barthian side of Niebuhr, Hauerwas breaks toward Barth. If we return to Kerr's image of a spectrum with Barth on one side and Troeltsch on the other, we might say that Niebuhr is halfway between the two with Gustafson shying toward Troeltsch, Hauerwas shying toward Barth, and Yoder perhaps even a little further toward Barth.[61] Yoder checks Niebuhr by helping Hauerwas to keep a focus on divine agency (or what Wells calls "narrative from above") even when he speaks of human agency (or what Wells calls "narrative from below").[62] In order to understand what Hauerwas does with human agency, it is necessary to understand the pragmatic dimension of his postliberalism.

---

[61]Further, we might even venture to suggest that Alasdair MacIntyre comes to replace Troeltsch as the historicist voice in Hauerwas's mature work. Over the years, many have questioned how Hauerwas can keep Yoder and MacIntyre in tension. I suspect that the answer lies in the fact that MacIntyre serves the historicist impulse without capitulating to the relativism that seems implied by Niebuhr's "inner history." For an excellent account of MacIntyre's historicism, see J. F. Gannon, "MacIntyre's Historicism," *CrossCurrents* 39, no. 1 (1989): 91-96. On historicism without relativism, see Jennifer A. Herdt, "Alasdair MacIntyre's 'Rationality of Traditions' and Tradition-Transcendental Standards of Justification," *Journal of Religion* 78, no. 4 (1998): 524-46.
[62]Wells, *Transforming Fate*, 46.

5

Barthian Postliberalism
Exemplified

Aт the outset, I suggested that we define the term *post-liberal* along the lines that Chad Pecknold does in *Transforming Postliberal Theology*. There he argues that early reception of George Lindbeck's *The Nature of Doctrine* overlooked the pragmatic dimensions of Lindbeck's proposal, preventing many from understanding the main thrust of the postliberal movement. Here I want to explore with greater depth the manner in which this type of postliberalism comes to influence Hauerwas's own theology and whether that theology is consistent with his Barthian impulses. In order to do that, I attend first to Hauerwas's use of performance as it is influenced by postliberalism. Then I will show how Hauerwas applies his postliberalism to his interpretation of Barth. Finally, I will argue that this move is not inconsistent with Barth's own theological impulses. In that regard, I take Hauerwas to be closer to the type of "directly influenced" Barthian that his critics deny him to be.

POSTLIBERALISM AS PRAGMATISM

Hauerwas initially notes the performative aspect of Lindbeck's *The Nature of Doctrine* in *Against the Nations*—a work published in the midst of Hauerwas's transition from Notre Dame to Duke. There Hauerwas draws on Lindbeck in order to suggest that theological claims are tested by the faithfulness of their performance: "Intelligibility comes from skill, not theory, and credibility comes from good performance, not adherence to independently formulated criteria."[1] Performance no longer means simply that in order to understand the Scriptures you have to perform them; it now also means for Hauerwas that the Christian moral life is capable of demonstrating the truthfulness of Christian convictions through embodied action. Indeed, it must. Hauerwas writes, "Christian ethics does not simply confirm what all people of good will know, but requires a transformation both personally and socially if we are to be true to the nature of our convictions."[2]

At first, Hauerwas's approval of Lindbeck's turn to performance brings charges of pragmatism and relativism. This forces Hauerwas to clarify how his emphasis on Christian practices differs from philosophical pragmatism. With his next publication, *Christian Existence Today* (1988), Hauerwas suggests that practicing Christianity differs from pragmatism because Christianity, at the end of the day, requires a sort of realism that most pragmatists would refuse.[3] In this way, he becomes a sort of pragmatist without wholesale adoption of a pragmatic theory of truth.

Hauerwas, in collaboration with James Fodor, further develops the theme of performance in the titular essay in *Performing the Faith* (2004). Hauerwas and Fodor mirror Lindbeck's typology in order to propose that the best image for thinking about Christian faith is neither the propositionalist-like image of the "deposit of faith" nor the expressivist-like image of experience, but instead the image of performance. Hauerwas and Fodor write, "Understanding Christian existence as a kind of performance helpfully encapsulates the sense in which both the intelligibility and the assessment of faith are of one piece."[4] In other words, faith is something that must be demonstrated, not explained, and further, faith is something that can be evaluated on the basis of that demonstration. For this reason, Hauerwas and Fodor claim, "The doing of theology is intrinsically performative."[5] Thus Hauerwas's focus on the lives of Barth, Bonhoeffer, and others is an attempt to demonstrate the truthfulness of the Christian faith by paying attention to

---

[1] George A. Lindbeck, *The Nature of Doctrine: Religion and Theology in a Postliberal Age* (Philadelphia: Westminster, 1984), 131, quoted in *AN*, 6.
[2] *AN*, 2.
[3] *CET*, 10.
[4] *PF*, 78.
[5] *PF*, 82.

their performances. Hauerwas invokes Wittgenstein in order to underwrite this move: "Wittgenstein observes, 'You cannot write anything about yourself that is more truthful than you yourself are.'"[6]

Hauerwas's recent publication *Approaching the End* (2013) ties performance and witness together even more explicitly. Writing on witness, Hauerwas and Charles Pinches claim, "Much of what we say is a sort of commentary on Wittgenstein's remark that 'a language-game must "*show*" the facts that make it possible.'"[7] Performance is a way to show what cannot be said, and witness is the form that showing takes for Christians, who often use story in order to help others see who God is. Hauerwas and Pinches point to Paul in the first century, who "often witnesses by telling his own story."[8]

Hauerwas's pragmatism, then, is not merely Lindbeck's scriptural pragmatism. Bruce McCormack is right to worry that Lindbeck simply repeats the neo-orthodox tendency to use the language of Scripture without concern for whether it really corresponds to reality.[9] Hauerwas's pragmatism, in contrast, is what Peter Ochs has called "theopractic reasoning"; that is, it is a combination of pragmatic and prophetic speech.[10] Christian performance is always for the sake of pointing to God.

The relationship between narrative and performance come together in the figure of a witness, someone who embodies the story of Christianity in her own life. Here, another influence begins to emerge from the background of Hauerwas's work: James McClendon. Hauerwas recalls first encountering McClendon's work early on at Notre Dame in a book coauthored with James M. Smith titled *Convictions* (1975).[11] One of the book's enduring influences on

---

[6]*PF*, 72 n. 49.

[7]*AE*, 42.

[8]*AE*, 47.

[9]This concern is also expressed by William C. Placher, *Unapologetic Theology: A Christian Voice in a Pluralistic Conversation* (Louisville, KY: Westminster John Knox, 1989), 164.

[10]Peter Ochs, *Another Reformation: Postliberal Christianity and the Jews* (Grand Rapids: Baker Academic, 2011), 94.

[11]*HC*, 245. Hauerwas first demonstrates knowledge of McClendon's published essay "Biography as Theology" in a couple of essays published in 1972 and 1973, see *VV*, 66 n. 31, and 72 n. 9; McClendon's "Biography as Theology" has recently been made available in *The Collected Works of James Wm. McClendon, Jr.*, ed. Ryan Andrew Newson and Andrew C. Wright (Waco, TX: Baylor University Press, 2014–2016), 2:153-72. By 1974, Hauerwas is familiar with McClendon's monograph *Biography as Theology* as well as his forthcoming 1975 publication *Convictions*, originally published by Notre Dame as *Understanding Religious Convictions* (see *TT*, 80-81, 223 n. 3, and 225 nn. 33 and 35).

Hauerwas's theology is the word *conviction*. Hauerwas prefers to talk about convictions instead of beliefs or values. When he does so, he is using the definition of *conviction* that he learned from McClendon: "a persistent belief such that if X (a person or community) has a conviction, it will not easily be relinquished and it cannot be relinquished without making X a significantly different person (or community) than before."[12] Convictions, then, are stronger than beliefs in the sense that they are *foundational* beliefs; they "make people what they are."[13] Theology, on this account, is attention to the particular convictions that make Christians who they are and make the church the community of people who hold those convictions.

Biography is significant for McClendon's account of religious convictions because the truthfulness of these convictions are tested by the actions of the people who hold them. In *Biography as Theology* (1974), McClendon writes, "Christian beliefs . . . are living convictions which give shape to actual lives and actual communities." Therefore, "the only relevant critical examination of Christian beliefs may be one that begins by attending to lived lives. *Theology must be at least biography*."[14] Convictions are tested and corrected in the context of the lives that people live who hold those convictions. McClendon examines the lives of Dag Hammarskjöld, Martin Luther King Jr., Clarence Jordan, and Charles Ives in order to demonstrate how each life was shaped by the common themes of suffering and reconciliation, which ultimately can be attributed to lives formed by the Christian doctrine of atonement.[15]

McClendon's use of biography initially relates to Hauerwas's use of narrative. This is not to suggest that narrative and biography are equivalent. The language of "narrative" and "story" dominate Hauerwas's writings, while the language of "biography" goes almost entirely unexplored.[16] Over time, however, Hauerwas comes to use witness and performance in a manner that functions synonymously with McClendon's use of biography. The truthfulness of Christian convictions becomes connected with

---

[12]James Wm. McClendon Jr. and James M. Smith, *Convictions: Defusing Religious Relativism*, rev. ed. (Valley Forge, PA: Trinity Press International, 1994), 5. See also *TT*, 214 n. 4.
[13]McClendon and Smith, *Convictions*, 7.
[14]James Wm. McClendon Jr., *Biography as Theology: How Life Stories Can Remake Today's Theology*, 2nd ed. (Philadelphia: Trinity Press International, 1990), 22 (emphasis mine).
[15]McClendon, *Biography as Theology*, 143-44.
[16]Samuel Wells, *Transforming Fate into Destiny: The Theological Ethics of Stanley Hauerwas* (Carlisle, UK: Paternoster, 1998; repr., Eugene, OR: Cascade, 2004), 45.

particular lives that exemplify those convictions through performing the faith. Further, those lives become witnesses to the overall truthfulness of Christianity.

In chapter two I suggested that Barth disappears from Hauerwas's written work for the large part of Hauerwas's career at Notre Dame, only reemerging with his move to Duke. This reemergence occurs subsequent to the publication of George Lindbeck's landmark *The Nature of Doctrine* in 1984. Shortly thereafter, Hauerwas publishes *Christian Existence Today*. There, he argues that the truthfulness of Christian convictions can be known only as they are demonstrated through the lives of the faithful. He acknowledges that this is a type of pragmatism, but insists that it is undergirded by an abiding sense of realism.

When, several years later, Hauerwas was invited to give the Gifford Lectures at St. Andrews, he decided to present the theological claims and the lives of three famous Gifford lecturers alongside of each other in order to demonstrate that it is Karl Barth whose theology best demonstrates how Christian convictions produce different lives than the convictions of liberal democratic societies. Thus, in *With the Grain of the Universe*, we see the fullest exemplification of what Hauerwas means when he speaks of "performing the faith." There the themes of biography, performance, and witness come together as Hauerwas reads Barth with attention to his own theological formation, the manner in which his theology "performs," and finally, how his life and his theology together are a witness to God.

A POSTLIBERAL READING OF BARTH

The first story I told—the story of Hauerwas's Barthianism (chap. 2)—goes something like this: Hauerwas learned a lot of things from Barth. Particularly, he learned to keep dogmatics and ethics together by rejecting the tendencies of Protestant liberalism. That lesson set Hauerwas on a course to emphasize how Christian ethics in North America could continue to be theological by continuing to be distinctly Christian. On that journey, however, Hauerwas came to a place where he needed to modify Barth's theological ethics in order to make them serve his purpose. To be sure, Hauerwas was always blazing his own trail—often in critical dialogue with Barth—but he imagined that his trail was one that was roughly parallel to the one Barth took in the 1920s and 1930s in Germany.[17] Eventually, however, Hauerwas came to a place where it seemed like he had to break with Barth's theology altogether.

Largely, the difference that emerges between the two theologians revolves around ecclesiology and the explication of church practices as a concrete means by which the church forms individual witnesses to the gospel. Instead of leaving Barth behind at this juncture, Hauerwas tries to renarrate Barth's theological agenda as a massive attempt to bear witness to the gospel through theological discourse as a church practice. In this section, I will return to Hauerwas's attempt to fix Barth's ecclesiology and narrate it through the lens of postliberalism. What emerges is a way of reading Barth that attends not so much to the content of Barth's theology but to how Barth does theology.

The basic problem with Barth's theological ethics, according to Hauerwas, is that it remains abstract because Barth fails to develop a concrete ecclesiology that can account for the means by which Christian disciples are formed. One of the ways that Hauerwas suggests we overcome this problem is by attending to the necessarily casuistical nature of theological ethics. Thus a clear difference emerges between Barth and Hauerwas at this point: where Barth rejects casuistry, Hauerwas embraces it. For Barth, casuistry is the attempt to gain purchase on God by predetermining certain fixed actions as obedience. This has the effect of ignoring God's freedom to issue a fresh command. For Hauerwas, in contrast, casuistry is necessary because it is the only means by which moral reasoning can obtain in the actual lives of individual Christians and, thus, become the sorts of performances that are necessary to bear witness to the truth.

What is utterly lacking in Barth's theology, from Hauerwas's perspective, is the sort of thick ecclesiology that accounts for how church practices train Christians to be saints. For Hauerwas, this is the place where Barth's rejection of Protestant liberalism reaches its limits. Reflecting on these deficiencies in Barth's ecclesiology, Hauerwas, writing with Will Willimon, writes, "Barth did not seem to have a way to run [his stand against the Nazis] into an account of the practices needed to sustain the church beyond its

---

[17]*HC*, 136.

confrontation with the Nazis."[18] The Swiss Protestant church, after all, was and remains just as accommodated to Western cultural assumptions as its European and American counterparts. Thus Hauerwas worries that Barth's ecclesiology cannot account for how to form people who are capable of resisting the temptations of the nation-state, late modern capitalism, and the corresponding problems of materialism and individualism.

Even though Barth's ecclesiology cannot account for the means by which the church forms disciples, according to Hauerwas, Barth himself is the product of just such a church. One of the major themes of Hauerwas's Gifford Lectures is that Barth's *Church Dogmatics* is a performance of theological speech that demonstrates how to worship God in a world which cannot understand that "those who bear crosses work with the grain of the universe."[19] Hauerwas writes that the *Church Dogmatics* "is Barth's way to provide a compelling account of God and God's redemption of creation in a world constituted by practices that have made Christian speech unintelligible."[20]

Barth's great achievement, then, is that he demonstrates what robust theological speech looks like over and against Gifford lecturers like William James and Reinhold Niebuhr who, for the most part, abandon God-talk and speak instead about religious experience and liberal democratic social orders respectively. Barth is "the great natural theologian of the Gifford Lectures" because he alone realizes that theology is most natural when it speaks about and from the perspective of a full doctrine of God.[21] With this argument, Hauerwas shifts focus from the content of *Church Dogmatics* to the manner in which it demonstrates that Barth's theology bears witness to the gospel.

The *Church Dogmatics* is Barth's attempt to show what theology must be if it is to bear witness "to the God who is the beginning and the end of all that is."[22] Because this God is the measure of all things, theology itself is a never-ending exploration of how to speak about this God. As such, the *Church Dogmatics* "with its unending and confident display of Christian speech" becomes a training manual for how to speak about God in a manner

---

[18] *WRAL*, 21.
[19] *WGU*, 17.
[20] *WGU*, 174.
[21] *WGU*, 20; *DT*, 208.
[22] *WGU*, 168.

disciplined by God's self-revelation in Jesus Christ.[23] Further, "Barth rightly saw that the truthfulness of Christian speech about God is a matter of truthful witness."[24] Following William Stacy Johnson, Hauerwas suggests that Barth's ethic of witness presses us toward pragmatism: "The proof of one's theology . . . must be made in the living."[25] In the final analysis, for Hauerwas, the *Church Dogmatics* is exemplary because with it "Barth taught us what it might mean not only to think but to live when God is acknowledged as the beginning and end of our existence."[26]

Reflecting on his reading of Barth in *With the Grain of the Universe*, Hauerwas exclaims, "I read Barth my way."[27] He further admits that "this way of reading Barth might have surprised Barth, as well as many who regard themselves as Barthians."[28] Hauerwas's way is one that he alternatively describes as "Aristotelianizing Barth"[29] and giving Barth a "Jamesian reading."[30] These comments are instructive for understanding what Hauerwas intends by focusing his analysis on how Barth's theology informs the way he lived.

First, consider Hauerwas's claim that he is "Aristotelianizing Barth." In some ways, Hauerwas's project has always been about Aristotelianizing Barth in the sense that he felt the need to shore up deficiencies in Protestant ethics with notions of character and virtue that came from Aristotelian and Thomist sources. What Hauerwas means in this particular case, however, is that he develops an account of Barth's theology as a means by which Christians use practical wisdom to learn how to speak truthfully about God. He often draws similarities between Aquinas's *Summa theologiae* and Barth's *Church Dogmatics* to suggest that both theologians intend their readers to undergo an apprenticeship in the faith.[31]

---

[23] *WGU*, 176, 179.

[24] *WGU*, 194.

[25] William Stacy Johnson, *The Mystery of God: Karl Barth and the Postmodern Foundations of Theology* (Louisville, KY: Westminster John Knox, 1997), 155, quoted in *WGU*, 193.

[26] *WGU*, 204.

[27] Stanley Hauerwas, "Hooks: Random Thoughts by Way of a Response to Griffiths and Ochs," *Modern Theology* 12, no. 1 (2003): 93.

[28] Stanley Hauerwas, "A Place for God? Science and Religion in the Gifford Lectures," *Christian Century*, February 21, 2006, 44.

[29] Stanley Hauerwas, "Faculty Forum with Stanley Hauerwas: Conrad Grebel University College," *Conrad Grebel Review* 20, no. 3 (2002): 70.

[30] Hauerwas, "A Place for God," 44.

[31] *WGU*, 175-76.

Second, consider Hauerwas's claim that he gives a "Jamesian" reading of Barth. According to Hauerwas, "William James rightly thought that lives matter. Unfortunately, he too often failed to understand how people who lived the lives he thought mattered actually meant what they said about the God who had made their lives possible."[32] In other words, James was correct to suggest that how people live their lives reflects the truthfulness of the convictions by which they live; he simply never imagined that the God who those convictions presupposed was real. James's detailed analysis of religious experience in *Varieties of Religious Experience* is supplemented in Hauerwas's reading by the pragmatism of James's *The Will to Believe*.[33]

Underlying both the "Aristotelian" and the "Jamesian" aspects of Hauerwas's reading of Barth is yet another important philosophical influence: Ludwig Wittgenstein. For Hauerwas, Wittgenstein, Barth, and Aquinas share important similarities. Particularly, each represents, in his own way, how to do "intellectual work as investigation," concerned more with the pursuit of truth than with having a "position."[34] Wittgenstein connects to Hauerwas's claim that he is "Aristotelianizing" Barth in the sense that Wittgenstein wanted his readers to become different people as they worked their way through his aphorisms.[35] Hauerwas learns from Wittgenstein how to "go on." Brad Kallenberg explains, "Wittgenstein's intention [is] to lead his readers on a conceptual journey rather than express once and for all by a single example all that it means to speak."[36] Hauerwas reads Barth in a manner that produces a similar result. Hauerwas writes, "Barth's [*Church Dogmatics*] is a performance, a witness, through which we learn the skills to go on in a way no doubt different from Barth."[37] To be a Barthian, then, is not simply to hold Barth's "position" on a particular theological point; instead, it is to reproduce the habits of thinking that always presses one further in the pursuit of a truthful witness to the triune God. As I suggested earlier, to be a Barthian

---

[32]*WGU*, 212.

[33]Hauerwas, "Hooks," 89; Hauerwas is particularly influenced by James's account of verification (*SU*, 3 n. 7).

[34]*HC*, 60-61.

[35]Brad J. Kallenberg, *Ethics as Grammar: Changing the Postmodern Subject* (Notre Dame, IN: University of Notre Dame Press, 2001), 33.

[36]Kallenberg, *Ethics as Grammar*, 47.

[37]*PF*, 25.

means graduating from Barth's school and going beyond him in a way that was not possible before him.

Similarly, Hauerwas reads James with Wittgenstein in mind. Particularly, where James focuses on the inner lives and experiences of individuals, Hauerwas attends to the actions of individuals and the communal contexts in which their actions make sense. In other words, Hauerwas attends to James's pragmatism while distancing himself from James's Cartesianism. Fergus Kerr explains the difference between James and Wittgenstein for us in a manner that clarifies Hauerwas's reading of James. In *Varieties*, James makes feeling foundational for religious belief. Wittgenstein's later work, by contrast, suggests that action is foundational. Thus James, the great pragmatist, seems to retreat to a "private and individualist" self while Wittgenstein emerges at this precise point as a religious pragmatist of sorts.[38]

Many scholars have suggested that the history of philosophy can be interpreted as an omega-shaped (Ω) path, in which the Enlightenment, typified by Descartes and Kant, represents a circuitous detour between the "epistemic modesty of Montaigne" in the sixteenth century and Wittgenstein in the twentieth century.[39] Hauerwas's reading of James presses him closer to Wittgenstein while simultaneously suggesting that Wittgenstein is in the same philosophical tradition as Aristotle and Aquinas in order to ensure an externalist reading of Barth.

The Barth that emerges is one who takes his place as a saint in Hauerwas's great cloud of witnesses, a cloud that includes John Howard Yoder, John Paul II, Dorothy Day, Dietrich Bonhoeffer, Rowan Williams, and others.[40]

---

[38]Fergus Kerr, *Theology After Wittgenstein*, 2nd ed. (London: SPCK, 1997), 157-58. James K. A. Smith has recently given further credence to this reading of Wittgenstein as a pragmatist. Smith argues that Wittgenstein, Richard Rorty, and Robert Brandom establish a lineage of pragmatism in Anglo-American philosophy. This sort of pragmatism, Smith relates, is "a kind of *therapeutic* philosophy—a critical, 'deflationary' philosophical tradition that punctures the balloons of our pretensions even as it topples the epistemological Babels of our own making, testaments of our attempts to claim heaven and achieve a God's-eye view" (*Who's Afraid of Relativism?*, 180-81).

[39]Kallenberg, *Ethics as Grammar*, 51-52. The omega-shape image is Stephen Toulmin's (see *Cosmopolis: The Hidden Agenda of Modernity* [New York: Free Press, 1990], 167). Roger Pouivet makes a similar argument in *After Wittgenstein, St. Thomas*, where he argues that Wittgenstein draws the "internalist interlude" of modern philosophy to a close with a return to an externalism and anti-individualism reminiscent of Thomas Aquinas (*After Wittgenstein, St. Thomas*, trans. Michael S. Sherwin [South Bend, IN: St. Augustine's, 2006], 1-5).

[40]On John Howard Yoder, John Paul II, and Dorothy Day, see *WGU*, 218-30; on Bonhoeffer, *PF*, 33-54; and on Rowan Williams, see *SU*, 209-13. Hauerwas's persistent defense of Yoder's exemplary

These saints, each in their own way, show us how to go on with the task of bearing witness to the gospel in a society where such behavior seems odd. The mere fact that they exist proves that God's Spirit is at work in the church.[41] Even though Barth's ecclesiology cannot adequately account for how he is able to make a stand against Protestant liberalism and the German Christians, his life proves that the church must be capable of producing such witnesses because people like Barth, after all, exist: *Barth acts, therefore, the church is.*

This reading of Barth also explains why Hauerwas ultimately decides that Yoder is the hero of the narrative of Christian ethics in America. Concerned with how Protestant liberalism and Roman Catholicism represent types of Monophysite ecclesiology—comingling divine and human agency through pietism and sacramentalism respectively—Barth's highly dialectical ecclesiology works in the opposite direction. Kimlyn Bender explains, "Barth's own position is to speak of the church as both divinely constituted and historically situated, a reality composed of both an inner mystery of the Spirit and a society of human persons in fellowship and joint activity."[42]

Here, Barth's ecclesiology is guided by his christological commitment to the Chalcedonian pattern. A merely visible church would succumb to the ecclesiological equivalent of adoptionism; likewise, a merely invisible church would be the ecclesiological equivalent of docetism. By holding both the visibility and the invisibility of the church together in a differentiated unity, Barth intends to maintain the invisible/visible dialectic without resolving the tension on one side at the expense of the other. Thus, for Barth, the church is both invisible and visible: invisible in the sense that the church is an event that is called into being by the work of the Spirit and visible in the sense that it is a historical institution. We see this most clearly in Barth's ethics of reconciliation, where he treats baptism with a formal distinction between Spirit baptism as God's action and water baptism as human response.[43]

---

witness in the face of abuse allegations has been deeply problematic. As late as 2010, he continued to point to Yoder as an example of church discipline in action (*HC*, 242-46). Only recently has Hauerwas publicly recognized that Yoder's actions and his persistent denial of their inappropriate nature remain problematic (*B*, 184; *MW*, 142-159).

[41] *WGU*, 207.

[42] Kimlyn J. Bender, "Church," in *The Westminster Handbook to Karl Barth*, ed. Richard Burnett (Louisville, KY: Westminster John Knox, 2013), 36.

[43] *CD* IV/4:2. For an excellent summary of Barth's mature treatment of baptism, see W. Travis McMaken, *The Sign of the Gospel: Toward an Evangelical Doctrine of Infant Baptism after Karl Barth* (Minneapolis: Fortress, 2013), 32-38.

For others, like Reinhard Hütter and Joseph Mangina, however, Barth's dialectical ecclesiology differentiates the Spirit's work from the church's practice in a manner that is almost Nestorian.[44] Similarly, for Hauerwas, Barth's invisible/visible church dialectic, with its asymmetrical emphasis on divine agency, undermines the church's participation in the proclamation of the gospel. In this regard, Barth makes the church accidental to the economy of salvation, to the point where "it is by no means clear what difference the church makes for how we understand the way the world is and . . . how we must live."[45]

Hauerwas differentiates himself from Barth in this regard, suggesting that his own ecclesiology is more "catholic" than Barth's because the church makes Christ known to the world.[46] In a North American context where the church is captive to capitalist, materialist, and liberal democratic tendencies—all of which suggest that war is the primary liturgical act of the nation-state[47]—Hauerwas worries that Barth has left the church with too few resources for understanding the difference that following Jesus Christ should make in their lives. In this regard, Yoder helps Hauerwas articulate a vision of the church as an alternative politics that offers the world a witness to the truthfulness of Christian convictions.[48] For Hauerwas, the church's main theological performance is the liturgy. Hauerwas writes, "Christians learn how to be praiseworthy people through worship."[49] The church's liturgy forms Christians to praise God in a manner that habituates praise into their daily lives. Ultimately, the liturgy becomes the means by which Christians learn to practice holiness: "The formation of Christians through the liturgy makes clear that Christians are not simply called to do the 'right thing,' but rather we are expected to be holy."[50] Thus Hauerwas's move "beyond Barth" is to attend to the liturgy as the means by which the church forms saints. This move seems to break with Barth because it poses a return to casuistry as the means by which Christians determine the measure of the

---

[44]For a summary of these concerns, see Kimlyn J. Bender, *Confessing Christ for Church and World: Studies in Modern Theology* (Downers Grove, IL: IVP Academic, 2014), 37-48.
[45]*WGU*, 193.
[46]*WAD*, 171 n. 2.
[47]A point Hauerwas makes forcefully in the introduction and first two chapters of *WAD*.
[48]*WGU*, 219.
[49]*IGC*, 154.
[50]*IGC*, 155.

good. I will argue in the next section, however, that it may in fact be the very move that demonstrates Hauerwas has truly understood Barth.

HAUERWAS AS AN INTERPRETER OF BARTH

Whether or not Hauerwas is a "Barthian" depends, according to McCormack, on whether Hauerwas has truly understood Barth's work. Many interpreters suggest that he misunderstands Barth just to the extent that he reproduces some of the liberal problems that Barth's theology seeks to avoid. In this regard, he may be "indirectly" influenced by Barth because he draws freely from Barth's work and allows his work to be inspired by Barth as he sees fit. Nevertheless, he cannot claim to be "directly" influenced by Barth, and therefore a Barthian in McCormack's sense of the term, because he reads Barth as a postliberal, that is, as a nonfoundationalist and a narrative theologian. This move perpetuates the problems that plague older neo-orthodox readings of Barth, especially an epistemological relativism that basks in Barth's retrieval of biblical concepts and imagery with little concern for whether there is a reality behind the text.

In this section, I will consider the possibility that Hauerwas's postliberal reading of Barth—a reading that attends to how Barth theologizes—is actually a legitimate reading of Barth, and therefore, a form of direct influence. In order to do so, I will appeal to a suggestion made by Danish theologian Bent Flemming Nielsen that Barth is deeply concerned with how his theology performed its task. Nielsen's suggestion presses the possibility that perhaps Hauerwas has actually understood one important aspect of Barth's work and has continued to work out his own theological ethics within that Barthian vein.

Nielsen suggests that scholars who misunderstand Barth often do so because they fail to go beneath the content of Barth's theological writings to the manner in which Barth is "acting theologically." Nielsen explains, "When reading Karl Barth, one often stumbles across sentences where Barth actually leaves behind the bare *semantic* level of language and introduces a sort of argument that I characterize as *pragmatic activity*."[51] Thus

---

[51]Bent Flemming Nielsen, "Theology as Liturgy? The Practical Dimension of Barth's Thinking," in *Dogmatics After Barth: Facing Challenges in Church, Society and the Academy*, ed. Günter Thomas, Rinse H. Reeling Brouwer, and Bruce McCormack (Leipzig: CreateSpace Independent Publishing Platform, 2012), 69.

Nielsen appeals to Barth's *Theologie treiben*, or his way of theologizing, as a crucial dimension of Barth interpretation.[52] Four examples clarify what Nielsen intends.

First, Nielsen appeals to Barth's 1922 lecture "The Word of God as the Task of Theology." There Barth argues that theology is always confronted with the same dilemma: "*As theologians, we ought to speak of God. But we are humans and as such cannot speak of God. We ought to do both, to know the 'ought' and the 'not able to,' and precisely in this way give God the glory. This is our plight.*"[53] Barth's solution to the problem, to glorify God, "willingly turns the answer (which won't be an answer) away from language's semantic level and into the very praxis of speaking."[54] A distinction is made here between "sentences about God" and "true speaking of God." In the case of the former, the human speaker retains authority over the words he speaks while in the case of the latter, the human speaker gives God glory by "renounc[ing] any authorship to *the truth* of his own speech."[55]

The distinction made here is not unlike the one that Hans Frei makes between first-order and second-order theological speech. First-order theology attends to the speech used in Christian worship and confession, while second-order theology concerns itself with the logic and grammar that is implicit in first-order speech.[56] While most theological discourse occurs at the level of second-order theology, what Nielsen—and Frei before him—suggests is that Barth's theological discourse is always pressing beyond second-order theology toward the first-order speech that occurs in Christian worship. For it is in worship that words about God are taken up by God and become the Word of God addressed to the people of God.[57] In other words, Barth is always interested to press the question of how our theological speech bears witness to God.

---

[52]Nielsen appeals to "Theologie treiben" as a description of Barth's understanding of how theology works. He roughly translates this phrase "making theology" or "acting theologically." I prefer to translate the term "theologizing."

[53]Karl Barth, "The Word of God as the Task of Theology, 1922," in *The Word of God and Theology*, trans. Amy Marga (London: Bloomsbury T&T Clark, 2011), 177 (emphasis original).

[54]Nielsen, "Theology as Liturgy," 69-70.

[55]Nielsen, "Theology as Liturgy," 70.

[56]Hans W. Frei, *Types of Christian Theology*, ed. George Hunsinger and William C. Placher (New Haven, CT: Yale University Press, 1992), 20-21.

[57]For Frei's understanding of how Barth moves between first-, second-, and third-order theology, see *Types of Christian Theology*, 43.

Second, Nielsen points to Barth's 1933 lecture "The First Commandment as an Axiom of Theology" as a clarifying example. There Barth argues that the first commandment—"I am the Lord *your* God. *You* shall have no other gods before *me*!"[58]—is axiomatic in the sense that it is the presupposition of all theology. Here Barth means "axiom" *not* as a premise from which you then surmise knowledge of God *but* as a command from God to which we must respond. On these terms, theology is always an act of response to God.

Third, Nielsen picks up the image of snake fighting that Barth uses in his rejection of Emil Brunner's natural theology (see chap. 3). Although Barth addresses Brunner's theology at a semantic level, a more compelling understanding of what Barth is doing occurs with his charge that Brunner has become preoccupied with the snake. The difference between a "true theology" and Brunner's natural theology is the difference between a theology that glorifies God through obedience (points one and two above) and a theology that maintains a certain level of human autonomy in our attempts to speak about God. Again, it is the difference between repeating the Word of God and utter reliance and confidence in our own words and potential.[59]

Finally, Nielsen points us towards Barth's book on Anselm. There Barth famously turns traditional readings of Anselm's *Proslogion* on their head. Many interpreters assume Anselm offers an ontological proof for the existence of God by drawing an analogy of being between the mental concept of God in the human mind and the reality of God. Barth, in contrast, argues that Anselm is actually demonstrating the limits of human knowledge about God. For Barth, then, "God is God" necessarily limits all human speech about God. Nielsen explains:

> God is the condition of the truth of all speech about God. If so, then the basic foundation for the truth of our god-talk is not our possession. Whatever "revelation" may mean, it doesn't mean the deposit of a container of truth that we might master in our thinking and talking. To the contrary, depending on God's truth we are bound to rely on actually obeying God's command in the execution of our theological praxis. In conclusion, theology is a very *practical* endeavor![60]

---

[58]Karl Barth, "The First Commandment as an Axiom of Theology," in *The Way of Theology in Karl Barth*, ed. H. Martin Rumscheidt (Eugene, OR: Pickwick, 1986), 65-66.

[59]Nielsen, "Theology as Liturgy," 71-72.

[60]Nielsen, "Theology as Liturgy," 74 (emphasis original).

All of this means that even from the start, Barth's theology was deeply interested in "the nexus of theory-praxis." Late in his life, Barth was particularly concerned to press the point that interpreting his work required attention to both the *movement* of his theology and the way it *moved* the interpreter. Near the end of his life, Barth emphasized this point in a conversation with Methodist pastors: "Yes indeed, doctrine is important to be sure, but the *lived doctrine* is important above all else."[61] Thus Nielsen argues, "[Barth] does not simply want what he says to be interpreted, he seeks an interpretation that is sensitive to what he is saying, to his activity when he says the things he does. He wants to be understood in the activity or praxis of writing and speaking, not just from the sentences on the page."[62]

A supreme example of what this might look like, according to Nielsen, is the liturgy. Theologizing, for Barth, "implies an inherent celebration . . . a doxological component." Thus "'Theologie Treiben,' then, to Barth would mean *liturgical acting*."[63] Barth at least made a comparison between the two in *Theological Existence Today*. He began that treatise by acknowledging that he was frequently asked how to respond to the German Church crisis and the rise of Nazism. His response was that he

> endeavour[ed] to carry on theology, and only theology [*Theologie und nur Theologie zu treiben*], now as previously, and as if nothing had happened. Perhaps there is a slightly increased tone, but without direct allusions: something like the chanting of the hours by the Benedictines near by in the *Maria Laach*, which goes on undoubtedly without break or interruption, pursuing the even tenor of its way even in the Third Reich. I regard the pursuit of theology as the proper attitude to adopt.[64]

For Nielsen, this suggests that theologizing is a liturgical act for Barth and, like the Benedictines, Barth must continue without interruption. To stop our theologizing to join some other cause, or to redirect the focus of theologizing away from God, is to make the same mistake that natural theology

---

[61]Karl Barth, "Conversation with Methodist Preachers (5.16.1961)," in *Barth in Conversation*, vol. 1, *1959–1962*, ed. Eberhard Busch, trans. Center for Barth Studies (Louisville, KY: Westminster John Knox, 2017), 125 (emphasis original).

[62]Nielsen, "Theology as Liturgy," 75-76.

[63]Nielsen, "Theology as Liturgy," 76.

[64]Karl Barth, *Theological Existence Today: A Plea for Theological Freedom*, trans. R. Birch Hoyle (1933; repr., Eugene, OR: Wipf and Stock, 2011), 9.

makes; it is to cease to glorify God because it means to presuppose that God's Word cannot prevail on its own.[65]

Nielsen's suggestion, namely, that we attend to how Barth theologizes, presses two important points. First, Barth is deeply concerned with whether theologizing glorifies God. Whether it is true theology depends on this point alone. The problem with natural theology and the like is that it risks glorifying human reason above God by suggesting that the Word of God needs our theologizing in order to make it speak to the pressing concerns of the world around us. Second, that theologizing glorifies God means that it is a liturgical act and therefore, like all liturgical action, has the ability to form us as liturgical animals (to borrow James K. A. Smith's memorable phrase).[66]

This means, among other things, that Hauerwas's postliberal, Jamesian, Aristotelian reading of Barth may not be that far off insofar as he concerns himself primarily with the question of how Barth performs the theological task in a manner that bears witness to the God who is wholly other. Hauerwas's account of Barth as the theologian who speaks most naturally of God because he does not allow himself to be distracted by Protestant liberalism's anthropocentrism appears, on Nielsen's reading of Barth, to understand Barth's way of theologizing. In this sense, we might say that Hauerwas is in fact a Barthian because he has done hard work to understand the *movement* of Barth's theology, and his own theological ethics are, in many ways, *moved* by Barth's theology.

One further point should be made. It is not a little ironic that the central passage for Nielsen's argument is the passage in *Theological Existence Today* in which Barth compares theology to the Benedictine liturgy. How does Hauerwas, who takes great inspiration from *Theological Existence Today*, fail to muster this text to his own service? Indeed, in *Christian Existence Today* Hauerwas clarifies and extends the logic of his understanding of the pragmatic aspects of theology while acknowledging Barth's influence on him at precisely this point. Later, however, when Hauerwas develops his idea that theological ethics should be taught with the liturgy, he misses the opportunity to connect this move to Barth's own theologizing in such an

---

[65]Barth, *Theological Existence Today*, 11-12.
[66]James K. A. Smith, *Desiring the Kingdom: Worship, Worldview, and Cultural Formation* (Grand Rapids: Baker Academic, 2009), 40.

explicit way. Indeed, for Hauerwas the liturgy represents his own move beyond Barth toward a more explicit ecclesiology. I think he could benefit from making this connection with his own work in order to show how his attempt to go "beyond" Barth was truly a move that extended the Barthian school of "theologizing."

Although Hauerwas will never be a "critically realistic dialectical theologian," he demonstrates a consistent willingness to learn from interpreters of Barth who are. More importantly, he makes a strong case that he has truly understood something about Barth's theology that is worthy of replicating in his own work. That he gives Barth a pragmatic reading suggests that there is at least one postliberal way of attending to Barth's work that does not simply regress into neo-orthodoxy. Even so, there are some remaining differences between Barth's and Hauerwas's theology that need to be reconciled if we are going to overcome the charge that Hauerwas's theology is liberal. For, if postliberalism is simply another name for liberalism, then Hauerwas's Barthianism is undermined from the start.

PART TWO

The Schleiermacher Thesis Examined

CENTRAL TO HAUERWAS'S BARTHIAN CLAIM is a twofold understanding of his own work. First, he understands his work to learn from Barth how to keep theological ethics theological by rejecting the liberal Protestant tendency to treat the question of ethics as a second and equal matter alongside the question of dogmatics. Second, he understands his work to "fix" problems in Barth's theology by developing a more robust ecclesiology that can produce people who have the moral formation to continue Barth's theological rejection of Protestant liberalism. Nicholas Healy and others have charged, instead, that it is at this point where Hauerwas's turn toward a concrete ecclesiology becomes "ecclesism," substituting the church for God as the very subject matter of theology. Thus Hauerwas's attempt to fix Barth actually threatens to undo Barth's rejection of liberalism and return to the theology of Schleiermacher. In part two, I will analyze whether Hauerwas's ecclesial ethics are truly an extension of Barth's insistence on keeping dogmatics and ethics together—an exploration of the *how* within the framework of the same *what*—or, whether Hauerwas actually changes the content of the *what*.

First, in chapter six, I will explore what "keeping dogmatics and ethics together" looks like in Barth's theological ethics. I will argue that at the heart of Barth's theological ethics is his reversal of the law and the gospel. This move results in his famous rejection of casuistry. Second, in chapter seven, I will give an introductory overview to Hauerwas's ecclesial ethics. At the heart of Hauerwas's ethics is the argument that the church's worship practices provide a rich casuistry for the formation of saints. The effect of Hauerwas's appeal to casuistry is to revive concerns that his theology actually perpetuates the liberal Protestant concerns that Barth rejects. Then in chapter eight I will explore whether Hauerwas's turn to casuistry after Barth is in fact a return to Protestant liberalism or if it is a move that shares a deeper affinity with Barth's critique of liberalism. Hauerwas's almost singular focus on the church's liturgy as a casuistry that morally forms Christians threatens, at this point, to validate the Schleiermacher thesis. To the contrary, I will argue that Hauerwas's understanding of casuistry operates within a basically Barthian set of theological commitments.

6

Karl Barth's
Theological Ethics

T HE PURPOSE OF THIS CHAPTER is to introduce the basic
structure and key themes in Barth's ethical sections of the *Church Dogmatics*.
First, I will attend to Barth's formal decision to keep dogmatics and ethics
together. Then I will explicate how this decision depends on Barth's insistence that the gospel precedes the law. Finally, in a third section, I will show
how Barth's rejection of casuistry in his special ethics of creation is a direct
correlate of his understanding of dogmatics and ethics.

These aspects of Barth's ethics are particularly relevant to a study of Hauerwas's ethics because (1) Hauerwas's narrative of how dogmatics and ethics
became divided depends heavily on the suggestion that the Protestant distinction of the gospel and the law plays a prominent role and (2) Hauerwas's
appeals to casuistry are part and parcel of his own attempt to "fix" Barth.
Whether Hauerwas represents a continuation of Barth's theological program or
a break with it will depend on how he attends to these aspects of Barth's thought.

DOGMATICS AND ETHICS

In a sense, the whole of Karl Barth's *Church Dogmatics* is ethical.[1] Nevertheless, there are particular sections at the end of each volume that are

---

[1]Hauerwas: "It is a mistake to identify Barth's 'ethics' only with those sections that he explicitly
identifies as such. All the volumes of the *Dogmatics* are Barth's 'ethics,' because Barth rightly saw
that the truthfulness of Christian speech about God is a matter of truthful witness" (*WGU*, 194).

explicitly concerned with ethics. Barth first elaborates his basic understanding of the relationship between dogmatics and ethics in a brief section
at the end of *Church Dogmatics* I/2. Then he formally treats ethics from the
perspective of each doctrinal locus. Thus, at the end of the doctrine of God,
ethics is treated as "the command of God" (*CD* II/2). Likewise with the
remaining sections: at the end of the doctrine of creation, "the command
of God the creator" (*CD* III/4), and at the end of the doctrine of reconciliation, "the command of God the reconciler" (*CD* IV/4).

Barth first addresses the theme of ethics in *Church Dogmatics* I/2, where
he clarifies his formal decision to treat ethics within his larger dogmatic
themes of God, creation, reconciliation, and redemption. Concerned to
keep dogmatics (God) primary and ethics (humans) secondary, Barth does
not give any material consideration to ethics until the end of his doctrine of
God in *Church Dogmatics* II/2. Only then can Barth properly speak of the
human agent without repeating the sort of Feuerbachian bait and switch he
wants to avoid.

The second section, *Church Dogmatics* II/2, introduces what Barth later
calls his "general ethics," beginning with "an upward look . . . to divine action"
with a view to understanding "good human action" as it is "effected by the
action of God in his command."[2] These "general ethics" correspond to the
"special ethics" of *Church Dogmatics* III/4 and the fragments of IV/4, which
Barth describes as an attempt to "look downwards . . . to the man who acts
. . . under the command of God."[3] In working from the general to the
special, Barth's "emphasis moves from the commanding position of God to
the commanded position of humankind, from the unquestionable goodness
of the divine action itself to the problematic goodness of human activity."[4]

In the "special ethics" of creation, reconciliation, and redemption, Barth
intends to consider the command of God as it encounters humanity specifically in the spheres in which humanity always exists: as creature, reconciled
sinner, and redeemed child. Thus the difference between general and special
ethics, for Barth, is the difference between a description of the moral space
in which all human action occurs—the covenantal relationship between

---

[2] *CD* III/4:4.
[3] *CD* III/4:5.
[4] Eberhard Jüngel, *Karl Barth: A Theological Legacy* (Philadelphia: Westminster, 1986), 126.

God and humanity—and a more sustained investigation into the manner in which the command of God confronts humanity in its "threefold determination" as creature, pardoned sinner, and child of God.[5]

The remainder of this section is devoted to a basic overview of Barth's treatment of the relationship between dogmatics and ethics in *Church Dogmatics* I/2 and II/2. A study of Barth's treatment of the relationship between the God who commands and the human who is commanded in II/2 necessarily leads to further exploration of the relationship between the law and the gospel and the rejection of casuistry. In this regard, this section sets the context for the remainder of the whole chapter.

From the beginning of *Church Dogmatics*, Barth is concerned to make sure that dogmatics and ethics remain together. Their division, according to Barth, is the result of post-Reformation Protestant theology's attempt to ground human goodness in anthropology instead of Christology. Unlike the Reformers, who understood that Christian holiness is "hidden with Christ in God" (Col 3:3 NRSV), these Protestant liberals set out to demonstrate that the good "can be directly perceived and therefore demonstrated, described and set up as a norm."[6] Grounded in general anthropology, ethics exerts its independence from dogmatics. Indeed, dogmatics becomes a bit of an embarrassment. Why appeal to the special knowledge of revelation when the general knowledge of reason can accomplish the same task? Barth's immediate predecessors, Hermann and Troeltsch, represent the culmination of this trajectory. They inherit a tradition, going back at least to Kant's *Religion Within the Limits of Pure Reason* and extending through Schleiermacher and Ritschl, that self-consciously dissolves dogmatics into ethics.[7]

Ethics independent of dogmatics loses focus, permitting "a fatal interchange of the subjects God and man."[8] Alternatively, Barth develops an account of dogmatics and ethics as a unity-in-distinction: "Dogmatics itself is ethics; and ethics is also dogmatics."[9] The subject of dogmatics is the

---

[5] *CD* II/2:549-50; Trevor Hart, *Regarding Karl Barth: Toward a Reading of His Theology* (Downers Grove, IL: InterVarsity Press, 1999), 82 n. 27.
[6] *CD* I/2:782.
[7] *CD* I/2:786. David Haddorff provides a particularly helpful summary of the manner in which Kant and Schleiermacher change the landscape of Protestant ethics. See *Christian Ethics as Witness: Barth's Ethics for a World at Risk* (Eugene, OR: Cascade, 2010), 37-42.
[8] *CD* I/2:790.
[9] *CD* I/2:793.

Word of God as it is addressed to humanity. When the Word of God addresses a person, she must hear it. For Barth, proper hearing is demonstrated by doing: "Only the doer of the Word is its real hearer, for it is the Word of the living God addressed to the living man absorbed in the work and action of his life."[10]

Here we are brushing up against two important aspects of Barth's theology: the Chalcedonian pattern and actualism. These two themes remain in the foreground for all of Barth's discussion of the relationship between God and humanity. Therefore, it is worth pausing to say a bit more about each.

First, Barth's thought in *Church Dogmatics* is deeply shaped by the decision he made at the outset to ground the whole christologically using the anhypostatic/enhypostatic distinction.[11] The Chalcedonian pattern uses the hypostatic union as an analogy for the manner in which divine and human action interact in much of Barth's work. This pattern is central to Barth's thinking; indeed, "there is virtually no discussion of divine and human agency in the [*Church Dogmatics*] which does not conform to this scheme."[12] According to George Hunsinger, the Chalcedonian pattern has three formal aspects: asymmetry, intimacy, and integrity. Human and divine action are *intimately* united in perichoresis such that each nature maintains its own *integrity* while the divine *asymmetrically* precedes and governs the human at every turn.

This analogy helps us to make sense of the "double agency" in Barth's thinking.[13] For Barth, there is no "zero-sum economy in which divine and human action compete with one another."[14] Instead, "Divine agency sets free genuine and effective human agency. God takes our action seriously—even to the extent that he lets his own action be 'co-determined' by our own."[15]

---

[10]*CD* I/2:792.

[11]Bruce L. McCormack, *Karl Barth's Critically Realistic Dialectical Theology: Its Genesis and Development, 1909–1936* (Oxford: Oxford University Press, 1995), 327-28.

[12]George Hunsinger, *How to Read Karl Barth: The Shape of His Theology* (Oxford: Oxford University Press, 1991), 187.

[13]Hunsinger, *How to Read Karl Barth*, 189.

[14]Gerald McKenny, *The Analogy of Grace: Karl Barth's Moral Theology* (Oxford: Oxford University Press, 2010), 203.

[15]Joseph Mangina, *Karl Barth on the Christian Life: The Practical Knowledge of God* (New York: Peter Lang, 2001), 175.

Second, Barth's thought presupposes actualism, or what Paul Nimmo calls Barth's actualistic ontology.[16] As Nimmo explains, "Barth, following the witness of Scripture, conceives of God and Jesus Christ, and (derivatively) of human beings as beings-in-action, existing in a covenant relationship."[17] Thus the human that is addressed by the Word of God is always a being-in-action; humans are essentially "doers."[18] Insofar as this Word of God really addresses this human being and anticipates a real reception, dogmatics will always be ethics if it seeks to speak about the reality of the Word of God.

These two themes are germane to a consideration of Barth's first material treatment of ethics. This occurs within his doctrine of God in *Church Dogmatics* II/2. There Barth distinguishes theological ethics from all other approaches to ethics. Specifically, he rejects (1) any form of ethics as apologetics, where theological ethics enters into the fray of philosophical ethics,[19] and (2) theological ethics as either partitioned from or correlated to philosophical ethics. In the case of the former, the subject matter of theological ethics is limited to a particular sphere, and in case of the latter, theological ethics is captive to both the starting point and the trajectory of philosophical ethics. Theological ethics, in contrast, always takes dogmatics as the basis and starting point for the ethical task. In this case, Barth has in mind the doctrine of election as a core theme of the doctrine of God.[20]

---

[16]Paul T. Nimmo, *Being in Action: The Theological Shape of Barth's Ethical Vision* (London: T&T Clark, 2007), 1. Nimmo is criticized by George Hunsinger for artificially constructing an "actualistic ontology" from Barth's work. Hunsinger is worried that Nimmo presents Barth as having a strong ontology that serves as the foundation for an entire ethical system (George Hunsinger, *Reading Barth with Charity: A Hermeneutical Proposal* [Grand Rapids: Baker Academic, 2015], 75-76). Instead, Hunsinger suggests Barth operates with a weak, or implicit, ontology and prefers to speak of Barth's "actualism" as one of a handful of significant "motifs" in Barth's work (*How to Read Karl Barth*, 30-32).

[17]Paul T. Nimmo, "Actualism," in *The Westminster Handbook to Karl Barth*, ed. Richard Burnett (Louisville, KY: Westminster John Knox, 2013), 1.

[18]Barth: "It is not as if man first exists and then acts. He exists in that he acts" (*CD* I/2:793).

[19]In CD II/2, Barth uses the term "general ethics" to speak of philosophical ethics or any attempt to ground ethics in something outside of dogmatics. Later, in III/4, he will confuse the matter a bit by referring to his own work in II/2 as his "general ethics" insofar as it expounds the basic covenantal framework in which ethical action always occurs. In order to avoid confusion, I will speak here of "philosophical ethics" where Barth speaks of "general ethics" in II/2.

[20]Barth's concern here is similar to his concern with natural theology. A Christian ethic that bases itself on a general anthropology instead of a christological anthropology exchanges its birthright for a mess of pottage. Trevor Hart points out that criticism of Barth on this point often is identical to criticism of Barth's rejection of natural theology (Hart, *Regarding Karl Barth*, 84).

Ethics belongs to the doctrine of God first and foremost because it pre-supposes the covenantal relationship that exists between the electing God and elected humanity. In this covenant between God and humanity, "the doctrine of the divine election of grace is the first element, and the doctrine of the divine command is the second."[21] In this regard, the structural arrangement of election and command in *Church Dogmatics* II/2 is the formal explication of what has become known as Barth's gospel-law thesis.[22]

The gospel-law thesis is a reversal of the traditional Protestant understanding of the relationship between the law and the gospel. Traditional Lutheran theology, for example, tends to present the law and gospel in a manner that emphasizes the subjective experience of the individual, who is first confronted by the law, learning of her insurmountable sin, and then confronted with the gospel message that she is forgiven. Barth, in contrast, reverses the priority of law and gospel, emphasizing instead the disposition of the God who saves us from sin and only subsequently the corresponding human disposition of obedience that is demanded by the law.[23]

To begin with the gospel means to begin with the doctrine of election: "The doctrine of election is," according to Barth, "the sum of the gospel."[24] In election, God wills to be for humanity and for humanity to be with God as his covenant partner.[25] Election makes a claim on the one elected in the form of the law.

What God wills from humanity is obedience, that is, for human agency to correspond to divine agency. As John Webster puts it, "Election is election to action."[26] Ethics is the name given to the process by which we learn to hear God's command as the gospel in the form of the law and respond to it with obedience, thereby joining our action to God's.

The remainder of *Church Dogmatics* II/2 addresses the command of God in terms of the *claim*, or demand, that God makes on humanity (§37), the *decision* that God makes for human action to correspond with divine action

---

[21]*CD* II/2:509.

[22]I borrow the term "gospel-law thesis" from McKenny. See the following section, The Gospel and the Law.

[23]Jüngel, *Karl Barth*, 118.

[24]*CD* II/2:3.

[25]This is Eberhard Busch's way of putting the matter: "The gospel speaks about God's will *for* us and the law tells us what God wills *from* us" (*The Great Passion: An Introduction to Karl Barth's Theology* [Grand Rapids: Eerdmans, 2004], 152).

[26]John Webster, *Barth's Ethics of Reconciliation* (Cambridge: Cambridge University Press, 1995), 49.

(§38), and the *judgment* that God renders by which we are reckoned righteous children of God (§39). Barth intends to return to the command of God as divine claim, decision, and judgment in each of his treatments on special ethics in order to account for how God's command confronts humanity in each sphere of human existence.[27]

Each aspect of Barth's ethics of the command of God—as in the preceding chapter on the election of God, and indeed, the whole of Barth's doctrine of God—is grounded in the knowledge of Jesus Christ. He is the basis, the form, and the content of the divine claim; he is God's sovereign, definite, and good decision; and finally, he is the presupposition, the execution, and the purpose of God's judgment. He both establishes and fulfills the divine command, representing sinful humanity before God's judgment on the one hand and representing God's desire to have us as his new creation on the other hand. We know Jesus through faith as the Holy Spirit enables us to pray to God and become truly obedient to God's command.

The decision to root all ethical reflection christologically is particularly dependent on a key move Barth makes early in *Church Dogmatics* II: the reversal of the relationship between the law and the gospel. Although I have provided a tentative explanation of that move here, greater attention to this feature of Barth's ethics is necessary to understand how Barth keeps dogmatics and ethics together. To that theme I now turn.

THE GOSPEL AND THE LAW

While Eberhard Jüngel is technically right that there is no section in Barth's ethics on gospel and law, it is the key theme that underlies much of Barth's general ethics in *Church Dogmatics* II/2.[28] This theme is so important, in fact, that Eberhard Busch calls it "the starting point of Barth's Christian ethics."[29] Gerald McKenny, in perhaps the fullest treatment of the theme to

---

[27]In some ways, this threefold explication of Barth's general ethics anticipates the structural features of Barth's special ethics: the claim of God suggesting the claim that the Creator has over his creatures as a demand for obedience, the decision of God suggesting that God decides to reconcile sinners to himself and to bring human action into correspondence to divine action, and the judgment of God suggesting that in the final judgment, God judges humanity as his own children and therefore already within the scope of his eternal kingdom. It seems like Jüngel is on his way toward this assertion but he does not flesh it out thoroughly. See *Karl Barth*, 126.

[28]Jüngel, *Karl Barth*, 111. Indeed, Gerald McKenny argues that II/2 is basically about the gospel-law reversal. See *Analogy of Grace*, 178.

[29]Busch, *Great Passion*, 152.

date, suggests that there are three main components to Barth's gospel-law thesis: (1) that the gospel and the law are one inseparable Word of God, (2) that the gospel is prior to the law, and (3) that the law is the form of the gospel.[30] First, Barth upholds the unity of gospel and law. Then he distinguishes the two asymmetrically, giving priority to gospel while maintaining the integrity of the law as such. In this regard, the relationship between gospel and law is reconciled along the lines of the Chalcedonian pattern.[31] This move has significant implications for the rest of Barth's theological ethics and warrants further explication.[32]

When Barth posits that the gospel and the law are inseparable and constitute the one Word of God, he intentionally challenges the predominant Lutheran understanding of law and gospel. Luther, in his own context, was fond of drawing a distinction between law and gospel, speaking of them as "two Words" that cannot be mixed together.[33] Jüngel's interpretation of Luther on the matter draws out two key implications to the separation of law from gospel, the first sociopolitical and the second personal.

First, in the case of the sociopolitical implication, Luther's "two Words" approach opposes what he perceives to be Catholicism's legalistic reduction of the gospel to the law on the one hand and the fanaticism of radical reformers like Thomas Müntzer, who parlayed the mandate to preach the gospel into a claim over the civil magistrate on the other hand. The problem, however, for Barth is that subsequent Lutheran theology overdetermines the difference between law and gospel in a manner that results in the eventual emancipation of ethics from dogmatics. Ethics becomes the explication of the law as the Word of God addressed universally to the public and/or secular sphere of existence, namely, the political and economic. Meanwhile, faith and dogmatics becomes the concern for the Word of God as gospel as it encounters humanity in the private sphere of religious experience.

---

[30]McKenny, *Analogy of Grace*, 167-68.

[31]Daniel Migliore, "Commanding Grace: Karl Barth's Theological Ethics," in *Commanding Grace: Studies in Karl Barth's Ethics*, ed. Daniel Migliore (Grand Rapids: Eerdmans, 2010), 11.

[32]John Hesselink is certainly right to say, "Barth's reversal of the law-gospel sequence touches on almost every aspect of his theology." See John Hesselink, "Law and Gospel or Gospel and Law? Karl Barth, Martin Luther, and John Calvin," *Reformation & Revival* 14, no. 1 (2005): 146.

[33]Jüngel, *Karl Barth*, 106. In another place, Jüngel seems to allow that Luther perhaps intends "two Words" to mean "two modes of the Word" (105).

Such was the basic state of theological ethics by the time Barth arrived on the scene. His professor Wilhelm Herrmann, for example, "based his thinking upon the view that the reality of the world is controlled by universally understandable laws that should guide our actions, whereas the province of religion is the individual inner life of the human person."[34] In this context, Barth's insistence that the gospel and the law are the one inseparable Word of God is a self-conscious determination to keep dogmatics and ethics together.

Barth is concerned that establishing the law as a separate Word of God apart from Jesus Christ means that you can have competing claims to what the Word of God commands: one based in universal laws and represented by worldly ordinances such as civil magistrates and the other based on God's self-revelation in Jesus Christ. A law independent of the gospel and an ethics independent of dogmatics threatens the freedom of the gospel itself, leaving us subject to "the worldly 'ordinances'" and "the 'competence of experts.'"[35] This was what Barth and the Confessing Church movement had specifically rejected eight years prior at Barmen:

> Jesus Christ, as he is attested to us in Holy Scripture, is the *one* Word of God which we have to hear, and which we have to trust and obey in life and in death. We reject the false doctrine, as though the church could and would have to acknowledge as a source of its proclamation, apart from and besides this one Word of God, still other events and powers, figures and truths, as God's revelation.[36]

Second, in the case of the personal implication, Luther distinguishes between law and gospel by suggesting that as law the Word of God addresses "a doer" while as gospel the Word of God addresses "a nondoer." As the law confronts "doers" they are forced to come to terms with the fact that they are lawbreakers who do not do what they are commanded. In contrast, the gospel is always addressed to the nondoer, or the one whose status before

---

[34]Busch, *Great Passion*, 154.
[35]Busch, *Great Passion*, 164.
[36]"The Theological Declaration of Barmen," in *The Book of Confessions: The Constitution of the Presbyterian Church (U.S.A.): Part I* (Louisville, KY: The Office of the General Assembly, 2007), 8.11-12 (emphasis added). See also Eberhard Busch, *The Barmen Theses Then and Now: The 2004 Warfield Lectures at Princeton Theological Seminary*, trans. Darrell and Judith Guder (Grand Rapids: Eerdmans, 2010), 19.

the gospel is not determined by action but by reception. In this regard, the law has to do with human action and the gospel has to do with human being.[37] With the being/acting distinction, Luther sows the seeds for what will be eventually known as "the introspective conscience of the West."[38] The second use of the law, as Lutherans would later call it, acts as a judgment on all our sinful doing and leads us to the truth of the gospel, that is, that our being is determined by our passive (nondoing) reception of God's grace. Human action becomes obsolete with regard to the question of human being. In this regard, personhood is now reconstituted along the lines of a sort of "inside-out" Cartesian dualism.

In contrast, Barth's insistence that the law and the gospel are the one inseparable Word of God registers as a strong protest against inside-out dualism.[39] For Barth, the person is constituted as a being-in-becoming, or a being-in-action. Barth's actualistic ontology means that human being is self-determined by human doing as it corresponds to divine action. God acts toward humanity in the gospel. Then, in a corresponding action, humans act in receiving the good news and responding with obedience to the law. The result is twofold. First, humans are given a real agency with regard to the gospel. Obedience to the law does not lead to God's grace, but it does arise as a genuine human response of gratitude to God's grace.[40] Second, this human agency corresponds analogously to divine agency, suggesting that human action and the question of its goodness (ethics) cannot be treated outside of a thorough treatment of God's action (dogmatics).[41]

---

[37] Jüngel, *Karl Barth*, 123.

[38] Krister Stendhal, "The Apostle Paul and the Introspective Conscience of the West," *Harvard Theological Review* 56, no. 3 (1963): 205-7.

[39] No doubt this is why the Lutheran theologian Helmut Thielicke counted Barth among the group of theologians he labeled "non-Cartesian," and why the Dominican theologian Fergus Kerr finds Karl Barth to be a natural ally to Ludwig Wittgenstein in the fight against Cartesians. See Helmut Thielicke, *The Evangelical Faith*, vol. 1, *Prolegomena: The Relation of Theology to Modern Thought Forms*, trans. Geoffrey W. Bromiley (Edinburgh: T&T Clark, 1974), 138-39; Fergus Kerr, *Theology After Wittgenstein*, 2nd ed. (London: SPCK, 1997), 8-9.

[40] Colin Gunton suggests that Barth follows Calvin's third use of the law in this regard (*The Barth Lectures*, ed. P. H. Brazier [London: T&T Clark, 2007], 126-27). Hesselink, in contrast, argues that Barth and Calvin share a more positive view of the law than Luther, but this is not equivalent to Calvin's third use. See Hesselink, "Law and Gospel or Gospel and Law," 140. I am more sympathetic with Gunton on this point. I see Barth's preference for the law as a form of the gospel to reflect the basic Reformed catechetical habit of addressing the law after questions of faith over and against the Lutheran catechetical habit of beginning with the law.

[41] Jüngel, *Karl Barth*, 121-26.

Thus Barth's refusal to separate law from gospel grounds his claim that ethics cannot be independent from dogmatics. This move immediately affects questions related to Christian social witness and divine and human agency. For Barth, both sorts of questions must begin with the subject of Christian dogmatics, the covenantal God who determines to be for humanity and who elects humanity to be with him.

This brings us to the two remaining components to the gospel-law thesis: the priority of the gospel to the law and the law as the form of the gospel. Both components differentiate the gospel from the law in the larger context of the unity they share as the one Word of God. To say that the gospel is prior to the law is to affirm that "the very fact that God speaks to us, that there is a Word of God, is grace."[42] In other words, to place the gospel before the law is to say that humans always encounter the Word of God in the context of the covenant of grace. Even when the one Word of God is law, it is law as the form of the gospel. That is to say, the law always confronts us from the perspective of what has been accomplished by Jesus Christ on our behalf. In this respect, the already-fulfilled law does not hang from our necks like a millstone. Unlike Luther's second use of the law, it does not accuse us or drive us to repentance;[43] instead, it demands that we "allow [Jesus'] fulfillment of the law . . . to count as our own."[44]

Jesus' fulfillment of the law, however, does not mean that Barth forecloses on human agency. To the contrary, the reversal of law and gospel "is at heart motivated by a desire to register a place for human agency."[45] Above I noted that a law which is separate from the gospel as a second Word of God risks appeals to competing sources of divine revelation. Similarly, a law that precedes the gospel always threatens to become an independent law (e.g., natural law) that points to an idol instead of the true God. A number of commentators see here a specific theological critique of the German Christians and Nazism.[46] After all, Barth's famous 1935 lecture "Gospel and Law" was delivered under protest by Karl Immer in Dahlem even as Barth himself

---

[42]Jüngel, *Karl Barth*, 111.
[43]Webster, *Barth's Ethics of Reconciliation*, 111.
[44]McKenny, *Analogy of Grace*, 197.
[45]Webster, *Barth's Ethics of Reconciliation*, 109.
[46]See, for example, Haddorff, *Christian Ethics as Witness*, 107-10; and Busch, *Great Passion*, 156.

was in the process of being expelled from Germany.[47] Recent interpretation, however, suggests that Barth had this theme in mind perhaps implicitly as early as his Romans commentary and explicitly at least as early as his 1927 lecture "Das Halten der Gebote."[48]

That Barth's prioritization of gospel over the law carries a large load in his criticism of Nazism and the German Christians is beyond dispute, but to suggest that the decision to reverse the two occurs entirely within the context of the *Kirchenkampf* risks missing a larger theological point. Reconstituting the law as the form of the gospel means to reconstitute human action as real and significant only as it corresponds to divine action. The law that is rejected is the law that suggests "we must do 'something' to make the gospel apply to us," while the law that is affirmed is the law that expects humans to do something on account of the fact that the gospel already applies to us.[49] This is why Barth's recharacterization of the law as the form of the gospel avoids Luther's original concern: works righteousness.

Luther's solution is to suggest that humans are utterly passive; humans do nothing, God does everything. For Barth, this solution is problematic. Busch explains, "What is wrong about works righteousness is not the fact that the human *does* something, so that in her passivity she would be in concordance with the grace of God. The wrong thing is that human action stands in contradiction to grace, competes with it rather than conforms to it."[50] The law as the form of the gospel creates space for genuine human action in correspondence to divine action, never suggesting that humans are the primary actors in their own obedience but suggesting that they are nevertheless real actors.

The prioritization of gospel over law follows Barth's determination to treat ethics within the context of dogmatics. As such, we are not surprised to see that he renders his understanding of ethics as the command of the Word of God christocentrically, giving an asymmetrical priority to God's gracious action and secondary consideration to human obedience to the command. This Chalcedonian pattern becomes paradigmatic of how Barth

---

[47]Merwyn S. Johnson, "Gospel and Law," in Burnett, *Westminster Handbook to Karl Barth*, 85.

[48]McKenny, *Analogy of Grace*, 179-80; and Alexander Massmann, *Citizenship in Heaven and on Earth: Karl Barth's Ethics* (Minneapolis: Fortress, 2015), 63.

[49]Busch, *Great Passion*, 164.

[50]Busch, *Great Passion*, 161.

treats the relationship of divine and human agency throughout the course of *Church Dogmatics*.

AGAINST CASUISTRY

Barth's formal decision to keep dogmatics and ethics together is, indeed, a rejection of the Protestant liberalism of his predecessors. This much is clear. Barth's general ethics are predicated on God's prior action in election. The indicative reality of God's election of humanity to be his covenant partner corresponds with the imperative of God's command as it confronts the human through Jesus Christ, the Word of God. Human action, then, is responsible to God and God alone. No independent or natural law can usurp the Word of God. As we turn to Barth's special ethics, we see that this explicitly means a rejection of casuistry.

In *Church Dogmatics* II/2, Barth prohibits theological ethics from depending on any sort of philosophical ethics for its foundation. In *Church Dogmatics* III/4, we see that this prohibition includes casuistry, or the formulaic application of general rules to particular cases. For Barth, the problem with casuistry is twofold. First, it threatens to sever the unity between dogmatics and ethics. Insofar as it seeks to provide humans with fixed moral principles or laws, it reverses the asymmetry between gospel and law, and divine and human agency. Second, it threatens to ossify the divine command, replacing the dynamic character of the ethical event with the static character of prescribed texts and principles.[51] This happens when humanity aspires to sit on God's throne, exercising judgment over good and evil, or when human judges wield God's command instrumentally, as a general law that requires human moral deliberation to render correct application. The end result is that genuine human freedom to respond to God is exchanged for a rote process of correlating general laws to specific circumstances.[52]

Barth is particularly concerned with the sort of casuistry that develops in rabbinic Judaism, the Roman Catholic sacrament of penance, and the Protestant field of biblical ethics.[53] Barth connects the rise of these types of casuistry in Christian theology to the development of books of penance,

---

[51]Migliore, "Commanding Grace," 6. See also Hart, *Regarding Karl Barth*, 82-83.
[52]*CD* III/4:10-15.
[53]McKenny, *Analogy of Grace*, 241.

which catalog varieties of sin and prescribe corresponding acts of repentance. Often these prescriptions are based in natural law, Scripture, or the
church's tradition.[54] For Barth, prescribing moral action in such a per-
functory manner represents an "effort to gain some purchase on sin" in the
form of human judgment.[55] The Protestant Reformation represents an
initial break with this sort of moral deliberation; however, the casuistry of
penance is eventually replaced with the casuistry of biblical ethics. In this
case, the command of God in Scripture—especially the Decalogue and the
Beatitudes[56]—becomes a set description of God's command with little
regard for its historical and narrative context as a specific command from
God to Israel or from Jesus to the disciples.[57]

    To say that Barth rejects casuistry is not to say, however, that Barth rejects
moral deliberation as such. Daniel Migliore warns against such a conclusion:
"The idea that Barth's critique of casuistry reflects a disdain of careful reasoning in the work of theology and ethics is entirely mistaken."[58] To the
contrary, Barth's ethics are an attempt to account for how a genuine moral
deliberation might occur as a human response to divine command. In this
regard, Barth continues to show a concern to give divine agency the priority
at every turn. This is what Barth is up to when he acknowledges that there is
"a practical casuistry, an active casuistry, the casuistry of the prophetic *ethos.*"[59]

    Barth envisions a sort of practical casuistry that each recipient of the
command of God must undergo as "the unavoidable venture . . . of understanding God's concrete specific command here and now in this particular
way, of making a corresponding decision in this particular way, and of sum-
moning others to such a concrete and specific decision."[60] When God's
command addresses a person, she must respond. This response is "the leap
of choice, decision and action."[61] This leap—this decision to respond in one

---

[54]*CD* III/4:7-8.

[55]Mangina, *Karl Barth on the Christian Life*, 121.

[56]Barth specifically addresses his concern with reading these texts as rules or moral guidelines in
    CD II/2. His concern here runs parallel to his larger concern of collapsing the Word of God into
    Scripture and imposing an external system of laws and precepts that stifle God's freedom (*CD*
    I/1:136-40).

[57]McKenny, *Analogy of Grace*, 242-43.

[58]Migliore, "Commanding Grace," 7. See also Haddorff, *Christian Ethics as Witness*, 249.

[59]*CD* III/4:9.

[60]*CD* III/4:9.

[61]*CD* III/4:16.

way and not another—is what Barth means by practical casuistry. The ethical agent undergoes moral deliberation and acts responsibly to God's command. At the same time, she can never have a certain prior knowledge that she is being obedient. She can only have the knowledge of God's previous commands and the manner in which human obedience corresponded to those commands; she can only have the "formed reference."

For Barth, God's command encounters the human agent vertically (from above); but it always encounters a human agent who exists horizontally (across time). Each new ethical encounter establishes a new "point in a linear pattern which may be traced" to record the history of God's command.[62] The formed reference is simply the ability of special ethics to reference the basic form in which God's vertical command intersects humanity's horizontal existence.

A formed reference is possible because all ethical events share the same two factors: God and humanity. First, the ethical event always has to do with "the commanding God as He is knowable to us in His own Word, in Jesus Christ."[63] This God "characterises Himself (in accordance with His inner trinitarian being) as Creator, Reconciler, and Redeemer."[64] Second, the ethical event always has to do with humanity as they relate to this God as creatures, reconciled sinners, and redeemed children of God. A "practical casuistry" is therefore possible as a commentary on the history of this God with this human as we identify the formed reference of the ethical event in these spheres and use it as guidance in our attempt to hear the command of God anew.

SUMMARY

Karl Barth's decision to keep dogmatics and ethics together is consistent with his theological break with liberalism. Concerned that ethics be grounded in divine action instead of human action, Barth set about to create space for genuine human agency as a response to divine agency. This leads

---

[62]Hart, *Regarding Karl Barth*, 98. To be sure, Barth also uses "linear" language (*CD* III/4:18), but I worry that this is a little too constrictive for what Barth intends. On Hart's account, we might imagine the ability to predict when, where, and how the next command of God will confront the agent. I would say that it gives a basic trajectory that enables us to discern some broader patterns in the way the command of God works without giving us predictive power over God's activity.
[63]*CD* III/4:24.
[64]*CD* III/4:25.

him to reconfigure the traditional Lutheran account of the law and the gospel in order to prioritize God's electing action as the gospel that commands a human response of obedience. At the same time, he rejects casuistry as the attempt to domesticate the commanding God by creating elaborate interpretive schemes that guarantee humans can know what God commands independent from and prior to God's actual command.

Hauerwas claims that he learns from Karl Barth how to keep dogmatics and ethics together. For this claim to hold, we should expect to see some of the same basic features in Hauerwas's theological ethics: a priority on divine action—particularly God's saving action in Jesus—combined with a rejection of human knowledge of the good from any source other than God's self-revelation in Jesus Christ. Instead, what we see is a reinvigoration of the project of casuistry in the context of the church's worship and witness to the triune God. This presses the question of whether Hauerwas really has learned from Barth how to keep dogmatics and ethics together.

7

Stanley Hauerwas's
Ecclesial Ethics

A BRIEF RECAPITULATION of my argument so far: Hauerwas learned from Barth to keep dogmatics and ethics together, thus rejecting the tendencies of Protestant liberalism. He then extended what he learned from Barth into his own context by arguing that Christian ethics in North America could continue to be theological by continuing to be distinctly Christian. Eventually, Hauerwas breaks with Barth's theology. At the crux of that break is a disagreement over the question of casuistry. For Barth, casuistry represents something like the fixed knowledge of God that Emil Brunner attempts to secure with natural theology. Hauerwas, sympathetic to Barth's critique of Brunner, attempts to rehabilitate casuistry as an ecclesial practice that reflects its basic theological commitment to God's self-revelation in Jesus Christ.

In this chapter, I will describe how Hauerwas attempts to redefine casuistry as a narrative-dependent practice that reflects a community's deepest convictions about reality, not fixed prescriptions for moral action. Then I will illustrate what this looks like in Hauerwas's own ecclesial ethics by showing how he uses the liturgy in order to frame ethical discourse within the church's worship of God. Finally, I will attend to the deeply christocentric convictions that underlie Hauerwas's ethics in the first place. This will set the stage for chapter eight, where I will evaluate whether Hauerwas's use of the liturgy as casuistry actually brings him into conflict with Barth's theological ethics.

CASUISTRY IN CONTEXT

The basic problem with Barth's theological ethics, according to Hauerwas, is that they remain abstract because Barth fails to develop a concrete ecclesiology that can account for the formation of disciples. One of the ways that Hauerwas suggests we overcome this problem is by attending to the necessarily casuistical nature of theological ethics. Thus a clear difference emerges between Barth and Hauerwas at this point: where Barth rejects casuistry, Hauerwas embraces it.

To be sure, Hauerwas resonates with Barth's concerns about casuistry. Hauerwas's own theological ethics are a rejection of traditional notions of casuistry that operate as a sort of applied ethics, where ethical theories and basic principles are applied to particular cases—an "ethic of doing," to borrow a memorable expression from Stanley Grenz.[1] Hauerwas concedes, "No doubt casuistry could denigrate into minimalistic ethics that were concerned primarily with avoiding evil rather than doing good."[2] Even so, Barth's rejection of casuistry seems wrongheaded to Hauerwas because it "fails to appreciate how religious communities have always generated informal as well as extremely sophisticated modes of moral reflection which can only be called casuistry."[3]

For Hauerwas, then, "the question is not whether to have casuistry or not to have casuistry, but what kind of casuistry we should have."[4] The type of casuistry a community has "depend[s] on prior communal presuppositions about the kind of people we should be."[5] Christian communities are particularly determined by the call to be new communities of holiness. Baptism, for instance, signifies the remission of sins and initiation into this new holy community. After baptism, Christians needed to develop other practices, like penance, to account for the forgiveness of sins and the continued pursuit of holiness. In this regard, the practice of baptism "provides the background for the understanding of the penitential practices that spawned the development of formal casuistical methods" in the Christian tradition.[6]

Casuistry, in the Christian community, then, is not determined by the desire to apply theories or principles to particular cases. Instead, the purpose of casuistry is to help the community to name the ways in which it falls short

---

[1]Stanley J. Grenz, *The Moral Quest: Foundations of Christian Ethics* (Downers Grove, IL: InterVarsity Press, 1997), 27; *PK*, 130; *IGC*, 170.
[2]*IGC*, 180.
[3]*CET*, 68.
[4]*PK*, 130-31.
[5]*CET*, 70.
[6]*IGC*, 179-80.

of its goal to be a community of holiness (confession) and to imagine a way forward (reconciliation). Hauerwas writes,

> What I mean by casuistry, then, is not just the attempt to adjudicate difficult cases of conscience within a system of moral principles, but the process by which a tradition tests whether its practices are consistent (that is, truthful) or inconsistent in the light of its basic habits and convictions or whether these convictions require new practices and behavior.[7]

One of the ways the community tests itself is by comparing its own actions to those of the saints—previous generations of Christians who embody what "well-lived and virtuous lives" look like.[8] Saints are people who lived "innovative lives that . . . help us know better what [Christian] convictions entail."[9] Casuistry involves studying the lives of the saints because convictions cannot simply be applied to our daily lives. In fact, the implications of our convictions cannot always be known in advance; they can only be worked out in the day-to-day lives of people who earnestly seek to be faithful to those convictions.[10] By attending to the lives of those the church designates as exemplars of Christian faithfulness, we can learn how particular convictions are embodied in the specific ethical actions of Christians in the past as well as anticipate what faithfulness might look like in the future.[11]

Saints do not "come out of nowhere." They are people whose moral character is formed over time in the context of particular religious communities. Those communities form the lives of their members as they participate in the practices that constitute the community's identity. In the case of Christian communities, this means participating in the worship of the triune God. For Hauerwas, the church's practices and liturgy become a type of casuistry as it retells the narratives in which casuistry is necessarily rooted. In this manner, it forms people who cannot help but think about their action in the world from the perspective of their worship of the triune God. The church's worship trains Christians to be friends with God as they seek to become "imitators of God" in their actions.[12]

---

[7]*PK*, 120.
[8]*PK*, 121.
[9]*IGC*, 181.
[10]*PK*, 120.
[11]*IGC*, 181.
[12]*IGC*, 180.

This crucial insight suggests that we should begin our assessment of Hauerwas's appeal to casuistry with a description of Hauerwas's mature theological ethics. Most scholars, including Hauerwas himself, gravitate toward *The Peaceable Kingdom* as the most complete expression of Hauerwas's theological ethics.[13] It is certainly a central text in Hauerwas's oeuvre and deserves attention; however, I worry that undue focus on *The Peaceable Kingdom* neglects the manner in which Hauerwas's theological ethics develops after his move from Notre Dame to Duke. Specifically, I am interested in how Hauerwas begins to teach Christian ethics to students who are preparing for ministry by attending to the liturgy as a means of moral formation. In this regard, I contend that the fullest expression of Hauerwas's theological ethics is the vision expressed in *The Blackwell Companion to Christian Ethics*, coedited with Samuel Wells.

To be sure, Hauerwas's work has always hinted at the liturgy. Early in his theological studies at Yale, Gregory Dix's *The Shape of the Liturgy* impressed him.[14] Later, at Notre Dame, he met Aiden Kavanaugh and Bill Storey—people who "thought it mattered how Christians actually worshiped God."[15] In *A Community of Character*, Hauerwas articulated the relationship between Scripture and liturgy as one of "performance" whereby the church performs the Scriptures through its liturgy in a manner that necessarily shapes how it interprets Scripture.[16] In this regard, he was "on the way" toward his mature theological ethics from the start.

With *The Peaceable Kingdom*, Hauerwas articulates an ecclesiology that bears the traditional Protestant marks of the church: proclamation, sacraments, and holy living. In that context, with a few short paragraphs, he gestures toward the ethical significance that the liturgy, especially the Eucharist, will hold in his later work:

> The sacraments enact the story of Jesus and, thus, form a community in his image. We could not be the church without them. For the story of Jesus is not simply one that is told; it must be enacted. The sacraments are means crucial to shaping and preparing us to tell and hear that story. Thus baptism is that

---

[13]Indeed, when Hauerwas moves to rebuff Healy's charge of ecclesiocentrism, he suggests that Healy did not sufficiently attend to the christological aspects of *PK*. See *WT*, 272-73.

[14]*HC*, 62.

[15]*HC*, 97-98.

[16]*CC*, 240 n. 9.

rite of initiation necessary for us to become part of Jesus' death and resurrection. . . . The eucharist is the eschatological meal of God's continuing
presence that makes possible a peaceable people. . . .

   [Baptism and eucharist] are the essential rituals of our politics. Through
them we learn who we are. . . . These liturgies *are* our effective social work.
. . . It is in baptism and eucharist that we see most clearly the marks of God's
kingdom in the world. They set our standard, as we try to bring every aspect
of our lives under their sway.[17]

Thus to suggest that Hauerwas first comes to the idea of liturgy after he ar-
rives at Duke would be a mistake. At the same time, Duke provides the
material conditions for the seeds of this idea to germinate.

   When Hauerwas arrived at Duke, having already published *The Peaceable
Kingdom,* he found himself coteaching the introduction to Christian ethics
course for students who were training for ministry. In conversation with his
colleague Harmon Smith, he decided to organize the course around the
liturgy. Hauerwas explains,

   The center of the ministry is word and sacrament. We were training people
   who would spend the rest of their lives presiding at the Eucharist. By orga-
   nizing the ethics course liturgically, we hoped to defeat any temptation students might have to ignore the fact that what they would do at the altar is
   determinative for the witness the church must make in the world.[18]

Nearly twenty years of teaching this course leads to the vision behind *The
Blackwell Companion.*

THE LITURGY AS MORAL FORMATION

Theological ethics, at its heart, is the investigation of human action from the
perspective that God acts first in Jesus Christ: "Ethics names the ways in
which disciples discern and embody Christ's life in the world." For Hauerwas and Wells, "The chief way [disciples] learn how to do this is through
worship."[19] Worship is the training ground where God's people learn to care
about the things he cares about, "to imitate [God] in habit, instinct, and

---

[17]*PK,* 107-8.
[18]*HC,* 195.
[19]*BCCE,* 26.

reflex," and to become living examples of God's love for the world.[20] In short, "Worship trains Christians to be saints."[21]

Of course, any human action that is oriented toward the glorification of God is properly considered worship. Hauerwas and Wells agree with the Westminster divines that humanity's "chief end" is "to glorify God, and to enjoy him forever."[22] But Hauerwas has in mind specifically the church's liturgy, and particularly the Eucharist, as a school for training. The liturgy is the place where Christians go with an expectation that God will meet them and make himself known. It trains them to enter each ethical event with a similar expectation.[23] For Hauerwas, the church's liturgy trains Christians to be Christians all the time; not merely to make "Christian decisions" when they are faced with moral dilemmas.[24]

The course Hauerwas developed at Duke follows the order of worship for most Christian worship services and unfolds in five movements.[25] Hauerwas and Wells title these movements: (1) Meeting, (2) Re-encountering the Story, (3) Being Embodied, (4) Re-enacting the Story, and (5) Being Commissioned.

In the first movement, Hauerwas and Wells emphasize "the social and political significance of the very fact that Christians gather at all."[26] Worship is political simply by virtue of the fact that it brings people together and asks them to see the world in a particular way. The practices that constitute "meeting" are gathering, greeting, confessing, and celebrating forgiveness. Christians are gathered together for the purpose of worshiping God, and in the process they are formed into a particular people. They learn to greet strangers as brothers and sisters in the gospel, to confess their sins to God and each other, and to celebrate their shared forgiveness by praising God. Particularly, The Blackwell Companion attends to the manner in which the church gathers people without distinction by gender, race, or nation and equips them each according to their callings. This means that Christians

---

[20]BCCE, 25.
[21]BCCE, 26.
[22]"The Shorter Catechism," Q1, in The Book of Confessions: The Constitution of the Presbyterian Church (U.S.A.): Part I (Louisville, KY: The Office of the General Assembly, 2007), 7.001; BCCE, 16.
[23]BCCE, 3.
[24]BCCE, 26.
[25]For a sample syllabus from one of Hauerwas's ethics courses at Duke, see IGC, 164.
[26]BCCE, 10.

have a particular political vision that informs questions of gender equality, racial reconciliation, and the like.

Second, Christians "re-encounter the story" of the God of Scripture. Through the liturgical practices of reading Scripture, preaching, reciting creeds, and the congregational disciplines of listening to the sermon and discerning the gospel, Christians are confronted each week with the "performed and enacted Word" of God.[27] These liturgical practices train Christians to recognize the authority of the Word of God and to name it for what it is—a liberating Word. It further trains them to practice moral reasoning as they deliberate what God's liberating Word means here and now.

Third, Hauerwas and Wells emphasize the liturgical practices that attend particularly to the idea that the community of believers is the one "body of Christ." This includes occasional practices like baptism and marriage as well as regular practices like intercession and passing the peace. Baptism marks the incorporation of new members into the body of Christ. It also makes particular claims about each Christian's body. In baptism, we confess that our bodies are not our own; they belong to God. Marriage bears witness to what it means to share your body with another. "My" body becomes "our" body. Intercession is the practice whereby the body of believers names the particular needs of some of the members of the body, acknowledging that the needs of one are the needs of all. Finally, passing the peace serves as a weekly reaffirmation that we can continue to trust each other to be the one body of Christ with each other. The ethical implications of proclaiming that Christians are the one body of Christ include questions related to human bodies: medical ethics, sexual ethics, poverty, social organization, and communal discipline.

Fourth, the liturgy climaxes with the Eucharist. In this, Hauerwas and Wells are in tune with the majority of the world's Christian traditions. The Eucharist is a rich practice that includes material, sacerdotal, and communal aspects. Particularly, they attend to the manner in which the Eucharist invokes the presence of the Holy Spirit, remembers Christ's sacrifice, calls us to communal participation in a shared meal, and evokes responses of thankfulness and service. These themes inform how Christians participate in the

---

[27] *BCCE*, 10.

church's witness through tithes and offerings, peacemaking, hospitality, and care for the disabled, among other things.

Finally, worship concludes in a benediction and dismissal. Christians are blessed and sent out into the world with a commission to trust God to provide and to bear witness to his good provision. This means trusting God for material provision as well as trusting God's providential rule of the world enough to have children and to raise them to trust God as well. By trusting God, Christians become living witnesses to the rest of the world that God is a God who provides for his people.

The Blackwell Companion is a collection of essays written by Hauerwas's former students and friends that largely conforms to the way that he ordered his ethics course at Duke. Indeed, after the publication of *The Blackwell Companion*, Hauerwas used it as a primary textbook.[28] As such, it is an important resource for understanding how Hauerwas thinks that specific worship practices provide the concrete conditions for the formation of disciples of Jesus and witnesses to the gospel. This aspect of the work is widely acknowledged.[29] What is less acknowledged, however, is that *The Blackwell Companion* also provides the clearest explication of what Hauerwas takes to be the basic theological commitments that inform his theological ethics. Hauerwas calls these basic theological commitments "convictions."

Certain theological convictions make Christian communities Christian and cannot be given up without changing the community to such an extent that it can no longer identify itself as Christian. For Hauerwas, there are at least three such theological convictions that run throughout his body of work: "the nature of God, the significance of Jesus, the eschatological fate of the world."[30] Christians come to learn these basic convictions as they participate in the Christian community, the church. The church is the community that lives by the gospel narrative that Jesus is Israel's Messiah: the incarnation of Israel's God in the flesh and the inauguration of that same

---

[28]I was a student in the first Christian Ethics class to use *BCCE* at Duke Divinity in the fall of 2004.
[29]See, for example, the following book reviews: C. C. Pecknold, review of *The Blackwell Companion to Christian Ethics*, ed. Stanley Hauerwas and Samuel Wells, *Journal of Theological Studies* 57, no. 1 (2006): 413-18; Michael Banner, review of *The Blackwell Companion to Christian Ethics*, ed. Stanley Hauerwas and Samuel Wells, *International Journal of Systematic Theology* 9, no. 1 (2007): 106-9; and Bernd Wannenwetsch, review of *The Blackwell Companion to Christian Ethics*, ed. Stanley Hauerwas and Samuel Wells, *Journal of Contemporary Religion* 21, no. 2 (2006): 264-65.
[30]*PK*, 13.

God's kingdom. The church is so formed by this narrative that its very existence bears witness to these convictions. Christian lives reflect their basic theological convictions and the truthfulness of those convictions is demonstrated in the performance of the lives that are shaped by them.

Convictions, then, for Hauerwas, are the metaphysical assumptions that Christians hold when they take the biblical narrative of God's dealings with Israel, Jesus, and the church to be true. These assumptions cannot be divorced from the narratives that make them intelligible. To wit: knowledge of God itself is rendered in the form of narrative because the triune God is a God who is always identified in relationship to the biblical narrative of the covenant he made with Abraham, renewed with Moses, fulfilled in Jesus, and continues in faithfulness to the church.[31] The very character of this God is discerned as his actions over the course of time prove to be consistent and trustworthy. The story is not important because it is a story, and therefore has the power to form us as any other story might; instead, the story is important because it is a story about God and, therefore, a claim about reality.[32]

This narrative-dependent knowledge of God necessarily implies a social ethic because the story of God's covenantal relationship with Israel and the church is also the story of God's calling a people out of the world to be his witnesses to the world. Such a vocation requires knowing, telling, and living the narrative in accordance with the basic theological convictions that make it intelligible and credible.[33] The church becomes a part of the story as it is drawn into God's ongoing relationship with his creation. In other words, the character of the God revealed in the story tells us something about how God's people should live.[34]

This is where accusations that Hauerwas is ecclesiocentric instead of theocentric really land. Hauerwas is certainly "ecclesiocentric" to the extent that the church becomes the stage on which Christian convictions are demonstrated. Hauerwas writes, "Christian beliefs about God, Jesus, sin, the nature of human existence, and salvation are intelligible only if they are seen against the background of the church."[35] Nevertheless, the church is not

---

[31]*PK*, 29.
[32]*CET*, 26.
[33]*CC*, 9.
[34]*CC*, 67.
[35]*AN*, 42.

itself one of the basic theological convictions that Hauerwas identifies (God, Jesus, the kingdom). Instead, the church is the embodiment of those convictions across time and space.

In this regard, I think scholars who accuse Hauerwas of being ecclesiocentric have often insufficiently attended to his claim that his theological ethics presuppose and are the outworking of these basic theological convictions. Scholars have long lamented that Hauerwas refuses to write his "big book" that "puts it all together."[36] Indeed, one of the long-standing criticisms of Hauerwas's work is that he has not done enough to make his theological presuppositions transparent, giving the impression that his theological ethics abandon God-talk and focus instead on church-talk. Robert Jenson, for example, exhorts Hauerwas "to parallel Barth also in metaphysical bluntness."[37] The persistence of these sorts of comments overlooks *The Blackwell Companion* in important ways.

Hauerwas, in a sense, did write his "big book."[38] He jokes that he was simply smart enough to convince others to write it for him. Unfortunately, his self-effacing humor overshadows the significance of the first two chapters of *The Blackwell Companion*. These chapters, cowritten by Hauerwas and Wells, are the clearest articulation of Hauerwas's basic theological convictions, and therefore must be considered in any examination of Hauerwas's theological ethics.

THE CHRISTOCENTRISM OF HAUERWAS'S ETHICS

The God of Christian ethics is the God revealed in Scripture. Particularly, for Hauerwas and Wells, he is the triune God of Jesus' baptism in Matthew 3. In this text, we have the actions of the trinitarian God setting the context for the human agency of Jesus. With Jesus' baptism, the heavens are open, the Holy Spirit descends, and the Father's voice reveals that Jesus is his Son. We know this triune God is the God of Israel because Jesus' baptism takes place in the Jordan River and thus recapitulates Israel's crossing during the exodus. Jesus himself becomes the true Israelite who obediently follows

---

[36] At least, Hauerwas regularly feels the need to explain why many of his books are not the "big book" that "pulls it all together." See *PK*, xvi; *STT*, 8; and *WGU*, 10.

[37] Robert W. Jenson, "The Hauerwas Project," *Modern Theology* 8, no. 3 (1992): 293.

[38] *BCCE*, 1.

Israel's God and, therefore, demonstrates what it means to "fulfill all righteousness."[39] Here we learn something about who God is and how we are called to live as followers of Jesus.

There is a real "gospel" message—a real good news—to Jesus' baptism: "God has acted decisively to change the context of life."[40] The heavens are open and God is listening to the prayers of his people; God's spirit is present and active in the world; and in Jesus Christ, God is revealing himself to his creation. The baptismal event is the epitome of God's gracious action, and in it "we have witnessed the foundation, the source, the context, and the content of Christian ethics."[41] The goal of Christian ethics is the same as the goal of Israel's baptism in the Jordan: liberation from slavery and friendship with God. This friendship is realized in the worship of God, principally in the Eucharist, where God shares table fellowship with his friends.

Hauerwas's theological ethics are christocentric in this respect: the baptism of Jesus is an event that at once remembers God's faithfulness to Israel, declares God's friendship with us in Jesus, and anticipates our eschatological companionship at God's banquet table. It is a demonstration that "God meets the needs of those who call upon him in need and expectation."[42] Christian ethics begins at the point of this expectation with the conviction that God has given us everything we need in giving us Jesus.

Hauerwas and Wells claim, "What God wants is for his people to worship him, to be his friends, and to eat with him."[43] In Jesus, he gives his people the gifts they need to accomplish these tasks: "Jesus epitomizes all of God's gifts."[44] Particularly, the classical doctrine of the threefold body of Christ provides the means by which God provides for his people. Jesus' historical body—the incarnation, life, death, resurrection, and ascension—is given to God's people in the gift of Scripture. Scripture is the story of God's faithfulness to Israel and Jesus' fulfillment of the righteousness that God expected from Israel. Guided by Scripture, the church worships God by praising him, giving thanks for his past faithfulness in Jesus, and petitioning

---

[39]*BCCE*, 14-15.
[40]*BCCE*, 15.
[41]*BCCE*, 16.
[42]*BCCE*, 16.
[43]*BCCE*, 13.
[44]*BCCE*, 16.

him for future intercession and the establishment of the kingdom of God. Between Christ's first and second coming, Christians live empowered by the Holy Spirit, who "trains God's people to recognize God's hand at work, shapes the ways in which they reflect God's character, and empowers them to express that character in the world."[45]

The second form of the body of Christ is the church. The church is the "people assembled . . . in the strength of Christ's coming and being among them."[46] God gives his people the church as the means by which they learn how to be friends with him. Through the many practices that constitute the church's worship of God, Christians are formed into the type of friends that God desires them to be by becoming reconciled to God and each other.

The third form of the body of Christ is the Eucharist. The Eucharist is a gift from God that differentiates God's people from the world around them by demarking a specific time, space, and action. It marks a specific time in the sense that it only happens when the church gathers together to celebrate Jesus' resurrection. It marks off a specific space because it makes the church that gathers around the table a visible church. Finally, it marks a specific action in the sense that it becomes identifiable as an act that is constitutive of the church's identity in the world. In sharing a meal with God and each other, the church receives the sustenance it needs to continue its mission in the world.

The relationship between the second and third form of the body of Christ holds center court in Hauerwas's theological ethics, to be sure. For Hauerwas the church is wherever the Eucharist is and it is constituted by whoever is gathered around the table. The Eucharist is the compendium of the church's liturgy. Hauerwas and Wells write,

> Celebrating the Eucharist means much more than eating bread. It means gathering, and thus becoming a visible people. It means being reconciled, and thus finding unity in Christ, rather than in "common humanity." It means listening and responding to the scriptural story, and thus sharing a tradition. It means remembering God's action and invoking the Spirit's presence, and thus being redirected to true power and unique sacrifice. It means being sent out to witness and serve, and thus being given a shape for living.[47]

---

[45]*BCCE*, 18.
[46]*BCCE*, 18.
[47]*BCCE*, 23.

But the church and the Eucharist are only these things as the body of Christ. "The church is not the limit of God's activity in the world," but it certainly is God's action, "bringing people out of slavery and exile" and reconstituting them as members of his body.[48]

The relationship between divine and human agency in the church requires further explication in Hauerwas's work. The church is God's action, and wherever the church is gathered around the Eucharist, God is present and active. And yet Christians have the responsibility to bear witness to the fact that God is at work. It does this primarily through *imitatio Christi*—bearing witness to the fact that it is the body of Christ by imitating Christ's earthly life, particularly his offices as prophet and priest.

The church imitates Jesus' prophetic office by living in the world as an alternative political community that is capable of speaking to and naming the idolatries of the world. Similarly, it imitates Jesus' priestly office by being an alternative political community as it gathers around the Eucharist and allows itself to be formed into a new people that is capable of seeing the world for what it is. It stops short in its imitation of Jesus at Christ's kingly office. Where the church attempts to imitate Christ's kingly office, it oversteps the limits of its human agency and tries to accomplish activity that belongs to God alone. Indeed, by trusting Jesus to exercise the office of king and establish his kingdom on earth, the church bears witness to the fact that God is providentially at work in the world, transforming it into his kingdom. The church primarily does this by demonstrating patience and nonviolence as it waits for God to act, exercising its priestly role through prayer for God's intercession and its prophetic role by proclaiming where and how God is present and active in the world.[49]

Central, then, to Hauerwas's claim that the liturgy forms saints is the argument that the church trains saints to imitate Christ's prophetic and priestly ministries even as it teaches them patience and nonviolence as a witness to Christ's kingship. The church has always done this, which explains why people like Karl Barth, Dietrich Bonhoeffer, Dorothy Day, John Howard Yoder, and Rowan Williams exist. For Hauerwas, however, Barth's own theology fails to attend to these concrete aspects of the church, and

---

[48]*BCCE*, 23.
[49]*BCCE*, 21-22.

therefore leaves the church without the resources necessary to go on training disciples in twenty-first-century America. At this crucial point, Hauerwas turns to thick description of church practices as a rich casuistry for the formation of saints.

8

Casuistry and Christology

Oᴸɪᴠᴇʀ O'Dᴏɴᴏᴠᴀɴ ʜᴀꜱ ʀᴇᴄᴇɴᴛʟʏ asserted that dogmatics and ethics are two discrete disciplines that require "a proper *vis-à-vis*."[1] He does so over and against the Protestant tendency to either collapse ethics into dogmatics or dogmatics into ethics. Whether O'Donovan threatens a Brunnerian return to the separation of the *how* from the *what* is not important here (although it is an interesting question); what is important is that on this description, the difference between Barth and Hauerwas is the difference between the tendency to imply the ethical within the dogmatic or the tendency to imply the dogmatic within the ethical. Interestingly enough, O'Donovan's suggestion concedes that Barth and Hauerwas at least share a tendency to hold dogmatics and ethics together in a manner that prevents the independence of each.

The difference between Barth and Hauerwas, however, is not irrelevant. Insofar as dogmatics endeavors to speak about God first, divine agency is given precedence. This is the fear that is ultimately expressed by the Schleiermacher thesis: that with Hauerwas's work dogmatics is collapsed into ethics and, therefore, humans become the measure of all things. On these terms, it would be better if Hauerwas gave dogmatics its own place alongside his ethics. For then, even if he risked severing them, he would at least be clear about the difference between divine and human action.

---

[1]Oliver O'Donovan, *Ethics as Theology*, vol. 1, *Self, World, and Time* (Grand Rapids: Eerdmans, 2013), 81.

The conflict between Barth's ethics as dogmatics and Hauerwas's dogmatics as ethics can be articulated in relation to the question of casuistry: Barth rejects casuistry; Hauerwas embraces it. While Barth worries that casuistry attempts to carve out a sphere where human agency can operate independently from and prior to the command of God, Hauerwas embraces it as a means to account for human agency as a reflection of God's agency. Such a strong emphasis on ethics threatens, at this point, to undermine Hauerwas's claim that he is Barthian in his attempt to keep dogmatics and ethics together.

In this chapter, I will take up the challenge made by the Schleiermacher thesis, that Hauerwas's theology substitutes the church for God as the subject of theology by collapsing dogmatics into ethics, divine action into human action. To the contrary, I will argue that Hauerwas's theological ethics, with its emphasis on casuistry, does not violate any of Barth's major concerns with casuistry. Indeed, Hauerwas changes the definition of casuistry in a manner that is more compatible with Barth's own attempts to treat moral deliberation. At the heart of Hauerwas's understanding of human agency are concepts of imitation and participation that resonate deeply with Barth's own thinking. Indeed, greater attention to the christological commitments of each theologian's ethics suggests a possible way forward.

CASUISTRY REDEFINED

For Hauerwas, casuistry is the means by which the church tests its behavior against its deepest convictions. It is not, in this sense, prospective but retrospective. Looking back on its actions, the church is able to determine whether its actions demonstrate faithfulness with its confessed convictions. In other words, casuistry for Hauerwas is not a prescriptive legalism but a self-reflective evaluation of the church's own faithfulness or sinfulness. Significantly, then, casuistry is not a matter of determining "the minimum" required to fulfill our duty to do "the right thing"; instead, casuistry is meant to point us toward "the maximal" in the sense of showing us how to pursue holiness.[2] Primary to Hauerwas's own account of holiness are the concepts of imitation and participation. For Hauerwas, these are both christological themes.

---

[2]B, 144.

Remember, Nigel Biggar charges that one key difference between Barth and Hauerwas is that Barth's Christology is Nicaean and Chalcedonian while Hauerwas's is Anabaptist. Behind this charge is the implication that Barth's Christology is high while Hauerwas's is low, attending to the life of Jesus but not the high christological themes of incarnation, atonement, resurrection, and the like. While Hauerwas has written a great deal to clarify his Christology since that time, Biggar at least had access to *The Peaceable Kingdom*.[3] A close reading of *The Peaceable Kingdom* demonstrates that Biggar's accusation fails to take Hauerwas at his word.

It is true that Hauerwas skewers "Christology" in *The Peaceable Kingdom*, suggesting, "Christian ethics has tended to make 'Christology' rather than Jesus its starting point."[4] He goes on to explain how doctrines like the incarnation, the atonement, and the two natures of Christ become the starting point for ethical reflection at the expense of the actual life and teachings of Jesus. Hence, Biggar's charge that Hauerwas's Christology is low and Anabaptist.

It is a mistake, however, to say that Hauerwas's Christology is not Nicaean and Chalcedonian. His point is not that ethics cannot begin with Christology; to the contrary, they must begin there. Instead, Hauerwas's point is that christological appeals in ethics are often made to doctrinal claims about Jesus that operate like wide-sweeping theories, replacing the biblical witness to Jesus. Thus, while incarnation is a doctrine that describes the biblical narrative of Jesus' conception, birth, and whole life, it becomes in the hands of some an abstract principle that is used with little concern for the actual content of the human life in which God came. In other words, Hauerwas's opposition to "Christology" is not against Christology itself, but against what it becomes when theology and ethics operate as "theory" and "praxis" and "God became human" becomes a principle that requires application.

Even so, this is not an endorsement of a low Christology.[5] Hauerwas is clear that a purely historical Jesus is a work of fiction. The only Jesus we have is the early church's Jesus as presented in the Gospels. Central to Jesus' life in these Gospel stories is the kingdom of God and the call to discipleship. Jesus is the *autobasileia*, the kingdom himself, and as such the call

---

[3]The most insightful of which is probably *CSC*.
[4]*PK*, 72.
[5]*PK*, 75.

to discipleship is a call to "locate our lives within God's life, within the journey that comprises his kingdom."[6] For Hauerwas, then, a proper Christology is one that balances the high christological claims of Christ's divinity with his life and teachings: "Jesus exemplified in his life the standards of that kingdom."[7] Again, this was a lesson Hauerwas learned from Hans Frei and developed in conversation with John Howard Yoder.

For this reason, *imitatio Christi* becomes an important aspect of Hauerwas's christological ethics. To locate our lives within God's kingdom requires "learning to be like God" by being like Christ.[8] Particularly, for Hauerwas, this means "Be perfect, therefore, as your heavenly Father is perfect" (Mt 5:48 NRSV). This is a perfection that is only possible as we attend to Jesus, the one human who is perfect.

This is neither the external *imitatio Christi* of the Franciscans nor the internal spirituality of the Modern Devotion movement. For Hauerwas, *imitatio Christi* means to become a disciple of Jesus Christ by becoming a member of the community that seeks to follow him. By imitating Jesus, we become imitators of God because Jesus is the Messiah, who fulfills Israel's threefold office of Prophet, Priest, and King: "Jesus' life was seen as the recapitulation of the life of Israel and thus presented the very life of God in the world."[9]

In short, Hauerwas's concept of *imitatio Christi* might instead be called *imitatio Dei* because it suggests that to be like Jesus means to become like God. This is important because this means that even Hauerwas's attention to Jesus' life is not, finally, about Jesus' humanity as an example of the good; instead, it is about what we can know of the divine life and how we are called to relate to God. Of course, for Hauerwas, central to this claim is the fact that in Jesus God faces the cross by choosing nonviolence, telling us something about God's very being. Thus Hauerwas's pacifism is christological from the start because it is rooted in a claim about who God is in Jesus Christ and only then, a subsequent call to imitate God's peacefulness in our own lives.

---

[6]*PK*, 75; on *Autobasileia*, see *CC*, 45.
[7]*PK*, 74.
[8]*PK*, 75.
[9]*PK*, 78.

Imitation is not the ultimate conceptual description in Hauerwas's christological ethics. By couching imitation within the existence of the church, Hauerwas effectively shifts from "imitation" language to "participation" language. After all, we become like God as we participate in and bear witness to his kingdom in the community of disciples established by Jesus.[10] This means, first, that we learn to see the world from the point of view of the resurrection and, second, that we "practice resurrection"—to borrow an expression from Wendell Berry—by becoming participants in the story of God's kingdom by practicing nonviolence, forgiveness, trust in God, hospitality, and so on.[11] Participation, for Hauerwas, means participating in the story of Jesus' kingdom by bearing witness to its presence in the world.

Here the liturgy becomes important for Hauerwas as the means by which we participate in the story of the kingdom. Particularly, "the sacraments enact the story of Jesus and, thus, form a community in his image."[12] Baptism makes us a part of the story, while Eucharist reminds us of how the story ends. Meanwhile, prayer invites God to be present in the world and opens our eyes to see his presence. Finally, preaching is the means by which we hear and tell the story, requiring that we encounter strangers as potential friends in Christ.[13]

That Hauerwas calls these things casuistry is, remember, based on the fact that casuistry means testing your actions against the convictions that make those actions intelligible. Further, those convictions are only known as they are received in narrative form. The liturgy is the primary place where Christians hear and learn to tell the story of God's kingdom. As such, it is the place where they learn to be like Jesus and to participate in his messianic ministry to the world. Thus, finally, for Hauerwas, the appeal to casuistry is an appeal to test our lives against the one whom we believe to be God's kingdom in the flesh and to seek to become more like God as we participate in the church's witness to him.

---

[10]A recent conversation between Brock and Hauerwas illuminates the relationship between imitation and participation in Hauerwas. For Hauerwas, participation is determinative for thinking about Christology and discipleship (*B*, 147).

[11]Wendell Berry, "Manifesto: The Mad Farmer Liberation Front," in *Collected Poems: 1957–1982* (New York: North Point, 1985), 151-52.

[12]*PK*, 107.

[13]*PK*, 108-9.

This, of course, places Hauerwas in tension with Barth. The tension is felt generally around the use of casuistry, but it heightens particularly around the notion of imitation. Ultimately for Barth, *imitatio Christi* is simply another type of casuistry, an attempt to have the command of God without listening for it.

Casuistry by Another Name?

There are two possible ways of dissolving this tension. The first is to simply say that Barth is wrong to reject casuistry and that his own ethics show this to be impossible in practice. The second is to demonstrate that each theologian's position shares similar concerns with casuistry and that each pivots, in his own way, toward Christology. I will consider both possibilities here.

The first line of argumentation is the one expressed by Hauerwas. He suggests that Barth's failure to recognize the necessarily casuistical nature of all moral reflection prevents him from giving greater expression to the manner in which his own theological ethics operate casuistically. With this criticism, Hauerwas joins a handful of Barth scholars who argue that Barth's own theological ethics operate casuistically in spite of his intentions.[14]

In essence, the question at hand is this: Is Barth's formed reference a return to casuistry? With Barth's transition from general ethics in *Church Dogmatics* II/2 to special ethics in III/4, one cannot help but feel the tension between his prohibition on casuistry and his own positive delineation of what he calls a "practical casuistry." This tension results in two competing interpretations of Barth's ethics.[15]

One line of interpretation occurs in the literature with Biggar's landmark study of Barth's ethics, *The Hastening That Waits*. Therein Biggar argues that Barth's rejection of casuistry is a rejection of closed ethical systems that operate as "a one-way movement from principles through rules to cases." In reality, however, most forms of casuistry are a more nuanced dialectical process that "constantly involves the modification of old rules

---

[14]*B*, 139. In addition to Biggar, I would also include William Werpehowski, whose work is referenced below. See Gerald P. McKenny, "Heterogeneity and Ethical Deliberation: Casuistry, Narrative, and Event in the Ethics of Karl Barth," *Annual of the Society of Christian Ethics* 20 (2000): 207.

[15]Alexander Massmann suggests there are two competing interpretations in the literature best represented by Nigel Biggar on the one hand and Paul Nimmo on the other. Massmann, *Citizenship in Heaven and on Earth: Karl Barth's Ethics* (Minneapolis: Fortress, 2015), xx-xxi.

and the generation of new ones in the attempt to give faithful expression to a given moral principle in reaction to new, morally significant data."[16] According to Biggar, Barth's own work tends to look more like this second type of casuistry, suggesting that he ends up developing a casuistry in spite of himself in the form of an open-ended ethical system. Biggar writes, "Barth concedes much more in practice to casuistry than his theory allows."[17] Thus Biggar's explanation of the tension is that Barth's theory is irreconcilable with his praxis.

Biggar's study is one of the first significant works on Barth's ethics, and his argument that Barth has an open-ended ethical system is particularly important against the backdrop of earlier interpretations of Barth as an act-deontologist whose command ethics leave no room for moral deliberation or development.[18] Among those scholars who lend support to Biggar is Joseph Mangina, who points out that Barth responds positively to the sort of detailed categorization of sin we see in Protestant scholasticism and even engages in "a practical exercise in 'handling sin'" with his formal treatments of sin as pride, sloth, and falsehood.[19]

Others, however, worry that Biggar unfairly injects fixed moral principles and casuistic themes into Barth's theology.[20] One such interpreter is David Haddorff, who agrees with Biggar that Barth's ethics work dialectically but disagrees about the two poles of the dialectic. For Biggar, the dialectic moves back and forth between fixed moral principles and the contemporary moral landscape and experience. For Haddorff, in distinction, Barth's dialectic "remains in constant movement 'back and forth' between God's free command and our responsible human action, as guided by ethical reflection."[21] Here

---

[16]Nigel Biggar, *The Hastening That Waits: Karl Barth's Ethics* (Oxford: Clarendon, 1993), 40-41.

[17]Nigel Biggar, "Barth's Trinitarian Ethic," in *The Cambridge Companion to Karl Barth*, ed. John Webster (Cambridge: Cambridge University Press, 2000), 222.

[18]Among the scholars whom Biggar is contradicting here are Robert Willis, James Gustafson, Reinhold Niebuhr, and Robin Lovin. Lovin particularly accuses Barth of act-deontology. See Biggar, *Hastening That Waits*, 21 n. 73.

[19]Joseph Mangina, *Karl Barth on the Christian Life: The Practical Knowledge of God* (New York: Peter Lang, 2001), 97, 121.

[20]Biggar himself later concedes that his work tends to push more in the direction that he thinks Barth should have gone instead of the direction Barth actually goes. Nigel Biggar, "Karl Barth's Ethics Revisited," in *Commanding Grace: Studies in Karl Barth's Ethics*, ed. Daniel Migliore (Grand Rapids: Eerdmans, 2010), 26.

[21]David Haddorff, *Christian Ethics as Witness: Barth's Ethics for a World at Risk* (Eugene, OR: Cascade, 2010), 249.

the poles are the divine and human agents; thus the dialectic is actually an asymmetrical relationship between two people. This is also the basic thrust of William Werpehowski's contribution to Barth studies, in which he argues that Barth is able to avoid casuistry because "he insists that the history in which persons are constituted is the history of a *relationship*."[22] With this, he clearly intends for the formed reference to mean the history of God's constancy and covenant faithfulness. The formed reference is not a new casuistry; it is the means by which Barth prevents his ethics from being deontological on the one hand and casuistical on the other.[23] No one has expressed this line of argumentation better than Paul Nimmo.

Nimmo represents the second line of interpretation, arguing that the formed reference is not a backslide into casuistry. With Werpehowski and Haddorff, he argues that Barth's actualism prevents anything like Biggar's fixed moral principles.[24] To the contrary, Barth's overall ethical scheme presupposes an actualistic ontology "in which, within the covenant of grace, the ethical agent as a being in action is called to correspond to the Being in action of God."[25] This means that the command always occurs within the broader context of the covenantal relationship—a relationship congruent to the Chalcedonian pattern.

In this regard, the tension between Barth's rejection of casuistry and his approval of a practical casuistry resolves in a more charitable conclusion:

> A sympathetic appraisal of this tension would be to suggest that in his general ethics, Barth is clearing away debris from the history of the discipline of theological ethics in order that the ethical agent might remain fully open to encounter with the command of God in the ongoing history of the covenant. With this unequivocal openness in place, Barth is then slightly more at liberty in his special ethics to explore the boundaries of the usefulness of the "formed" reference.[26]

Knowledge of the formed reference gives rise to the possibility of "a non-casuistic special ethic" because it allows us to specify "the constancy and

---

[22]William Werpehowski, *Karl Barth and Christian Ethics: Living in Truth* (Burlington, VT: Ashgate, 2014), 30.

[23]Paul T. Nimmo, *Being in Action: The Theological Shape of Barth's Ethical Vision* (London: T&T Clark, 2007), 51 n. 86; Werpehowski, *Karl Barth and Christian Ethics*, 31.

[24]Nimmo, *Being in Action*, 54, 60.

[25]Nimmo, *Being in Action*, 1. See also Nimmo, "Actualism," in *The Westminster Handbook to Karl Barth*, ed. Richard Burnett (Louisville, KY: Westminster John Knox, 2013), 1.

[26]Nimmo, *Being in Action*, 58.

continuity" with which the vertical command of God always intersects the horizontal creaturely existence. The starting point for all knowledge of the formed reference is the history of Jesus Christ. In Christ, we have both the commanding God and the obedient human. His life, death, and resurrection is, therefore, a reference point—although nothing more—for our own attempts to discern what obedience to God looks like in each new ethical encounter.[27]

Thus Barth's prohibition of casuistry is not, as some early interpreters of Barth suggest, the elimination of moral deliberation on the part of the ethical agent. Instead, it is consistent with his larger concern to keep ethics theological by always speaking about God's action before human action and about human action only as it corresponds to God's action. Much like his decision to prioritize the gospel over the law, here Barth wants to emphasize the relationship that exists between the God who elects and elected humanity first, and only subsequently specific ethical commands and the form that obedient responses might take. Again, we see the extent to which the Chalcedonian pattern governs how Barth thinks about divine and human action.

Hauerwas tends to agree with those Barth scholars who argue that Barth does casuistry in spite of himself. I, on the other hand, tend to agree with Nimmo that Barth's "practical casuistry" is not really casuistry in the classical sense of the term. Barth never permits something like Biggar's fixed moral principles. This was, after all, Brunner's criticism of his rejection of natural theology. Nevertheless, Barth clearly does have a vested interest in accounting for moral deliberation—how it occurs, and what reference points it takes in any act of deliberation.

It is precisely at this point that the language of casuistry itself breaks down. On the one hand, Barth says he is not doing "casuistry" because casuistry is the human attempt to sit on the judgment seat of God and declare prospectively what actions are good and right. Barth's deepest worry is that casuistry justifies human action not by faith but by work. That is, for Barth each human act is ventured as an act of faith, and the absolute rightness of the act cannot be secured beforehand. Again, this does not mean that Barth has no sense of moral deliberation; he actually spends a great deal of energy

---

[27]Nimmo, *Being in Action*, 44-46.

delineating the patterns of a "practical casuistry" that is christologically determined by the formed reference. In this sense, our actions are always ventured by faith in and as a reflection of Jesus' obedience.

On the other hand, Hauerwas distances himself from the definition of casuistry that Barth rejects—rules applied to specific cases—in order to suggest that there is a different type of casuistry that makes judgments about actions retrospectively, enabling us to make sense of our moral lives. These judgments are rendered in accordance not with fixed moral prescriptions but with the story of Jesus Christ and the kingdom he inaugurates. Thus both theologians agree that the traditional notion of casuistry is problematic and that the solution lies in refocusing moral deliberation on Jesus Christ.

Is it possible to dissolve the tension by simply saying that both theologians want similar things? I think mostly so. For one thing, it is certainly the case that both theologians are reacting to a way of doing casuistry that gives it a law-like independence. In Barth's case, he worries that the law operates independently and antecedent to the gospel, so he reverses the order, meaning that we are confronted with the law of God in and through the gospel of Jesus Christ. As we hear God's command anew, we can return time and time again to the formed reference of Jesus in order to begin a fresh attempt to hear and respond faithfully. In Hauerwas's case, this means doing casuistry almost as a third use of the law, where the pursuit of holiness becomes a process of testing our actions retrospectively against the story of Jesus and the people of God in order to be honest with ourselves about our shortcomings. Indeed, I think a great deal of the tension could be relieved if Hauerwas would simply give up the language of casuistry and use instead the language of wisdom or discernment.[28]

For another thing, there is an affinity between what Hauerwas means by *imitatio Christi* and how Barth understands imitation. To be sure, we cannot simply equate Barth's formed reference to Hauerwas's use of *imitatio Christi*. For Barth, there are certain aspects of discipleship that will include *imitatio*, but strictly speaking *imitatio Christi* is another sort of casuistry, fixing certain moral principles based on Jesus' own life. Jesus' call to "follow me" sometimes becomes, in the hands of casuists, the totalization of commands

---

[28]*B*, 141.

like, "take up one's cross," "deny oneself," and "leave all." When this happens, specific historic commands Jesus gave to specific historic people become generalized into universal prescriptions that lead to "escapism, asceticism, ethical rigorism and the like." In contrast, Barth argues that "follow me" means that the disciples "are to be with [Jesus], to abide with him."[29] To follow Jesus means to open yourself up to the possibility that all of these and more will be commanded because Jesus himself is Lord of your life.

For Barth, imitating Jesus cannot mean repeating every aspect of his historical life. For then we would no longer need Jesus himself, only his example. Instead, for Barth, Paul's language of imitation is meant to suggest that we ought to imitate God's grace as it is revealed in Jesus. This is something like having the mind of Christ Jesus (Phil 2:5). Instead, imitating Christ means being the *imago Dei* by corresponding to God's grace. In short, what we are called to imitate is Jesus' obedience to God's command. The formed reference is a pattern of obedience to God's command that gives us an idea of what future obedience should look like—not in the particulars of the case necessarily, but in the manner that it corresponds to God by reflecting his grace to the world.

For Hauerwas, it is not so much reflecting God's grace as it is reflecting God's holiness. His own use of imitation and participation is couched in the language of sanctification and perfection, suggesting that ultimately what it means to imitate Jesus is to become holy. This means that the tension cannot be dissolved entirely. Here Hauerwas presses toward an account of imitation as a part of a larger process of deification, a suggestion that Barth would reject outright.[30] Even so, the unresolved difference between Barth and Hauerwas on this point is not one that differentiates between a Barthian and a liberal Protestant perspective; instead, it is the difference between a Reformed and a Wesleyan perspective. The Reformed tradition follows Calvin in emphasizing "union with Christ" by the power of the Holy Spirit, meaning that humans "participate" in Christ's divinity spiritually but not ontologically.[31] In contrast, Wesley was influenced by the Eastern church fathers,

---

[29]Barth, *CD* II/2:569-70.

[30]Barth, *CD* II/2:577.

[31]The best account of "participation in God" in Calvin's thought is J. Todd Billings, *Calvin, Participation, and the Gift: The Activity of Believers in Union with Christ* (Oxford: Oxford University Press, 2007).

leading many to suggest that Wesley's doctrine of Christian perfection, or entire sanctification, is akin to the Orthodox doctrine of deification.[32]

CONCLUDING REMARKS

What is undeniably similar between the two is the grounding of both the formed reference and *imitatio Dei* in Christology with particular concern for what Christ's humanity tells us about our own human agency. In Barth's case, Christ's humanity is expressed as obedience in response to divine agency. For us, this becomes a paradigm of what obedience looks like even if it does not provide an exhaustive example. Meanwhile, in Hauerwas's case, Christ's humanity reveals his divine nature and therefore shows us what it means to become like God. Indeed, Douglas Harink has made a compelling case that Hauerwas's use of imitation is deeply Pauline and therefore reminiscent of Barth on this point.[33]

Both Barth's outright rejection of casuistry and Hauerwas's redefinition of casuistry share a common concern from the start: to reject the attempt to have ethics without Christ; or, to reject natural theology. Barth's deep concern is that ethics becomes an "other task of theology" that claims a separate and equal authority to God's self-revelation in Jesus Christ. Similarly, Hauerwas's problem is a strand of Protestant theological ethics that seeks to ground Christian ethics in something that is called "creation" that operates alongside of Christ. In Hauerwas's case, this is a position that occurs in H. Richard Niebuhr's modalist trinitarianism and is perpetuated by James Gustafson and a number of contemporary Reformed thinkers, especially Max Stackhouse.[34] Where it occurs, it argues that an ethic based on Jesus must be relativized to an ethic of creation, or an ethic of the first article.

Where Hauerwas's ethics turn toward Christology, even a Christology that is determined by our participation in the church, we see a deeper

---

[32]Randy L. Maddox, "John Wesley and Eastern Orthodoxy: Influences, Convergences and Divergences," *Asbury Theological Journal* 45, no. 2 (1990): 39-40. It is worth mentioning that some theologians have tried to argue that Calvin's theology is compatible with deification, but this is a minority position and is rejected by some of the most reputable Calvin scholars. See Sung W. Park, "The Question of Deification in the Theology of John Calvin," *Verbum et Ecclesia* 38, no. 1 (2017): 1-5.

[33]Douglas Harink, *Paul Among the Postliberals: Pauline Theology Beyond Christendom and Modernity* (Grand Rapids: Brazos, 2003), 82-83, 94-95.

[34]Harink, *Paul Among the Postliberals*, 95 n. 44.

christocentrism behind and presupposed in his ecclesiocentrism. For Hauerwas, the church never becomes the subject matter of theology because the church is always the church that recognizes Christ's lordship. Sam Wells has recently made this point with great clarity:

> The church does not have to do Christ's work for him. The world has been saved. Its destiny does not hang in the balance, waiting for the church's decisive and timely intervention to tip the scales. The church must not talk or act as if God were dependent on its faithfulness or initiative. The church does not make the difference. The church lives in the difference Christ has made.[35]

All of this suggests that advocates of the Schleiermacher thesis are at least wrong to the extent that they posit the difference between Barth and Hauerwas as theocentrism versus ecclesiocentrism. At the heart of both is Jesus Christ. In Barth's case, he is interested in the God who is revealed in Jesus Christ while in Hauerwas's, he is interested in the church that is founded by Jesus Christ to be a witness to the God who is revealed in him. And yet, it is precisely at this point, where the tension between Barth and Hauerwas is partly alleviated, that we encounter the possibility that John Webster is right to suggest Hauerwas's ethics is reminiscent of the theology of Ritschl.

---

[35]Samuel Wells, "The Difference Christ Makes," in *The Difference Christ Makes: Celebrating the Life, Work, and Friendship of Stanley Hauerwas*, ed. Charles M. Collier (Eugene, OR: Cascade, 2015), 18.

PART THREE

The Ritschl
Thesis Examined

A͟T͟ ͟T͟H͟E͟ ͟H͟E͟A͟R͟T͟ ͟O͟F͟ ͟J͟O͟H͟N͟ ͟W͟E͟B͟S͟T͟E͟R͟'͟S͟ ͟C͟H͟A͟R͟G͟E͟ that Hauerwas's theological ethics reproduce Ritschl's moralistic theology is the claim that Hauerwas's Christology, with its disdain for metaphysics, reduces Jesus to an ethical exemplar we should seek to imitate. I've already demonstrated above that Hauerwas's Christology cannot be so simply dismissed. In Webster's hands, however, the ecclesiocentrism charge is reinvigorated around the question of a theology of Scripture. Webster makes a compelling case when he suggests that Hauerwas's theology of Scripture as the church's book shifts "the centre of gravity . . . away from God's activity and towards the church."[1] For Webster, the solution is to return Scripture to its proper theological locus: the doctrine of revelation. In other words, Webster sees Hauerwas's doctrine of Scripture as being representative of Ritschlian theology while Webster's own doctrine of Scripture approximates Barth, locating Scripture within the doctrine of revelation instead of the doctrine of the church.

Webster's criticism is reminiscent of Nigel Biggar's. Remember, for Biggar, Hauerwas's use of Scripture is sociological in nature, attending to the function of Scripture in the moral formation of the church's identity, while Barth's use of Scripture is theological in nature, attending to the reality of the God about whom it speaks. It is the purpose of part three to investigate these claims. I will accomplish this by constructing two test cases for

---

[1]John Webster, *Holy Scripture: A Dogmatic Sketch* (Cambridge: Cambridge University Press, 2003), 43.

evaluating the difference between Barth and Hauerwas's use of Scripture. In the first test case (chap. 9), I will explore the formal relationship between Scripture and the church in each theologian's work. In the second test case (chap. 10), I will explore how each theologian actually reads Scripture by comparing how they exegete a common scriptural pericope. In both cases, Biggar's claim is confirmed, suggesting that Hauerwas is indeed ecclesiocentric in a manner that differs from Barth. In a final chapter, I will briefly explore whether Hauerwas's proven ecclesiocentrism necessarily equates to Protestant liberalism. I will suggest, to the contrary, that Hauerwas may yet be able to escape Webster's charge that he is a Ritschlian.

9

The Church's Book

T HE DIFFERENCE BETWEEN BARTH and Hauerwas with regard to Scripture, both John Webster and Nigel Biggar suggest, is the difference between Scripture as a witness to the God whose revelation it repeats and as a witness to the church's nature and mission in the world on behalf of that same God. On the surface, Hauerwas's theology seems to confirm this line of criticism. Hauerwas, after all, has famously rejected *sola Scriptura*, choosing instead to emphasize the manner in which the Scripture is "the church's book."[1] Provocatively, Hauerwas writes, "When *sola scriptura* is used to underwrite the distinction between text and interpretation, then it seems clear to me that *sola scriptura* is a heresy rather than a help in the Church. . . . It assumes that the text of the Scripture makes sense separate from a Church that gives it sense."[2] A deeper investigation of each theologian's work certainly confirms differences along these basic lines.

I will conduct such an investigation by attending first to Barth's understanding of the relationship between Scripture and the church as expounded in his "Threefold Word of God." Second, I will synthesize an account of Hauerwas's understanding by exploring three texts that span Hauerwas's theological career. Finally, I will compare the two in order to confirm Biggar's thesis that Hauerwas's use of Scripture is "sociological" and therefore ecclesiocentric.

---

[1]This is David Kelsey's way of putting it. See David H. Kelsey, *The Uses of Scripture in Recent Theology* (Philadelphia: Fortress, 1975), 94.
[2]*US*, 27.

KARL BARTH AND THE THREEFOLD WORD OF GOD

When Karl Barth restarted his dogmatic project, he changed the title from *Christian Dogmatics* to *Church Dogmatics* in order to acknowledge explicitly that the dogmatic task of theology is essentially *pro ecclesia*. For Barth, the entire theological enterprise must be done as "a function of the Church" for the "self-examination" of the church's confession of God.[3] In this sense, it is proper to say that Barth's dogmatic project is ecclesiocentric because theology is done *in* and *for* the church.

The relationship of the theological task to the church in Barth's thought is clear: theology and the theologian serve the church, testing the church's confession that Jesus Christ is Lord. The most significant way that dogmatics challenges church proclamation comes through testing it against Scripture. In this sense, Barth's ecclesiocentrism—that is, his insistence on the centrality of the church for dogmatics—is qualified by the claim that the church is centered on Scripture. And yet it is not enough to stop there; for the Scriptures are not themselves the center of the Christian faith either. In fact, Jesus Christ is the center, and Scripture becomes central to the church when it finds Christ as its center. Thus to say that Barth's theology is ecclesiocentric requires that we immediately qualify ecclesiocentrism with a prior christocentrism. Barth writes, "God in Jesus Christ is the essence of the Church";[4] or again, "Jesus Christ is the being of the Church."[5]

Barth explicates the relationship between church, Scripture, and Jesus Christ with the claim that the Word of God has a threefold form: the Word of God preached, the Word of God written, and the Word of God revealed. The Word preached refers primarily to the church and its proclamation of the gospel. The church's proclamation is commissioned by God, has God as its theme, is judged by God, and is the event whereby God joins his Word to human words.[6] The church's proclamation, however, is not in and of itself the Word of God. Alongside the church, and external to its own being, stands Scripture.

The relationship between the church and Scripture—between the preached Word and the written Word—is a relationship that is best highlighted by

---

[3] *CD* I/1:3-4.
[4] *CD* I/1:12.
[5] *CD* I/1:42.
[6] *CD* I/1:88-99.

similarity and difference. The church and Scripture share a "similarity of phe-
nomena" and can "be set initially under a single genus" as proclamation:
"Scripture as the commencement and present-day preaching as the continuation of one and the same event, Jeremiah and Paul at the beginning and the
modern preacher of the Gospel at the end of one and the same series."[7]

There is, however, "dissimilarity in order" between Scripture and the
church's preaching. Scripture is the *norma normans*, while the church's proclamation is the *norma normata*. The content of the Scripture is what gives it
priority over the church. Scripture is the proclamation of the prophets and
apostles: "[People] who yearned, waited and hoped for this Immanuel and
who finally saw, heard and handled it in Jesus Christ." As such, this
Scripture—this word of the prophets and apostles—"must confront the life
of the church . . . as a criterion which cannot be dissolved into the historical
life of the church."[8] It is only because Scripture as the written Word of God
stands over the church and confronts it that the church is able to be the
church that preaches the Word of God. Thus the preached Word is derivative of the written Word.

While the preached Word is derivative of the written Word, the written
Word is not the Word of God in and of itself either; it bears witness to the
revelation of the Word of God, but it is not itself the revelation of God's Word.
In fact, "revelation is originally and directly what the Bible and the Church
proclamation are derivatively and indirectly, i.e. God's Word." The relationship between the three is as follows: "Proclamation is real proclamation
. . . only as the repetition of the biblical witness to past revelation, and the
Bible is real witness . . . only in its relation to this past revelation attested in
it."[9] The Word of God revealed is the Word of God *in se*. More precisely, the
Word of God revealed is Jesus Christ, "The Word became flesh."[10]

The relationship between the church's proclamation, the Bible's witness,
and the revealed Word of God may be one of derivation, but it is also more
than that. Revelation "underlies the other two," and "we know it only indirectly, from Scripture and proclamation." But when we encounter the Word

---

[7]*CD* I/1:102.
[8]*CD* I/1:108.
[9]*CD* I/1:117.
[10]*CD* I/1:119.

of God in its mediate forms, it is *really* the Word of God. Revelation, Scripture, and church proclamation are unified in the threefold form of the Word of God. In this unity, we really and truly encounter the Word of God.[11]

Barth's distinction between the church's preaching and Scripture as derivatives of the revealed Word of God places the church under the authority of Scripture and Scripture in the position of pointing beyond itself to the Word of God as the source of its authority. And yet the three are unified such that Barth can shift focus on the interrelationships between church, Scripture, and revealed Word without misplacing priority:

> The revealed Word of God we know only from the Scripture adopted by Church proclamation or the proclamation of the Church based on Scripture.
>
> The written Word of God we know only through the revelation which fulfills proclamation or through the proclamation fulfilled by revelation.
>
> The preached Word of God we know only through the revelation attested in Scripture or the Scripture which attests revelation.[12]

In summary, with regard to Scripture's relation to the church, Barth makes three main points. First, Scripture points the church to the Word of God and speaks to the church as the Word of God through the power of the Holy Spirit.[13] Second, the Word of God in Scripture exercises authority over the church, and the church's own authority is undergirded by its submission to Scripture.[14] Third, Scripture stands in freedom over and against the church. The church is only free insofar as it is grounded on Scripture.[15]

Before we move on, I think it particularly germane to my dialogue with Hauerwas to pause and address two matters that occupy Barth in his section on the threefold Word of God: (1) Barth's position on Scripture and the church as it specifically relates to his concerns with Roman Catholic doctrine, and (2) the manner in which Barth discusses the relationship of the individual to Scripture and the church. By exploring these two concerns at length, I will be in a position to see the similarities and differences between Barth and Hauerwas.

---

[11]*CD* I/1:121.

[12]*CD* I/1:121. It is worth noting that Barth claims there is an analogy between the "basic determinations and mutual relationships" demonstrated here and the doctrine of the Trinity.

[13]*CD* I/2:457.

[14]*CD* I/2:538.

[15]*CD* I/2:661.

First, Barth clearly distinguishes a Protestant view on Scripture and the church from Roman Catholicism in §2. Primarily, this distinction regards theological starting points. In the Reformation, "the doctrine of the sole normativeness of Holy Scripture" was given primary importance in the theological prolegomena of Philipp Melanchthon and John Calvin. Barth contrasts this with the tendency in Roman Catholic prolegomena to place Scripture and tradition on equal footing. Specifically, he points to "the definitions of the dignity of Church tradition alongside or even in preference to Holy Scripture at the head of the rulings of the Council of Trent."[16] Thus, for Barth, the difference between Protestant and Roman Catholic formulations of the relationship between Scripture and church remains determined by *sola Scriptura*.

Later, in §20, Barth more precisely identifies the concern he has with Roman Catholic doctrine. It is the same concerns he has with Protestant liberalism. For Barth, Scripture must hold primacy, exercising authority over the church and for the church. In both Roman Catholicism and the pietistic modern Protestantism of Schleiermacher, Barth sees a problematic understanding of divine revelation. In both, divine revelation is portrayed as something that the church inherently possesses. Thus the church is able "to declare with certainty where and what revelation is and therefore where and what the witness of revelation is."[17] As such, the church becomes a material authority in and of itself as opposed to a church that stands under the authority of Scripture.

Protestant pietism and Tridentine Roman Catholic theology come together in the figure of Johann Möhler.[18] Möhler and his predecessors in the Catholic Tübingen school, under the influence of Hegel and Schleiermacher, suggest that the church today is the place where revelation occurs. In the transition from the apostolic to the postapostolic age, "the doctrine of Scripture now becomes the doctrine of the Church. . . . So tradition is the extended self-impartation of the original divinely spiritual life-force once and for all posited

---

[16]*CD* I/1:35.
[17]*CD* I/2:542.
[18]Roger Haight provides an insightful explanation of how the Romanticism of Schelling and Schleiermacher comes to influence the Tübingen Catholics, especially Drey and Möhler. See Roger D. Haight, SJ, *Christian Community in History*, vol. 2, *Comparative Ecclesiology* (London: Continuum, 2005), 337.

with the founding of the Church."[19] For Barth, the final demonstration of the fact that Roman Catholic doctrine relativizes Scripture to the church is the First Vatican Council, in which the pope takes his place as an infallible authority alongside of and perhaps in contradiction to Scripture.[20]

Thus the difference Barth draws between evangelical and Roman Catholic—and, notably, Protestant liberal—views on the relationship between Scripture and the church is complete. On the one side, Scripture stands over the church and the church exercises authority under its witness. On the other side, the church stands equal to Scripture and in some ways superior to it because the church interprets Scripture. As such, the church (and finally the pope) claims for itself an authority that comes directly from the Word of God, unmediated by Scripture. Finally, this is Barth's concern with Catholic ecclesiology: the church bypasses Scripture in its reception of divine revelation.

Second, it is worth exploring in greater detail Barth's understanding of the relationship between the individual, the church, and Scripture. I want to focus specifically on comments made in §§7 and 19 in order to clarify how Barth perceives the three as interrelated. In §7 Barth anticipates the relationship between Scripture and the church that he develops more fully in §§19-21. In clear, succinct language, Barth claims, "The Church rests . . . on the recollection and the expectation that God in fact has spoken and will speak the Word to us in the Bible."[21] Without the Bible functioning as God's Word to the church, the church's proclamation is reduced to a conversation with itself. In contrast, when the church chooses to be the church of Jesus Christ in submission to the Bible (whose subject matter is Jesus Christ), then individuals are capable of hearing the Bible as God's Word.[22]

The church and the individual both stand under Scripture and are called to be obedient to it. The concomitant obedience of the church and individuals demonstrates how Barth understands the relationship between the two under Scripture. The Bible directs us to the Word of God and answers

---

[19]*CD* I/2:561-62.

[20]*CD* I/2:569. It is with some humor that Barth points out that the papal authority granted by Vatican I results from a council that was characterized by papal initiation, papal oversight, and finally, papal proclamation.

[21]*CD* I/1:255.

[22]*CD* I/1:261.

our questions about God's revelation. Nevertheless, individuals do not receive the answers to these questions alone. Barth elaborates in §19: "Of course, we could not have received this answer, if as members of the Church we had not listened continually to the voice of the Church, i.e., if we had not respected, and as far as possible applied the exposition of the Bible by those who before and with us were and are members of the Church."[23] In the first sense, then, obedience to Scripture means a relationship of obedience between individuals and the church's historical and current exposition of Scripture.

In the second sense, obedience to Scripture involves a relationship of obedience between the individual and Scripture itself. In order to even hear the church's voice as the exposition of the Scriptures, one must accept a personal responsibility for seeking correct exposition. Only through obedience in these two ways can an individual hear the Word of God in Scripture.

Finally, the relationship between Scripture, church, and individual comes into full focus in Barth's thought:

> But just as we should ask Holy Scripture in vain about the revelation of God, if we were to sidetrack the exposition of the Church, or to try to spare ourselves the trouble of individual exposition, what is equally necessary, and even more so, is that it should be Scripture which actually does and alone can answer us. The Church can expound, and we can expound, and there is authority and freedom in the church, only because Scripture has already told us what we are asking about when we ask about God's revelation. The statement that the Bible is the witness of divine revelation is not, therefore, limited by the fact that there is also a witness of the church which we have to hear, and in addition witness is also demanded of us. The possibility of both the witness of the Church and of our own witness is founded upon the reality of which that statement speaks. Yet all statements which we have still to formulate about those secondary definitions of our obedience to Scripture, all the statements about the necessary authority and equally necessary freedom in the Church itself, can only be expositions of the basic statement that there is a Word of God for the Church: in that it receives in the Bible the witness of divine revelation.[24]

---

[23]CD I/2:462.
[24]CD I/2:462.

The church's witness and the individual Christian's witness are contingent on the witness of Scripture. Under Scripture, church and individual relate to each other dialectically. The individual hears the Word of God in the witness of the church to Scripture. At the same time, the individual is responsible to test the witness of the church against Scripture in order to see if Scripture has been exposited correctly. In both cases, Scripture takes primacy. Thus the Protestant *sola Scriptura* is maintained.

STANLEY HAUERWAS AND THE CHURCH'S BOOK

It is notoriously difficult to articulate Hauerwas's "position" on just about anything. After all, Hauerwas claims that he does not believe in having "positions."[25] This is certainly true for his views on Scripture. In order to synthesize an account of the relation between Scripture and the church, I will attend to three different works that span a thirty-year period in Hauerwas's career: a 1981 essay titled "The Moral Authority of Scripture," the book *Unleashing the Scripture* (1993), and his 2008 response essay to Richard Hays's *The Moral Vision of the New Testament*, titled "Why 'the Way the Words Run' Matters." By so doing, I hope to offer a sympathetic and accurate overview of Hauerwas's thought.

First, in "The Moral Authority of Scripture," Hauerwas explores "how scripture does and/or should function ethically."[26] Particularly, he challenges the idea that an individual can independently read Scripture and discern ethical imperatives that are universally applicable. This notion presupposes that a text bears a meaning independent of the community that calls it Scripture. In order to make this argument, Hauerwas turns to the work of John Howard Yoder and David Kelsey.

Hauerwas first appeals to Yoder in order to suggest that a "free church understanding of the significance of the community" is what is needed in order to fully appreciate the moral authority of Scripture.[27] Yoder challenges both the Protestant emphasis on "the perspicuity and objectivity" of Scripture and the magisterial Catholic position that provokes it, suggesting, "The free church alternative to both recognizes the inadequacies of the text of Scripture standing alone uninterpreted and appropriates the

---

[25]*HC*, 60.
[26]*CC*, 53.
[27]*CC*, 54.

promise of guidance of the spirit through the ages, but locates the fulfillment of that promise in the assembly of those who gather around Scripture in the face of a given real moral challenge."[28] In correspondence with Yoder's claim, Hauerwas argues that Scripture asserts authority within the context of a community called the church.

Similarly, David Kelsey emphasizes the inherently communal nature of moral claims regarding the authority of Scripture. Kelsey, and Hauerwas in turn, challenges the theological project of "translation" whereby theologians assume "that if scripture is to be meaningful it must be translated into a more general theological medium."[29] The entire project of modern theology, from which Christian ethics was born, is one that historically divorces Scripture from the community and then leaves scholars and experts to extrapolate relevant information from the Scriptures *for* the community.

What Hauerwas gleans from Kelsey is the fact that the way Scripture is used in the church is often different from the way it has come to be used in theological discourse. Kelsey ultimately sees the relationship between church, Scripture, and theology to be some form of a hermeneutical circle. Particularly helpful, then, is the way that Kelsey explains "the influence the church has on how we construe scripture."[30]

What Hauerwas finds problematic with Kelsey is also significant. In the end, "Kelsey's analysis fails to do justice to the ways in which Scripture morally shapes a community."[31] To emphasize the way a community influences Scripture without equally emphasizing the way that Scripture shapes a community is a problem that Hauerwas wants to avoid.

In short, two key points are worth noting from this early essay. First, it is notable that Hauerwas attempts to navigate between what he deems to be extreme Protestant views on the perspicuity of Scripture and equally extreme Roman Catholic views on submission to the authority of the magisterium. Second, Hauerwas finds Kelsey insufficient insofar as he does not balance his account of how community *informs* Scripture with an account of how Scripture *forms* a community.

---

[28]John Howard Yoder, "Radical Reformation Ethics in Ecumenical Perspective," *Journal of Ecumenical Studies* 15 (fall 1978): 657, cited in *CC*, 54.

[29]*CC*, 55.

[30]*CC*, 65.

[31]*CC*, 65.

In our second text, *Unleashing the Scripture*, Hauerwas takes a line of criticism that runs opposite to the concerns he expressed with Kelsey's proposal. Here, Hauerwas expresses a concern that American Christians fail to submit their individual readings of Scripture to the authority of the church. For Hauerwas, the root of this problem is the Protestant doctrine of *sola Scriptura*.

Hauerwas's controversial thesis is that "the Bible is not and should not be accessible to merely anyone, but rather it should only be made available to those who have undergone the hard discipline of existing as part of God's people."[32] This assertion derives from the observation that North American Christians "read the Bible not as Christians . . . but as democratic citizens who think their 'common sense' is sufficient for 'understanding' the Scripture."[33] American individualism combined with Scottish common-sense philosophy leads to a situation where the Bible becomes the possession of the individual, not the church. "Freeing the Bible" from the church in this way does not actually lead to a "free bible." Instead, the Bible is enslaved to any number of ideological positions, the most concerning for Hauerwas being nationalism.[34]

Corollary to Hauerwas's thesis is the assertion that *sola Scriptura* is a heresy. The Protestant Scripture principle "joined to the invention of the printing press and underwritten by the democratic trust in the intelligence of the 'common person,' has created the situation that now makes people believe that they can read the Bible 'on their own.'"[35] This assertion is polemically overstated, and Hauerwas concedes as much.[36] But the point he presses is that "the problem is not how *sola scriptura* was used by the Reformers but how it is used now."[37]

Revisiting a point he made (by way of Kelsey) in "The Moral Authority of Scripture," Hauerwas protests the idea that the biblical text makes sense without the church.[38] This is the very same presumption that both fundamentalists and

---

[32]*US*, 9.

[33]*US*, 15.

[34]*US*, 29-32.

[35]*US*, 17.

[36]Hauerwas heeds the advice he receives from Reinhard Hütter: "*sola scriptura* does not make the Church superfluous; rather it implies the Church since it functions as intra-ecclesial criterion" (*US*, 153 n. 17).

[37]*US*, 27.

[38]*US*, 27.

historical-critical scholars hold. Indeed, Hauerwas argues that fundamentalism and higher criticism are but two sides to the same Enlightenment coin.[39] These extreme positions objectify the Bible in a way that bypasses the role the church has in reading and interpreting it.

This critique of *sola Scriptura* sets the stage for Hauerwas to make his key claim: in order to understand Scripture one must become a disciple of Jesus Christ in the community that is called the church. For Hauerwas, the obvious counterexamples to Protestant individualism are the Roman Catholic and Orthodox Churches. Both of these traditions emphasize the church's essential role as an "interpretive community."

Particularly, Hauerwas appeals to the Vatican II document *Dei Verbum* to demonstrate the contemporary Roman Catholic position. *Dei Verbum* claims that Scripture and tradition together make up "one sacred deposit" of the Word of God. The task of interpretation of the Word of God belongs to the teaching office of the church, which is not above the Word but serves it. Tradition, Scripture, and the teaching office of the church "are so linked and joined together that one cannot stand without the others."[40]

The force of Hauerwas's appeal to *Dei Verbum* suggests that Hauerwas's rejection of *sola Scriptura* is at once ecumenical and Catholic. Read from this perspective, *Unleashing the Scripture* is Hauerwas's attempt to correct an extreme version of Protestantism that is married to liberal democratic ideals. Indeed, for Hauerwas, the problem may not really be Protestantism in and of itself.[41] Instead, the problem is that Protestantism in America has become more American than Protestant. We see Hauerwas make a similar argument with American Roman Catholicism. He is concerned that Roman Catholicism in America follows Protestantism in adopting liberal democratic presuppositions at the expense of its deepest theological convictions.[42]

Our third Hauerwas text is an essay Hauerwas wrote in response to Richard Hays. *Unleashing the Scripture* received a great deal of criticism from both biblical scholars and theologians. One of the most significant

---

[39]*US*, 18.

[40]"Dogmatic Constitution on Divine Revelation," in *US*, 22.

[41]Although Hauerwas suggests at numerous points that Protestantism is a doomed project. See, for example, *AE*, 87-97.

[42]Stanley Hauerwas, "The Importance of Being Catholic: A Protestant View," *First Things*, March 1990, 23-30.

critiques comes from Hays. In his *The Moral Vision of the New Testament*, Hays considers Hauerwas's "hermeneutical strategy" alongside Reinhold Niebuhr, Karl Barth, John Howard Yoder, and Elisabeth Schüssler Fiorenza. Hays's assessment is that Hauerwas does not really have a hermeneutical strategy but instead operates with a "freewheeling approach" that makes it difficult if not impossible to hold "a coherent hermeneutical position."[43]

Hays distinguishes Yoder from Hauerwas, claiming that Yoder emphasizes the way in which the New Testament shapes the life of the church while Hauerwas emphasizes the necessity of the church in order to read the New Testament correctly. Thus Hays can remark, "Hauerwas is less inclined to exposit the text than to propose conditions that must be met in order for the text to be understood."[44] Most problematic for Hays is Hauerwas's understanding of the authority of Scripture in relation to tradition. In Hauerwas, "The classic Protestant idea that Scripture can challenge and judge tradition" is not possible.[45] Finally, Hays makes his concern clear: "The logic of Hauerwas's hermeneutical position should require him to become a Roman Catholic."[46]

Hauerwas did not address Hays's criticism until 2008, when he was invited to contribute to a festschrift in Hays's honor. On the heels of his recently published theological commentary *Matthew*, Hauerwas thought the timing and occasion were finally right to respond to his friend and colleague. In "Why 'the Way the Words Run' Matters," we see that Hauerwas is not merely responding to Hays's critical remarks on *Unleashing the Scripture*, but he is responding generally to the entire guild of biblical scholarship.[47]

Hauerwas's argument begins with a quote from Yoder. This move has a twofold effect. First, it echoes the same move he made in "The Moral

---

[43]Richard B. Hays, *The Moral Vision of the New Testament: A Contemporary Introduction to New Testament Ethics* (San Francisco: HarperSanFrancisco, 1996), 254.

[44]Hays, *Moral Vision*, 259.

[45]Hays, *Moral Vision*, 263.

[46]Hays, *Moral Vision*, 265.

[47]A symposium on *M* was published by *Pro Ecclesia* in 2008. It included two very critical reviews by Markus Bockmuehl and Luke Timothy Johnson. The review by Bockmuehl is particularly scathing. Johnson's is more polite but no less critical. Johnson's review is especially interesting when considered alongside his positive review of *US*. Compare Luke Timothy Johnson, "Unleashing the Scriptures: Freeing the Bible from Captivity to America," *Modern Theology* 11, no. 2 (1995): 283-85; and Johnson, "Matthew or Stanley? Pick One," *Pro Ecclesia* 17, no. 1 (2008): 29-34.

Authority of Scripture." Second, it undermines part of Hays's criticism because it identifies him closely with Yoder. He emphasizes Yoder's claim that we need to understand how the Holy Spirit is linked to the church's practice of binding and loosing in order to understand the authority and use of Scripture. Then Hauerwas acknowledges Hays's criticism of his rejection of *sola Scriptura* and his Roman Catholic leanings.[48] Finally, he defends himself by appealing to Markus Bockmuehl's work. Bockmuehl argues that Scripture itself, in both the Old and New Testament, implies that it addresses itself to a "disciple"—a "witness" to God—and therefore presupposes an ecclesial location.[49] Hauerwas ends the essay with a summation of the relationship between Scripture and the church: "Scripture, vivified by the Holy Spirit, is the heart of the Church."[50]

In summary, between 1980 and 2008 there does not appear to be a significant shift in the overall tenor of Hauerwas's portrayal of Scripture and the church. He follows Yoder's attempt at a middle road between extreme Protestant and Catholic positions. In the first essay, written while he was teaching at the Catholic Notre Dame, he finds that it is important to balance Kelsey's claim that the church *informs* the way we read Scripture with Yoder's more Protestant reminder that Scripture *forms* the church. Later, when teaching at the Methodist Duke, Hauerwas shifts the emphasis in the other direction, reminding his Protestant students and colleagues that the church stands between the individual and Scripture, proclaiming the Word of God and making disciples who are capable of being witnesses to the truth of Jesus Christ proclaimed in Scripture. Finally, in his response to Hays, he harkens back to his earlier suggestion about the manner in which Scripture morally forms the church. This has the effect of reminding Hays that his focus on the relationship between individuals and the church in *Unleashing the Scripture* is conditioned by his polemic against North American Protestantism. As a result, the Reformation emphasis on the authority of Scripture sometimes takes a back seat to the claim that the church is the only place where the biblical text can be read and performed as Scripture.

---

[48] *WWW*, 95-98.
[49] *WWW*, 103-6.
[50] *WWW*, 112.

OBSERVATIONS

The effect of Hauerwas's alternating polemic is a bit of a seesawing between emphasizing the moral authority of the text over the community and the necessity of the community for correct performance of the biblical text: here challenging the church to be formed by Scripture and there challenging the individual Christian to remember that the church is the community in which one receives formation from Scripture. In both instances, however, Biggar's charge that Hauerwas resorts to a sociological use of Scripture is somewhat confirmed. He is entirely preoccupied with questions related to how the Scripture relates to the community and how it becomes truthful when a community that believes it is true embodies it.

Barth is not uninterested in these sorts of questions. Indeed, as we have seen, he can adequately account for how both the church and individual Christians relate to Scripture and participate in its witness to God. At the same time, he grounds Scripture theologically in his Christology. Scripture's primary function is not the moral formation of the community for which it is authoritative; its primary function is to bear witness to God's self-revelation in Jesus Christ, the Word of God incarnate. Undoubtedly, then, Biggar's ecclesiocentrism thesis is at least confirmed with regard to the formal explication of the relationship between Scripture and the church. Likewise, we must admit that Webster's insistence that Scripture belongs within the doctrine of revelation instead of ecclesiology is clearly reflected in Barth's theology while his description of Ritschl's doctrine of Scripture finds affinity with Hauerwas. On Hauerwas's side, however, there is an open question regarding whether his "sociological" use of Scripture equates to Protestant liberalism. From Hauerwas's perspective, his polemic against *sola Scriptura* is meant to challenge liberal Protestant assumptions about common sense in American Christianity. I will revisit this point in chapter eleven. First, however, let's explore a second test case.

Salvation Belongs
to Our Church?

In THE PREVIOUS CHAPTER I examined the formal relationship between Scripture and the church in the theologies of Barth and Hauerwas. In this chapter I will explore how each theologian actually reads Scripture. Exegetical practice will give us a better sense of how each theologian understands the Scripture to "bear witness." In order to draw out the differences between the two, I will compare how each theologian interprets the rich man text in Matthew 19:16-30 and Mark 10:17-31. Again, Nigel Biggar's thesis that Barth points to God while Hauerwas points to the church will be confirmed. Even more, Hauerwas's reading of Scripture seems to push the question of salvation itself into ecclesiology. At this point, finally, John Webster's charge that Hauerwas's theology is reminiscent of Ritschl's has to be taken with great seriousness.

WHAT MUST I DO TO INHERIT ETERNAL LIFE?

Hauerwas's reading of the rich man comes in the context of his commentary on Matthew for the Brazos Theological Commentary on the Bible series. Hauerwas makes a number of preliminary claims regarding the purpose of the commentary and the Gospel itself that shape the overall commentary and, therefore, his reading of the rich man. Two in particular are worth stating. First, Hauerwas is convinced that as an interpreter of Scripture he must come alongside the writer of Matthew and "write with" him "in and for our time."[1] This decision means that Hauerwas both minimizes the role that historical-critical work does and opens space for analogical and moral readings of the text.[2] One prime example: in Hauerwas's reading of the Gospel, Herod becomes a cipher for "the politics of death"[3]—political orders that maintain the fragile illusion of power through violence and fear. Ultimately, for Hauerwas, this includes America.[4] This theme recurs when Herod's son, Antipas, throws a banquet in which he is forced to behead John the Baptist in order to satisfy his guests with a demonstration of power. Hauerwas contrasts this with Jesus' subsequent feeding of the five thousand in order to suggest that the politics of this world are contrary to the politics of Jesus.[5] The moral sense of the text is that true power is life-giving, not life-taking.

This segues nicely into the second preliminary claim. According to Hauerwas, "Matthew's gospel is meant to train us to be disciples of Jesus."[6] This discipleship training has both soteriological and sociopolitical implications. To be trained as a disciple of Jesus means that we must learn "to recognize that the salvation wrought in the cross is the Father's refusal to save us according to the world's understanding of salvation, which is that salvation depends on having more power than my enemies."[7] We learn to read Matthew in this way when we are "guided by the presumption that the church is the politics that determines how Matthew is to be read."[8] In other words, Hauerwas's reading of Matthew presupposes that it is a textbook that only accomplishes its pedagogical purpose in the ecclesial classroom. These preliminary claims help us to make sense of Hauerwas's reading of the rich man text in Matthew 19:16-30.

A number of critical passages in Hauerwas's commentary read as an extended conversation with influential theologians. For example, Hauerwas's entire commentary on the Sermon on the Mount is an extended dialogue with Dietrich Bonhoeffer, with John Howard Yoder occasionally interjecting.

---

[1] *M*, 18.
[2] *M*, 21.
[3] *M*, 18.
[4] *M*, 37.
[5] *M*, 138-39.
[6] *M*, 19.
[7] *M*, 27.
[8] *M*, 30.

Similarly, Hauerwas's engagement with the rich man text is a three-way conversation between Pope John Paul II, Karl Barth, and himself. The result is a portrayal of salvation as becoming Jesus' disciple through membership in the visible community called the church.

We might break the text into two parts. In the first part, a young man, whom we later learn is rich, comes to Jesus and asks him what he must do to have eternal life. When Jesus tells him to obey the commandments, he proudly declares that he already does so. Jesus then commands him to sell everything he has, give the money to the poor, and follow Jesus. To which the man responds with sorrow and leaves. The second part of the text begins at this point. As the rich man walks away, the disciples marvel at how hard it is to be saved. Seeking assurance of their own salvation, they ask Jesus what they will receive for following him. He assures them that anyone who follows him will receive eternal life.

In Hauerwas's commentary on the first part, John Paul II speaks first to remind us that the fact that this man even poses the question suggests he is on the right track because he knows "there is an essential connection between the moral good and the fulfillment of our destiny."[9] Even so, Hauerwas reminds us that Jesus responds, "There is only one who is good" (Matt 19:17 NRSV). This suggests the rich man is not aware that Jesus is himself the source of all goodness.

Barth takes over the conversation at this point with an exploration of the command of God. The command of God is both love of God and love of neighbor. Jesus' explicit reference to the second table of the commandments means that the command of God here confronts the rich man in "its external aspect" as "a concrete doing or not doing." Even as the rich man has superficially kept all of the commands of the second table, he must be confronted with the fact that he has not been truly obedient to the command of God. Jesus' exhortation to sell his possessions and give all his money to the poor unmasks the twofold fact that (1) as long as he has many possessions he will not be truly free for God and (2) as long as he does not give his wealth to the poor he will not be truly free for his neighbor. He will only truly love God and neighbor if he chooses to follow Jesus.[10] Here John Paul II gets the

---

[9]*M*, 173.
[10]*M*, 174.

last word, echoing Barth's conclusion by reminding us that following Jesus (i.e., discipleship) is the necessary basis of all Christian ethics.

In his commentary on the second part of the text, Hauerwas focuses on Jesus' response to the disciples' question, "Then who can be saved?" (Mt 19:25). Worried that most middle-class American Christians hear Jesus' response that "for God all things are possible" (Mt 19:26) as an antinomian exhortation to continue pursuing materialistic lives, Hauerwas claims that Jesus' reply challenges "our very conception of salvation." He goes on to describe what salvation means:

> To be saved, *to be made a member of the church through baptism*, means that our lives are no longer our own. We are made vulnerable to one another in a manner such that what is ours can no longer be free of the claims of others. As hard as it may be to believe, Jesus makes clear that salvation entails our being made vulnerable through the loss of our possessions.[11]

This definition of salvation is undergirded by an appeal to the story of Ananias and Sapphira in Acts 5.[12] This intertextual reading reminds us that "it is our possessions that encourage us to lie, making impossible the trust necessary to be Jesus' disciples." We must be saved from our possessions by becoming a truthful people. Hauerwas again defines salvation: "To be saved, *to be part of the body of Christ*, is to participate in a people who make truthful speech with one another not only possible but necessary."[13]

The commentary on this section concludes with another lengthy word from Barth, who sees that the disciples have in fact done what the rich man could not. Their positive witness is possible because they have learned to depend on Jesus himself to provide. Jesus' final comments about the last and the first transition Hauerwas into a commentary on the parable of the vineyard workers where the first hired represent Israel and the last hired are Gentile Christians.[14]

---

[11]*M*, 174 (emphasis added).

[12]It is worth noting at this point that the connection Hauerwas makes between the rich man and Ananias and Sapphira is not a new exegesis of this text. He came to this connection at least as early as 1981 (*RA*, 129-31), when he connects the Lukan version of the text to Acts 5. Indeed, it seems that Hauerwas makes this exegetical appeal whenever he is working through questions of wealth and material possession (*WRAL*, 27).

[13]*M*, 175 (emphasis mine).

[14]*M*, 176-77.

Hauerwas's reading of Matthew 19, then, juxtaposes the rich man with the disciples in order to demonstrate that salvation entails becoming Jesus' disciple by leaving everything behind, becoming dispossessed, and learning to trust God for everything in a manner that makes one truly free to love God and neighbor. The rich man went away sad and therefore turned away from the salvation that confronted him in Jesus. The disciples, in contrast, will receive eternal life because they bear witness to the very salvation that Jesus offers through a life of dispossession and trust. At both points, Hauerwas draws on Barth in order to clarify the meaning of the text. In the first instance, he uses Barth to demonstrate how the rich man's claims of obedience are rendered false by a failure to truly hear and understand God's command. In the second instance, he uses Barth to juxtapose the obedience of the disciples to the disobedience of the rich man, and therefore to suggest that the answer to the question in Matthew 19:16, "What good deed must I do to have eternal life?" is "become a disciple of Jesus," which in Hauerwas-speak means "to be made a member of the church through baptism." It is precisely at this second point where Hauerwas's use of Barth becomes questionable.

FOR MORTALS IT IS IMPOSSIBLE

Barth's treatment of the rich man comes in *Church Dogmatics* II/2. This two-part volume is divided into two corresponding chapters, on the election of God and the command of God. Ethics is treated as the command of God and belongs to the doctrine of God first and foremost because it presupposes humanity as God's elected covenant partner. In the covenant between God and humanity, "the doctrine of the divine election of grace is the first element, and the doctrine of the divine command is the second."[15] In election, God wills for humanity to be God's covenant partner. But this "will for" also necessarily includes a "want from." What God wants from humanity is obedience. This happens when human response corresponds to divine command, thereby bearing witness to God's action with a "self-determination which corresponds to [the divine] determination" of God's electing action.[16] In other words, ethics is the name given to the process by which we learn to hear God's command and respond to it in obedience.

---

[15]*CD* II/2:509.
[16]*CD* II/2:510-11.

Barth treats three themes in his chapter "The Command of God": the command of God as God's *claim* on humanity (§37), *decision* about humanity (§38), and *judgment* on humanity (§39). Barth's reading of the rich man text occurs in §37, on the command of God as God's claim. Therefore, it is worth revisiting the major points of this section.

Jesus Christ is the basis, content, and form of the divine claim that God's command makes on us. This means that first, in Jesus, God claims human nature as his own. When we confront Jesus, we confront the basis of the claim that God's command makes on our lives. Second, Jesus is also the content of the divine claim. Jesus' life demonstrates what it looks like to receive God's command and to respond with obedience. Finally, Jesus is the form of the divine claim because Jesus' obedience becomes normative for our own obedience.

It is in the context of the question of the form of the divine claim that Barth exegetes the rich man text from Mark 10. For Barth, this story instantiates the form of the divine claim as both the rich man and the disciples come face-to-face with the command of God in the person of Jesus. Parallel to Barth's doctrine of election, the command of God receives both negative and positive witness in this story as the rich man demonstrates disobedience while the disciples demonstrate obedience.[17]

Barth's treatment of the first half of the story, that pertaining to the rich man, can be described in four movements.[18] In the first, Barth treats the rich man's action in coming to Jesus as "rang[ing] himself with the disciples" in the sphere of the *Regnum Jesu Christi*, the kingdom of Christ.[19] Both the rich man and the disciples bear witness to their objective membership in the kingdom of Christ, and there is no withdrawal from this kingdom. It objectively defines their relationship to Jesus. The rich man's arrival on the scene further demonstrates that he knows at least implicitly that he is encountering the command of God in Jesus.

---

[17]Barth emphasizes that this parallel is intended, pointing to the negative witness of Israel and the positive witness of the church in the election of the community (*CD* II/2:627).

[18]Here it must be acknowledged that I am imposing a certain form on the text that is not explicit in Barth. I find that reading this text in four movements reveals the asymmetrical relation between the command of God and the human response. The rich man's confrontation with the command of God (second movement) and his subsequent disobedience (third movement) is encapsulated by the presupposition of his election (first movement) and inclusion in the kingdom of Christ (fourth movement).

[19]*CD* II/2:613.

The second movement centers on the rich man's question, "What must I do to inherit eternal life?" (Mk 10:17), and Jesus' response. That the rich man believes he has kept the commandments means that even as he implicitly acknowledges the command of God in Jesus, he misses it. He misunderstands what it means to be obedient, and therefore he misunderstands who Jesus is. Jesus appeals to the second table of the commandments—the external commandments—in order to confront the man with the challenge of meeting God in the neighbor.[20]

In the third movement, the rich man's disobedience is laid bare. He knows that he objectively stands under the command of God, yet he rebels against God's authority.[21] Thus, when Jesus elaborates that the man should sell everything, give to the poor, and follow him, the rich man is confronted with the fact that he has not truly obeyed the command of God. Because he cannot sell his possessions and become free for loving his neighbor, it is revealed that he has not truly heard the liberating command of God. Further, that he is not free to love his neighbor demonstrates that he is not free to trust that he inherits everything he needs from God as a child from his father. Because he does not recognize the command of God in Jesus, he will not follow Jesus and, therefore, will not become free for God and neighbor.[22]

In the fourth movement, Barth reiterates the objective reality of the rich man's place in the kingdom of Christ. Barth picks up on Mark's claim that Jesus looked on the rich man and loved him, using it to establish that even in his disobedience the rich man is claimed by God.[23] The rich man's disobedience is his confession that he is unable to be obedient. His disobedience occurs at the edge of the abyss that is eternal damnation. But it is precisely at this point where God establishes the boundaries for his kingdom. The man who is sinking into the abyss will be continually confronted with the God who will not tolerate his rebellion.[24]

This point is made even more poignantly in Barth's comments on the second half of the story. Again, we can describe Barth's treatment of the disciples as the positive witness to God's command with four movements.

[20]*CD* II/2:615-17.
[21]*CD* II/2:617.
[22]*CD* II/2:619-22.
[23]*CD* II/2:617-18.
[24]*CD* II/2:623.

First, we are reminded that even though these disciples have chosen to follow Jesus, they are still within the same realm as the disobedient rich man. Even as the command of God distinguishes the obedient from the disobedient, it does so without dividing them: "It remains a Word of judgment even to the obedient, and a Word of promise even to the disobedient."[25] Barth claims that as Jesus looks on the disciples, he is looking past them toward the one who has gone away.

In the second movement, we see that the disciples are in solidarity with the rich man as they ask Jesus, "Then who can be saved?" (Mk 10:26). God's command has confronted them anew, and they stand again where the rich man stands at the abyss. Indeed, we feel the weight of Jesus' words, "For mortals it is impossible, but not for God; for God all things are possible" (Mk 10:27). The solidarity that the disciples share with the rich man is twofold. First, they both stand under the judgment of God. In this position, they are condemned by the claim that "no one can be saved—in virtue of what [humanity] can do." Second, they both stand under the mercy of God. In this position, they both stand objectively within the kingdom of Christ, liberated by the claim that "everyone can be saved—in virtue of what God can do."[26]

Barth makes explicit what differentiates the disciples from the rich man in the third movement. Whereas the third movement in the first half of the story emphasized the rich man's unmasking as one who has not truly kept the commands, here the disciples' positive witness becomes plain. The disciples are the ones who are truly free to leave everything behind, trusting that Jesus will become for them what they cannot be for themselves. He provides for them as they leave their possessions behind; he becomes obedient for them as they recognize that they cannot be obedient on their own. The disciples become apostles of the living Lord as they learn what it means to rest in Jesus' ability instead of their own inabilities.[27]

Again, the fourth movement reemphasizes the equal footing beneath both the obedient disciples and the disobedient rich man. Indeed, Barth takes the opportunity provided by the text to remind us that the "first will be last, and the last will be first" (Mk 10:31). Ultimately, the primary description for the

---

[25] CD II/2:624.
[26] CD II/2:625.
[27] CD II/2:626-27.

difference between the positive witness and the negative witness is not saved and lost, within and without, participants and nonparticipants; instead, the primary description is first and last. The disciples, who demonstrate obedience as they depend on Jesus' obedience, are the firstfruits of the kingdom of Christ, while the rich man, who demonstrates disobedience as he continues to rely on human inability, becomes the last to enter the kingdom. Even this difference is relative, however, as Barth is quick to remind us that those who are last today might become first tomorrow. God never withdraws from the rich man, and therefore the rich man always remains within the kingdom of Christ.

To summarize, the rich man text demonstrates for Barth the manner in which the command of God lays claim on everyone it encounters, both those who are obedient to it and those who are disobedient to it. Indeed, in the command, God exercises a prior claim on humanity, objectively placing all humanity within the kingdom of Christ. There is nothing that humans can do that can remove them from God's saving action. They may remain among the last fruits of the kingdom, but they still belong to the kingdom. Thus the overall thrust of Barth's exegesis is not, as Hauerwas suggests, that salvation depends on a response of obedience to Jesus' call to discipleship. Instead, for Barth, salvation depends on the obedient response of Jesus alone, who includes all of humanity within his response. Salvation objectively describes all of humanity as it is claimed by the command of God prior to and independent of all subsequent human responses of obedience or disobedience. In this regard, Hauerwas's appropriation of Barth is either deceptive or misguided. Either way, Hauerwas edits Barth's voice and presents it in harmony with John Paul II and himself in a manner that obscures the main thrust of Barth's reading.

OBSERVATIONS

When these two readings of the rich man text are placed side by side, Biggar's critique is again vindicated. First, notice the main objective the Scripture serves in each reading. For Barth, the text points us to Jesus as the one who confronts us as the command of God and the means by which we receive eternal life. For Hauerwas, however, the overwhelming thrust of his reading is that the Scriptures point us to the church as the place where we become trained to see Jesus as the command of God. In the end, it must be acknowledged that a fundamental difference exists regarding the relationship between Scripture and the church.

Second, notice the direction the discussion of salvation moves in each theologian. For Hauerwas, the question, "What good deed must I do to have eternal life?" (Mt 19:16) forms the basic theme of the passage, with church membership being a necessary part of the answer. For Barth, on the other hand, the main accent is not on what must be done but the fact that "for mortals it is impossible." In other words, while Hauerwas's soteriology assimilates to his ecclesiology, Barth's soteriology assimilates to his doctrine of God.

Without a doubt, then, we can say that Biggar's charge that Hauerwas's theology is ecclesiocentric obtains at least insofar as both the task of interpreting Scripture and the very means by which one comes to a saving knowledge of God are ecclesially mediated. For Barth, the Scriptures refer the reader to God; for Hauerwas, at least in this text, the Scripture points the reader to God's people. This suggests that Webster is right to worry that Hauerwas follows Ritschl in giving ecclesiology its own secondary focal point within his theology. Indeed, Hauerwas's account of salvation itself seems to reflect a priority of the community over Christ. Is this, in the end, a return to Protestant liberalism after all? I don't think so; however, it does require a great deal of explanation.

11

Ecclesiocentrism
Without Liberalism

My comparisons of Barth and Hauerwas regarding Scripture (both their doctrines of Scripture and their actual exegesis of Scripture) demonstrate that Nigel Biggar's claim regarding Hauerwas's sociological use of Scripture is a fair point. This divergence is felt in two important places. First, as Richard Hays suggested, Barth relies heavily on the Protestant doctrine of *sola Scriptura* to emphasize the manner in which Scripture stands over and against the church, while Hauerwas prefers instead a more Catholic expression of the continuity of authority between Scripture and the tradition. We cannot simply chalk this up to a difference between Protestantism and Catholicism, however, because from the beginning Barth ties his misgivings of Catholicism to the Protestant liberalism of Schleiermacher.[1] Thus for Hauerwas to break with Barth on this point suggests that those who claim Hauerwas is more like Schleiermacher than Barth would be right. In order to reassert Hauerwas's Barthian bona fides, we will have to, instead, suggest that Hauerwas's tempering of *sola Scriptura* is not a return to liberalism but a move toward postliberalism.

Second, as John Webster suggested, Hauerwas's understanding of salvation bears a strong resemblance not to Barth but to Ritschl. Hauerwas, worried that personal salvation comes at too cheap a price, emphasizes the central role the church plays in mediating salvation to the individual

---

[1]This seems clear from the very beginning of *CD*; see I/1:34.

Christian. This communal aspect to salvation leaves open the possibility that Hauerwas's theology looks more like Ritschl's ellipsis, with a second ecclesial focus alongside the first christological one. For Hauerwas to overcome this difficulty, he will have to answer for his insistence that salvation means incorporation into the church. Does this claim presuppose the sort of christocentrism featured in Barth's ecclesiology, or does it in fact introduce an alternative definition of salvation that gives the church a soteriological agency beyond Christ's saving work?

Without a doubt, Hauerwas's use of Scripture is ecclesiocentric, and scholars like Biggar who worry about this tendency in his thought have a real bone to pick with him; however, whether Hauerwas's ecclesiocentrism is equivalent with Protestant liberalism, as Webster and others go as far as to suggest, remains an open question at this point. To be sure, his criticism of *sola Scriptura* and his insistence on the church's centrality in the definition of salvation leave him open to the charge that he cannot be "Barthian" because he asserts a number of positions that Barth himself would have thought problematic. In this chapter, I will argue that he sees these moves not as a break with Barth but as an extension of Barth's rejection of Protestant liberalism.

SOLA SCRIPTURA AND ECCLESIOCENTRISM

Consider, first, Barth's reliance on *sola Scriptura* over and against Hauerwas's appeals to Roman Catholic and Orthodox positions privileging the church's role in interpreting Scripture for the community of faith. Barth's appeal to *sola Scriptura* functions within his doctrine of revelation as an insistence that while the church is the continuation of the apostolic teaching it still sits under the authority of the apostolic witness recorded in Scripture. The church does not replace Scripture as the ultimate mediator of the Word of God.

Hauerwas's break with Barth on *sola Scriptura* fits the pattern I previously recognized in his relationship to Barth's theology overall. For Hauerwas, rejecting *sola Scriptura* is about rejecting the manner in which it is co-opted by Protestant liberalism in America in order to undergird projects like fundamentalism and higher criticism. Thus Hauerwas's priority of the church over Scripture tends to focus more on prioritizing the community over individuals in the process of interpreting Scripture.

Indeed, Hauerwas's criticism of *sola Scriptura* in its post-Enlightenment form might be just the sort of thing that Barth would affirm. Barth had no sympathy for the rationalism that invaded Protestant theology in the seventeenth and eighteenth centuries. He made this much clear in his lectures on the theology of the Reformed confessions. Consider, for example, Barth's rebuke of the English Congregationalists, "who have elevated to the level of principle the idea of freedom over against one's own ecclesial past."[2] Or again, consider Barth's harsh words against the American Presbyterian revision of the Westminster Confession of Faith: "It is typical modern bungling when the *Revision of the Westminster Confession* of the American Presbyterians (1902) changes [the confession] to read that God reveals himself in nature, in history, and in the hearts of men."[3] With this adaptation, the Presbyterians changed the confession from speaking of a "light of nature" that was subsequent to Scripture to speaking of a natural knowledge of God that precedes Scripture. For Barth, then, the Enlightenment ideals of the freedom of the individual and a commonsense rationality guided by the laws of nature are problematic. Over and against them, he asserts both the authority of tradition and the priority of Scripture. These are the exact same concerns that Hauerwas expresses in *Unleashing the Scriptures* when he rejects *sola Scriptura*. This suggests that there is at least room in the space between Barth and Hauerwas to find a middle ground in the common rejection of Protestant liberalism.

Admittedly, the shared rejection of Protestant liberalism seems to be the limit of the common ground between the two theologians at this point. One of the most interesting features of Barth's lectures on the Reformed confessions is his persistent criticism of the Scottish Presbyterians for adopting the Westminster Confession of Faith and abandoning the Scots Confession.[4] Along these lines, we might expect that Barth would comment on the differing placement of Scripture in the Scots and the Westminster respectively.

The Scots, on the one hand, addresses Scripture toward the end of the confession and in the context of its articles on the church (chap. 19). This,

[2]Karl Barth, *The Theology of the Reformed Confessions*, trans. Darrell L. Guder and Judith J. Guder (Louisville, KY: Westminster John Knox, 2002), 26.
[3]Barth, *Theology of the Reformed Confessions*, 48.
[4]Barth, *Theology of the Reformed Confessions*, 151-52.

perhaps, suggests that the proper place for a doctrine of Scripture is within ecclesiology after all. On the other hand, the Westminster moves the doctrine of Scripture to the preamble (chap. 1), placing it before even the doctrine of God, suggesting its foundational significance and authoritative status. However, where one might see an affinity with Hauerwas's concern about the role of Enlightenment rationalism on the Protestant *sola Scriptura*, Barth demurs. To the contrary, Barth pauses in his Gifford Lectures on the Scots Confession to insist that although the confession does not deal with Scripture at the beginning, "it is not, however, false to its spirit to insert a short note at least at this point on the *knowledge* of revelation."[5] Then, later, in his commentary on the Scots' treatment of the government of the church, Barth reasserts the authority of Scripture over and against the church.[6]

In this regard, we must admit that the similarity between Barth and Hauerwas at this point is limited to a shared identification of the problem: Protestant liberalism. Nevertheless, this is a real similarity. Both Barth, with his doctrine of revelation, and Hauerwas, with his rejection of *sola Scriptura*, intend to challenge post-Enlightenment liberal Protestant assumptions about Scripture. When Barth relativizes Scripture to Christ, he is protecting against the same types of problems that Hauerwas has in mind when he relativizes Scripture to the church: fundamentalism and scientific criticism, namely, Enlightenment rationality.

Both theologians are engaged in a theological rejection of Protestant liberalism. Barth, concerned with the domestication of divine revelation, insists on divine freedom over and against any type of "Babylonian captivity."[7] Hauerwas, concerned with intellectual, political, and economic forces that seek to isolate the individual from the web of relationships and narratives that make revelation intelligible, insists on the necessarily communal aspect

---

[5]Karl Barth, *The Knowledge of God and the Service of God According to the Teaching of the Reformation: Recalling the Scottish Confession of 1560: The Gifford Lectures Delivered in the University of Aberdeen in 1937 and 1938*, trans. J. L. M. Hare and Ian Henderson (1938; repr., Eugene, OR: Wipf and Stock, 2005), 66.

[6]Barth, *Knowledge of God*, 178.

[7]"Babylonian captivity" is Barth's term for any sort of anthropocentrism. For example, in *Evangelical Theology*, Barth writes: "If theology wished to reverse this relationship, and instead of relating man to *God*, related God to *man*, then it would surrender itself to a new Babylonian captivity. It would become the prisoner of some sort of anthropology or ontology that is an underlying interpretation of existence, of faith, or of man's spiritual capacity" (*Evangelical Theology: An Introduction* [Grand Rapids: Eerdmans, 1992], 8 [emphasis original]).

of God's self-revelation. The Word of God is always the Word of God *for the people of God.* For this reason, suggesting that Hauerwas's ecclesiology necessarily reduces to Protestant liberalism seems facetious.

One final tension can be relieved at this point. Remember, for Barth, the problem with the Catholic view of Scripture and the church revolves around the concern that the church and Scripture become one uninterrupted revelation, with the church claiming authority over Scripture by virtue of its contemporaneity. This was a problem he also attributed to Schleiermacher and Protestant liberalism. On the surface, this seems to lend credence to those who might argue that Hauerwas's appeal to Catholic doctrinal positions on the relationship between church and Scripture on this point is another example of how his theology skews toward Schleiermacher. To do so, however, fails to appreciate that Barth's concern is primarily with the Kant-infused Catholicism of the Tübingen school.

A more sympathetic reading of Hauerwas is that his turn to the church is a postliberal move—a move that shares Barth's concerns with Protestant liberalism yet recognizes the necessarily communal dimension of the doctrine of revelation. Thus Hauerwas's "Catholic" understanding of the relationship between Scripture and the church is not equivalent to Protestant liberalism because it is a self-critical attempt to buttress against one of the more pernicious effects of Protestant liberalism: individualism.[8]

From Hauerwas's perspective, this is going beyond Barth and "fixing" some idealist tendencies in Barth's theology by appealing to a more concrete and more Catholic ecclesiology. Joseph Mangina helpfully summarizes Barth's idealism and Hauerwas's fix. For Mangina, Barth's problem is that his depiction of the church's use of Scripture "is not construed as part of a practice that *takes up time* in the world."[9] Barth fears that doing so would make revelation conditional on human activity. For Hauerwas, in contrast, "Scripture functions as the norm that tells us who the God of

[8]Hauerwas would probably recognize his own view of the relationship between Scripture and the church to be closer to the Roman Catholic position developed by Matthew Levering, who depends on *Dei Verbum* to argue that "we cannot cordon off the truth of the gospel (let alone Scripture or its interpretation) from the truthfulness of the Church" (Matthew Levering, *Engaging the Doctrine of Revelation: The Mediation of the Gospel through Church and Scripture* [Grand Rapids: Baker Academic, 2014], 4).
[9]Joseph Mangina, "Bearing the Marks of Jesus: The Church in the Economy of Salvation in Barth and Hauerwas," *Scottish Journal of Theology* 52, no. 3 (1999): 281.

Jesus Christ is—the God who both judges and forgives our sin—but the norm does actual work only when it is employed as a script by the Christian community."[10] This move offers at once a more concrete account of how Scripture works in the community and a more Catholic ecclesiology in the sense that the church becomes the mediator of revelation. This move is essentially postliberal in the sense that it is an attempt to recover a Catholic emphasis on the church's role in revelation while retaining a Barth-like skepticism of modern Catholicism and the manner in which it parrots Protestant liberalism. Thus, at least with regard to the differences between Barth and Hauerwas's doctrine of Scripture, it is possible to articulate Hauerwas's ecclesiocentrism as a postliberal ecclesiocentrism instead of a return to Protestant liberalism.

Before we move on to an examination of the differences in exegetical practice, it is perhaps worth pausing to emphasize that this is a point Hauerwas seems to have won. Among those who have contributed to the field of theological interpretation of Scripture in the last couple of decades, almost all agree that the role the community plays in the transmission and interpretation of Scripture was vastly under-recognized in the Protestant tradition.[11] Even those who join Jeffrey Siker in worrying that Hauerwas ultimately replaces *sola Scriptura* with *sola ecclesia* find they must at least say something more positive about the relationship between Scripture and the church than was previously said.[12] In particular, those who press for adherence to the traditional Reformed mark of *sola Scriptura* tend to shore up their theologies of Scripture with a stronger ecclesiology in order to avoid the sort of concerns Hauerwas identifies with American Protestant liberalism.[13] To wit: Kevin Vanhoozer's recent attempt to recommend the five

---

[10]Mangina, "Bearing the Marks," 297.

[11]See, for example, The Scripture Project, "Nine Theses on the Interpretation of Scripture," in *The Art of Reading Scripture*, ed. Ellen F. Davis and Richard B. Hays (Grand Rapids: Eerdmans, 2003), 1-8, see especially theses 2, 6, and 7.

[12]Jeffrey S. Siker, *Scripture and Ethics: Twentieth-Century Portraits* (Oxford: Oxford University Press, 1997), 123. For an example of someone who continues to disagree with Hauerwas but must account for the church in greater depth in light of the concerns Hauerwas expresses, see John Webster, *Holy Scripture: A Dogmatic Sketch* (Cambridge: Cambridge University Press, 2003), 42-67.

[13]Two clear examples of attempting to have *sola Scriptura* plus a postliberal, or Hauerwasian, view of Scripture's relation to the church are Kevin J. Vanhoozer, *The Drama of Doctrine: A Canonical-Linguistic Approach to Christian Theology* (Louisville, KY: Westminster John Knox, 2005); and

solas of Protestantism requires him to retrieve and redefine the concept of the priesthood of all believers as "a virtual sixth sola: *sola ecclesia.*"[14]

In the end, the distinction between Barth and Hauerwas as it relates to the formal relationship between the church and Scripture is not evidence of Hauerwas's vestigial liberalism. Instead, it is a postliberal awareness of the relationship between Scripture and the church with which Protestant theology is just now coming to terms. We need not drive a wedge between Barth and Hauerwas on this point. As Angus Paddison notes, "If we think we face a dilemma whether to speak of Scripture out of attention to God or attention to the church, we have made a misstep."[15] This is not to say, however, that Hauerwas's tendency toward ecclesiocentrism is entirely innocuous. To the contrary, I worry that the manner in which he actually reads Scripture, as demonstrated in my examination of his exegesis, truly threatens to obscure the scriptural witness to divine agency by focusing on human agency.

EXTRA ECCLESIAM NULLA SALUS AND ECCLESIOCENTRISM

A second problem emerged when I considered the way Barth and Hauerwas actually read a common piece of Scripture. It is not simply that Hauerwas insists that knowledge of God is ecclesially mediated; he actually goes as far as to suggest that salvation itself is ecclesially mediated. For Hauerwas, again, this is a return to a more Catholic expression of salvation. Simply put, the difference between Barth and Hauerwas on this point is a difference between how to understand *extra ecclesiam nulla salus*, "outside the church there is no salvation." This difference can again be explained in terms of a shared criticism of Protestant liberalism. At the same time, Hauerwas's reading of the rich man text presses the possibility that Webster is right to worry that Hauerwas's theology resembles Ritschl's. It is not merely the case that salvation is ecclesially mediated for Hauerwas; instead, he redefines what the gospel is and what salvation entails in a manner that threatens to posit a second ecclesial focus alongside his self-proclaimed christological center.

Stanley J. Grenz and John R. Franke, *Beyond Foundationalism: Shaping Theology in a Postmodern Context* (Louisville, KY: Westminster John Knox, 2001).

[14]Kevin J. Vanhoozer, *Biblical Authority After Babel: Retrieving the Solas in the Spirit of Mere Protestant Christianity* (Grand Rapids: Brazos, 2016), 29.

[15]Angus Paddison, *Scripture: A Very Theological Proposal* (London: T&T Clark, 2009), 3.

I observed above that while Hauerwas's soteriology assimilates to his ecclesiology, Barth's soteriology assimilates to his doctrine of God. Essentially, this is a difference regarding how to interpret *extra ecclesiam nulla salus*. For Barth, *extra ecclesiam nulla salus* is true provided that we recognize that the church has its origin and being in the Word of God. Barth writes, "*Extra ecclesiam nulla salus* necessarily means: that by belonging to Christ we belong to all who belong to Him."[16] Here, Barth's understanding of the relationship between Christ and the church takes the form of the Chalcedonian pattern.[17] The asymmetry between Christ and the church ensures that the saving action is always the work of Christ. Thus, for Barth, to say that there is no salvation outside the church is equivalent to saying that there is no salvation outside of Jesus Christ.

This way of conceiving things concerns Hauerwas because it risks making ecclesial agency superfluous.[18] For this reason, he emphasizes the necessary role that the church plays. In *After Christendom*, Hauerwas writes, "Salvation is a political alternative that the world cannot know apart from the existence of a concrete people called church. Put more dramatically, you cannot even know you need saving without the church's being a political alternative."[19]

We can interpret Hauerwas's insistence on the church's mediation of salvation in a similar manner that we interpreted his rejection of *sola Scriptura*. Here, Hauerwas is again polemical, taking aim at individualistic and pietistic notions of salvation that accommodate capitalist and liberal cultural assumptions and depoliticize the church's witness. Nevertheless, the overall effect is to put Hauerwas at odds with Barth because he again inserts the church between God and salvation. On these terms, we might join with Bruce Hamil in worrying that Hauerwas domesticates salvation within the life and practices of the church.[20]

---

[16]*CD* I/2:217.

[17]Barth describes the church's existence as both determined by Jesus Christ and the upstart arbitrariness that results from human effort. This he compares to the relationship between Christ's divinity and humanity: "The nature of the Church cannot be gathered from man's upstart arbitrariness in it. Just as, similarly, Jesus Christ cannot be understood from the standpoint of man's nature and kind, which He assumed and adopted, and which are only too familiar to us" (*CD* I/2:214).

[18]*WGU*, 145.

[19]*AC*, 35.

[20]Bruce Hamill, "Beyond Ecclesiocentricity: Navigating Between the Abstract and the Domesticated in Contemporary Ecclesiology," *International Journal of Systematic Theology* 14, no. 3 (2012): 278.

The most robust expression of this concern is the one raised by the Ritschl thesis, namely, that Hauerwas's ecclesiocentrism posits a second ecclesial focus within his theological ethics that operates alongside of his christological commitments. It is not merely that the church somehow stands between the individual and God; Hauerwas's ecclesiocentrism actually alters his definition of what the gospel is and what salvation entails. If Hauerwas is a Barthian, he will have to overcome this suggestion that his ecclesiocentrism distorts his theological project by compromising the sort of Barthian christological commitments he claims to possess.

In his reading of the rich man, Hauerwas defined salvation alternatively as being "made a member of the church through baptism" and being "part of the body of Christ."[21] This suggests that Hauerwas's ecclesiocentric explication of salvation presupposes the christological expression that the church is the body of Christ. In other words, while Hauerwas emphasizes the church's agency in mediating salvation, it is not necessarily the case that ecclesiology operates independently and alongside of Christology in his thought, à la Ritschl. Nevertheless, the complete lack of any language of divine agency feels incredibly un-Barthian. A comparison of Barth and Hauerwas on the question, What is the gospel? presses this point.

Karl Barth's understanding of the gospel is best captured in the focus sentences at the beginning of *Church Dogmatics* II/2:

> The doctrine of election is the sum of the Gospel because of all words that can be said or heard it is the best: that God elects man; that God is for man too the One who loves in freedom. It is grounded in the knowledge of Jesus Christ because he is both the electing God and elected man in One. . . . Its function is to bear basic testimony to eternal, free and unchanging grace as the beginning of all the ways and works of God.[22]

The good news is that God is the sort of God who chooses to be "God for humanity" and to be "humanity with God" in the incarnation of Jesus Christ. Indeed, everything that can be said about this God conforms to the knowledge of God we have in Jesus Christ. Jesus Christ is the very content of the gospel because "God's decision in Jesus Christ is a gracious decision."[23]

---

[21]*M*, 174-75.
[22]*CD* II/2:3.
[23]*CD* II/2:10.

For Barth, Jesus Christ is both the God who elects and the human who is elected to be with God. In Jesus, we see that God is not God without us, but God *with* us and *for* us.

This God is known "by way of [his] self-testimony." For Barth, we hear this testimony through the voices of the church as they conform their message to the voice of Scripture. Both Scripture and the church, in turn, are governed by "the voice which reigns, the voice by which we are taught by God Himself concerning God, . . . the voice of Jesus Christ."[24] In other words, for Barth, we learn about the God who elects to be for us and with us as he reveals himself in the threefold Word of God. For Barth, the gospel is that Jesus Christ is the Word of God, God's self-testimony to his gracious decision to be God *for* us. This Word is a word that is repeated as it is anticipated by the Old Testament prophets and attested by the New Testament apostles in Holy Scripture, and as it is proclaimed by the church today. The church's proclamation must conform to Scripture and bear witness to Jesus for it to truly be the gospel, the Word of God.

When we turn to Hauerwas, we see some similarities in his understanding of the gospel. But we also see a striking difference. Albert Mohler once asked Hauerwas, "What is the gospel?" Hauerwas responded:

> That through Jesus Christ, very God and very man, we Gentiles have been made part of the promise to Israel that we will be witnesses to God's good care of God's creation through the creation of a people who once were no people that the world can see there is an alternative to our violence. There is an alternative to our deceptions. There is an alternative to our unfaithfulness to one another through the creation of something called church. That's salvation.[25]

Thus, for Hauerwas, the gospel is grounded in the work of Christ, which is (notably) connected to his personhood and his two natures. The good news is that in Christ we are included in God's covenant people. Here election runs toward ecclesiology and, therefore, away from Barth's claim that the doctrine of election belongs to theology proper. For Barth, the doctrine of election is the sum of the gospel because it is the divine decision to be God *for* humanity.

---

[24]CD II/2:4.

[25]Albert Mohler, "Nearing the End: A Conversation with Theologian Stanley Hauerwas," Albert Mohler website, April 28, 2014, http://www.albertmohler.com/2014/04/28/nearing-the-end-a-conversation-with-theologian-stanley-hauerwas/.

For Hauerwas, election means being brought into the political community of the people of God and given a vocation to bear witness to the world. This is an election to be "with God" to be sure, but it is also an election to be God's witnesses in the world. Whereas for Barth the accent is on God's divine agency and the indicative reality that it creates for elected humanity, for Hauerwas the accent is on human responsibility, taking the force of an imperative.[26]

Particularly, Christians bear witness to God's providential care for creation by being a community that lives peaceably and trusts God to provide. When Christians do so, they bear witness to the "peaceable kingdom," a kingdom that is embodied in Jesus' very life, death, and resurrection. Jesus does not just proclaim the kingdom; he is the kingdom, the *autobasileia* (the kingdom himself).[27] Thus salvation means participating in Jesus' kingdom as its very embodiment in the world. This makes Christians "resident aliens" in the world around them. Hauerwas does not obviate the centrality of the cross; to the contrary, he often says that the world was changed in AD 33 with Jesus' crucifixion and resurrection. But the salvation that is wrought on the cross is not reduced to forensic or economic metaphors of sacrifice, punishment, or debt. For Hauerwas, the cross is both exemplary of the extent to which Christ calls us to live nonviolently and the means by which Christ claims victory over the powers of sin and evil and establishes his kingdom. "Being saved" means becoming a part of the kingdom and bearing witness to its reality through participation in the church's worship.[28]

Among those similarities that Hauerwas shares with Barth, then, is the centrality of Jesus' person and work. But for Barth, Jesus is the gospel himself, and he bears witness to the God who chooses us to be with him. The church proclaims the gospel, but it only does so truly when it conforms to God's self-testimony in Jesus. Meanwhile, for Hauerwas, the gospel is the word about what Jesus has done for us. Namely, Jesus has incorporated us into his body, and he gives us a mission to be his body in the world: the embodiment of an alternative political reality called the kingdom of God. In short, the gospel according to Barth is that Jesus reveals the gracious and electing God

---

[26]*MW*, 260-63.

[27]*CC*, 44.

[28]Nobody has better encapsulated Hauerwas's thoughts on atonement and salvation than Victoria Lorrimar, "Christ and Church in the Work of Stanley Hauerwas," *Ecclesiology* 11 (2015): 310-18.

who is for us, while the gospel according to Hauerwas is that Jesus makes us participants in God's election of a people who are witnesses to his kingdom in the world—that Jesus makes us into the church.

Even here, then, Hauerwas's ecclesiocentric soteriology is deceptive. It does not repeat Ritschl's aversion to high Christology, as Biggar and Webster have suggested; instead, it claims high christological doctrines like Christ's two natures as presuppositions in its explication of the church's being as participation in Christ's election and mission to the world. Further, to say that you have to be a member of the church to read Scripture correctly is not to say that the church has authority over Scripture; it is, instead, to insist that the individual has no authority over Scripture. Indeed, it emphasizes that the individual only learns how to hear Scripture from those who have come to terms with Scripture's authority: the community of believers. And finally, Hauerwas's emphasis on the church's mediation of salvation is not to say that the church is the primary agent in our salvation. To the contrary, the question of who saves (God) is presupposed. Instead, the question that interests Hauerwas is the question, What does salvation entail? or, How are "the saved" supposed to act? In this sense, Hauerwas's theological ethics is truly an attempt to follow Barth's maxim that the *how* question must be treated within the context of the *what*. For Hauerwas, the *how* becomes the church's worship, as I have demonstrated above. In worship, Christians receive moral formation that enables them to act in the world in a manner that bears witness to the God who saves. Those who charge that Hauerwas is a liberal Protestant often assume that the *how* operates independently from the *what* or that it replaces the *what* altogether. And this is simply not the case.

Conclusion

OVER THE COURSE OF THIS BOOK, I have considered the question, Is Hauerwas a Barthian or is he a Protestant liberal? I have tried to be as sympathetic as possible to Hauerwas's self-understanding as a Barthian, on the one hand, while also acknowledging the truth of the Protestant liberalism concerns, on the other. Hauerwas is most certainly a Barthian in the sense that he learns from Barth the importance of keeping theology and ethics together and rejecting natural theology. I have expressed this in Barth's terms as the attempt to treat the *how* questions of theology within the context of the *what* question. Further, I have argued that for Hauerwas particularly, the *how* is always grounded in Christology; a Christology that certainly attends to the question of Christ's humanity more so than Barth but one that nevertheless presupposes all of the same high christological doctrines and, even further, appeals to a similar Pauline understanding of imitation. Finally, I have suggested that even Hauerwas's postliberal attempt to "fix" Barth's ecclesiology might be Barthian at the end of the day because (1) it fits within Barth's expectation that his students will go beyond him, and (2) it attends to what Bent Flemming Nielsen has called Barth's *Theologie treiben*, or how Barth theologizes. Both of these aspects of Hauerwas's postliberalism suggest that his reading of Barth pushes beyond the simple nonfoundationalism and intertextuality that Bruce McCormack thinks problematic.

At the same time, I have tried to temper my reading of Hauerwas's Barth by acknowledging and explicating Hauerwas's own postliberalism as much as possible. I have argued that Hauerwas's postliberalism operates predominantly as a type of Christian pragmatism. Thus, for Hauerwas, the question that presses him beyond Barth is not, What would Barth say about X? but, What does it look like to live as if X is true? In this sense, I have intentionally differentiated Barth's influence from postliberalism in Hauerwas's thinking. Although some have suggested that Barth is the father of postliberalism, I have tried to locate the origin of postliberalism in H. Richard Niebuhr's neo-orthodoxy and a Troeltschian concern for history.[1] This move intentionally concedes something of the liberal Protestant criticism by acknowledging (1) that Hauerwas's own theological origins are unmistakably liberal in nature, and (2) that even Hauerwas's rejection of Protestant liberalism is only intelligible against the backdrop of how his postliberalism returns to the questions of liberalism from a more Barthian angle. In this sense, I have acknowledged the truth of the similarities between Hauerwas and Schleiermacher or Ritschl, but I have argued that he cannot simply be reduced to a pale imitation of their work. Instead, his theology often takes up questions that press the relationship between divine and human agency and the *how* of theology only after presupposing that Barth's account of the *what* is largely true.

While I take this to be the case with Hauerwas's work, I think that people often misinterpret him because of a combination of challenges that come with engaging his work. Hauerwas's body of work is massive, and outsiders are often uncertain where he said what and how to make connections across the work in a manner that achieves a holistic and sympathetic account of his thinking on any particular theme. To compound the problem, Hauerwas's work is an exercise in what Barth would call irregular dogmatics, meaning that his theology is not a "detailed systematics" but instead is a "free dogmatics" that "does not cover the whole ground" of theology and is, therefore, "a fragment."[2] In other words, irregular dogmatics is not a scholastic theology. For Barth, this is not a problem; to the contrary, it is the more common of the two forms of dogmatics. It simply means that scholars who wish to take up Hauerwas's irregular dogmatics should heed Barth's words that "it will have to be evaluated as such."[3] Comparisons between

---

[1] Douglas Harink, *Paul Among the Postliberals: Pauline Theology Beyond Christendom and Modernity* (Grand Rapids: Brazos, 2003), 18.
[2] *CD* I/1:277.
[3] *CD* I/1:277.

Barth and Hauerwas sometimes break down where the expectations are that Hauerwas should have been more comprehensive, like Barth.

Because of Hauerwas's irregularity, scholars often limit themselves to a few key essays or works (especially *PK*) for the sake of convenience. This means that readers have not yet really taken Hauerwas at his word when he presses them to consider his sermons and prayers as serious theology. Hauerwas is a postliberal, which means that he draws a distinction between first-order and second-order language. First-order language is the church's speech about God that occurs in its worship of God, and therefore as speech not just *about* God but *with* and *to* God. Second-order theological language is reflection on that first-order language. Scholars often limit themselves to Hauerwas's essays, which are second-order language, and neglect the first-order language in his sermons. Thus, when they complain that Hauerwas disdains metaphysics or refuses to make his metaphysics clear, they miss an important point, namely, that his metaphysical presuppositions are on display in his first-order theological work because that is where he thinks that it is proper to speak so boldly *to* and *about* God.[4]

It is my greatest hope that scholars will come to see that for Hauerwas the *how* is always connected to the *what*. In this regard, I think that there are a few things that Hauerwas—or those who might want to further my case—can do in order to make this point more obvious. First, I think that Hauerwas should try and situate his own ecclesiology in closer proximity to Barth's christological ecclesiology as it is described by Kimlyn Bender. Second, I think that Hauerwas should engage some of the work that is being done by Darrell Guder and the missional theology movement. Let me say a little bit more about each of these suggestions.

First, Hauerwas would benefit from reconsidering how his own theological ethics relate to Barth's ecclesiology. Bender's study of Barth's ecclesiology particularly presses this point. Indeed, Hauerwas has recently preempted me on this point, writing in a footnote:

> I have in several places suggested my ecclesiology is more robust than Barth's account of the church. But I have now read Kimlyn Bender's *Karl Barth's Christological Ecclesiology*. . . . Bender has certainly convinced me that my

---

[4]This point has recently received greater focus (*B*, 273-83).

understanding of the church as a community that participates in the very life
of Christ is not a position foreign to Barth.[5]

One wishes that Hauerwas would expand this thought beyond a footnote
and into a full-blown reconsideration of Barth's ecclesiology. What, particularly, is it about Bender's account that has changed Hauerwas's mind? For
one thing, Bender opens up the possibility that to be "ecclesiocentric" does
not mean to be anti-Barthian or liberal. Let me explain.

For Bender, Barth's ecclesiology has a necessarily christocentric logic.
This logic is composed of three primary elements: the Chalcedonian pattern,
the patristic distinction between *anhypostasia* and *enhypostasia*, and the
positive articulation of human action as correspondence to divine action.
First, the Chalcedonian pattern regulates all divine and human relationships in analogy to the hypostatic union. This means that Barth's ecclesiology has both theological and sociological aspects; yet the theological is
always given an asymmetric priority. Second, the *anhypostatic/enhypostatic*
distinction further clarifies the extent to which the being of the church is
entirely dependent on divine action while it still has a real and creaturely
existence. Finally, the notion of correspondence allows for Barth to speak
of divine action and human action existing in a real relationship to each
other without placing the two on equal footing. Ecclesiologically, this
means that for Barth "the church is to attempt and bear within its life and
in the life of each member 'an imitation and representation of the love with
which God loved the world.'"[6]

These three elements are seen clearly in Barth's ecclesiology in his exploration of three specific relationships: the relationship between the Spirit and
the church as it pertains to the church's origin and nature, the relationship
between Christ and the church as it pertains to the church's order and form,
and the relationship between the church and the world as it pertains to the
church's ordination and mission. As Bender explains, we might consider
Barth's ecclesiology as comprising three concentric circles. The innermost
circle is Christ, while the middle circle is the church, and the outer circle is
the world. Both church and world are centered on Christ. The Spirit-church

---

[5]*WT*, 273 n. 16.
[6]Kimlyn J. Bender, *Karl Barth's Christological Ecclesiology* (Eugene, OR: Cascade, 2013), 3-7.

relationship and the Christ-church relationship both follow the christo-centric logic of Barth's ecclesiology to the extent that the human action is always centered on and has its being from the divine center. The church-world relationship, however, can be distinguished by virtue of the fact that "now the church takes the place of the first term in the relation."[7] This does not mean that the church replaces Christ and therefore becomes the center. Nevertheless, the church, predicated on its Christ center, becomes, in a manner, central in its relation to the world.

If Bender is right about Barth's ecclesiology, then it does not necessarily seem to be the case that Hauerwas's ecclesiocentrism places him at odds with Barth's christocentrism. Indeed, it is more likely the case that Hauerwas presupposes a Barth-like christocentrism and tries to work out the church-world relationship from this center in his own American context. That his ecclesiology ultimately looks different from Barth's is not in dispute. But this need not prevent him from calling himself a Barthian if he does in fact presuppose a christocentric logic like the one Bender describes.[8] I have suggested here that such a similarity in Christology exists in each theologian's work where it is focused on the concepts of imitation and participation, conceiving of human agency as reflecting God to the world. Therefore, while those who have pointed out that Hauerwas's work is ecclesiocentric have definitive evidence that this is true, they have perhaps overstated their case by suggesting that Hauerwas is a pre-Barthian liberal masquerading as a Barthian.

Particularly, the Ritschl thesis suggests that Hauerwas's ecclesiology operates as an independent theological focal point outside of his Christology, making Hauerwas's theology elliptical like Ritschl's. Bender provides a way to say that Hauerwas is indeed ecclesiocentric with regard to his focus on the church-world relationship and yet that does not contradict Barth's christocentrism. Instead of two theological foci, there remains one—Christ—and the church is an intermediate concentric circle between Christ and the world.

---

[7]Bender, *Karl Barth's Christological Ecclesiology*, 8-10.

[8]Bender himself leaves the door open for this conclusion: "Hauerwas's ecclesiology may be an attempt to provide the rich historical description that Barth lacks. One would not want to overestimate the differences between them" (Bender, *Confessing Christ for Church and World: Studies in Modern Theology* [Downers Grove, IL: IVP Academic, 2014], 63).

Conclusion

At the same time, this certainly does not mean that the two simply become one. Theologians who "wonder where the Spirit went" in Barth's theology often point to Hauerwas's ecclesiology as a potential remedy.[9] Indeed, there is a tendency among some scholars to imply the Holy Spirit in Hauerwas's ecclesiology at places where Hauerwas himself demurs.[10] This was one of the main concerns that Sam Wells expressed with Hauerwas's theology in *Transforming Fate Into Destiny*.[11] So when Hauerwas recently published about the Holy Spirit in a few places, there were high hopes that this lacuna would finally be filled.

Historically, Hauerwas explains, he was reticent to speak too much of the work of the Spirit because he feared pietistic reductions of the Spirit to personal experience; he preferred instead to emphasize the relationship between the work of the Spirit and the church.[12] Interestingly, Hauerwas ties this move to his Barthianism. Barth's rejection of Protestant liberalism taught him to distrust theologies grounded in experience because they are probably just some form of Feuerbachian projection.

Recently, Hauerwas has tried to speak of the work of the Spirit by locating it between his Christology and his ecclesiology. In relation to Christology, Hauerwas insists that "whatever we say about the Holy Spirit must be tested by and congruent with the life, death, and resurrection of Jesus."[13] At the same time, however, he claims that "Jesus can be known only through the connections the Spirit makes possible."[14] That is, the distinct work of the Holy Spirit in the gospel is that the Spirit comes to rest on Jesus, "and by doing so, manifests the love that constitutes the relation of the Father and the Son."[15]

The Spirit's work is recapitulated with regard to ecclesiology. The Holy Spirit—who is "intensely communitarian, relational, and embodied"—gives

---

[9]Robert W. Jenson, "You Wonder Where the Spirit Went," *Pro Ecclesia* 2, no. 3 (1993): 296-304.

[10]I am thinking predominantly of Hütter and Mangina; however, I would say that this also applies to the Orthodox ethicist Vigen Guroian. See Guroian, *Incarnate Love: Essays in Orthodox Ethics*, 2nd ed. (Notre Dame, IN: University of Notre Dame Press, 2002), 52-53.

[11]Samuel Wells, *Transforming Fate into Destiny: The Theological Ethics of Stanley Hauerwas* (Carlisle, UK: Paternoster, 1998; repr., Eugene, OR: Cascade, 2004), 98.

[12]*WT*, 35.

[13]*HS*, x.

[14]*WT*, 39.

[15]*WT*, 43.

birth to the church.[16] Further, the Spirit is God's gift to the church, sustaining and sanctifying it until Christ comes again. It comes and rests on the church, Christ's body, and guides its mission to bear witness to Jesus.[17] The church's activity—word, sacrament, and ministry—is taken up by the power of the Holy Spirit and becomes the means by which Christ is present to his church.[18] In this sense, the Spirit "is the link between the earthly offering of praise and the eternal liturgy of the Trinity."[19]

For Hauerwas, then, the Holy Spirit is the one who draws us into the life that the Father shares with the Son by first pointing us to Jesus and then helping us to point others to him. While he is careful not to collapse his pneumatology into his ecclesiology, he nevertheless speaks of the church's liturgical action as being taken up by the Spirit. This is where Hauerwas's ecclesiology obviously breaks with Barth's.

For Barth, the church's agency is purely human, and it never cooperates with divine agency in a manner that confuses the two. In his famous treatment of baptism this is obviously clear where he distinguishes between spirit baptism and water baptism as separate but corresponding actions. If we return to Bender's treatment of Barth's ecclesiology, we see that one clear difference between Barth and Hauerwas will be the question of the relationship between divine and human agency in the church's practices. To say that Barth's ecclesiology needs to be fixed by developing a more concrete account of church practice is not the same thing as saying that the church's agency in those practices is cooperating with the Spirit's agency. Thus, while Bender will help Hauerwas to account for the church's action in the world as a consistent and logical outworking of a Barthian Christology, Hauerwas still must come to terms with how his pneumatological account of church practices fits with his earlier intuition that speaking of the Spirit's work too concretely risks the liberal Protestant collapse of the Spirit into the church. Hauerwas has Catholic and postliberal resources that might enable him to do this, but he has to break with Barth on this point in order to do so.

---

[16] *HS*, x.
[17] *WT*, 40.
[18] *HS*, 49.
[19] *WT*, 46.

Second, Hauerwas might benefit from engagement with the missional theology movement. On first blush, this idea seems counterintuitive. After all, John Flett has pointed out that Hauerwasian phrases like "let the church be the church" trace their origins back to Protestant Christianity's mid-twentieth-century abandonment of mission talk.[20] Indeed, the great difference between how Hauerwas often uses the term *witness* to speak of Christian ethics and how Flett and the missional theology group uses the term to speak of Christian mission probably owes something to Protestant liberalism itself. Christian ethics and social action emerged in the early twentieth century in mainline American Protestantism in conjunction with two trends. One is the sobering awareness of the extent to which global missions was tied to colonialism. The other is a loss of confidence in the church's proclamation of the gospel. The result was that the church abandoned "mission" talk and chose instead to focus on "social work." Even today, often the difference between liberal Protestant and evangelical conceptions of the church's relation to the world reflects the language of social ethics versus mission.

Missional theology, drawing on the work of Lesslie Newbigin, couches the church's witness in the world within the "missionary God." Thus the church's missional agency reflects and participates in God's missional activity. In this regard, the relationship between the church and the triune God is one that is deeply Barthian, with both mission and ethics fitting more broadly into what Barth calls the church's proclamation of the gospel.

Even though Flett seems to close the door on a similarity between Hauerwas and missional theology because he sees little room for ecclesiocentrism in mission, Darrell Guder has recently suggested otherwise. In his Shenk Lectures, delivered at Associated Mennonite Biblical Seminary, Guder claims that a missional hermeneutic begins with the question, "How did this particular text continue the formation of witnessing communities then, and how does it do that today?"[21] In so doing, a missional hermeneutic is also critical of Christendom, which reduces salvation to an individual personal decision, ignores the kingdom of God,

---

[20]John G. Flett, *The Witness of God: The Trinity, Missio Dei, Karl Barth, and the Nature of Christian Community* (Grand Rapids: Eerdmans, 2010), 267-68.

[21]Darrel L. Guder, *Called to Witness: Doing Missional Theology* (Grand Rapids: Eerdmans, 2015), 92.

and reduces the church to a partner with the State whose main purpose is to "save souls."[22]

One does not have to strain to hear the echoes of Hauerwas's voice. Hauerwas's attention to important themes like how Scripture forms communities to be disciples, the communal aspect of salvation, Christ's kingly lordship, and the church's captivity to the nation-state all clearly resonate with Guder's project. We should not be surprised. Guder himself concedes that "there is probably more groundwork for a missional interpretation of Scripture in Anabaptist writings about the theology of scriptural authority than in the other streams of the Reformation."[23]

Again, this is not to say that Hauerwas's work is completely compatible with missional theology. For one thing, Guder's missional hermeneutic "invests the Reformation's *sola scriptura* with great urgency," a prospect that would certainly give Hauerwas pause.[24] For another, missional hermeneutics is grounded in the missional theology movement's origins in "the paradigm shift in twentieth century missiology . . . away from the ecclesiocentric understanding of mission shaped by Christendom to the theocentric and ultimately Trinitarian understanding of mission as the actual implementation by God's grace."[25] In other words, missional theology is grounded on a rejection of a Christendom account of mission as the church's agency. While Hauerwas's own theology shares a rejection of Christendom, it mostly follows the tradition of Christian ethics in America. This means that it speaks of ethics instead of mission and where it does so it continues to speak about the church's own actions, not God's. While I have argued that this does not necessarily mean that Hauerwas's work capitulates to Protestant liberalism, Hauerwas would benefit from probing the similarities and differences between his own work and the missional theology movement. I suspect he would find there a more Barthian way to speak about God's agency in his own theological ethics.

---

[22]Guder, *Called to Witness*, 95-96.
[23]Guder, *Called to Witness*, 93. Jeppe Bach Nikolajsen's recent comparison of Newbigin and Yoder presses my point even further. See Nikolajsen, *The Distinctive Identity of the Church: A Constructive Study of the Post-Christendom Theologies of Lesslie Newbigin and John Howard Yoder* (Eugene, OR: Pickwick, 2015).
[24]Guder, *Called to Witness*, 93.
[25]Guder, *Called to Witness*, 99.

These two suggestions—that Hauerwas should reconsider how Barth's ecclesiology relates to his own and that Hauerwas should engage the missional theology movement—demonstrate that I have barely scratched the surface of the theological relationship that Hauerwas's ethics have to Barth. In that sense, I hope that this work will be received as the beginning of a conversation. It is certainly not the last word.

Bibliography

Banner, Michael. Review of *The Blackwell Companion to Christian Ethics*, edited by Stanley Hauerwas and Samuel Wells. *International Journal of Systematic Theology* 9, no. 1 (2007): 106-9.

Barth, Karl. "An Answer to Professor von Harnack's Open Letter." In *The Beginnings of Dialectic Theology*, edited by James M. Robinson, 1:175-85. Richmond: John Knox Press, 1968.

———. *Barth in Conversation*. Vol. 1, *1959–1962*. Edited by Eberhard Busch. Translated by the Center for Barth Studies. Louisville, KY: Westminster John Knox, 2017.

———. *Church Dogmatics*. Edited by G. W. Bromiley and T. F. Torrance. Translated by G. W. Bromiley. 4 vols. in 13 parts. Edinburgh: T&T Clark, 1956–1975.

———. *The Epistle to the Romans*. Translated by Edwyn C. Hoskyns. Oxford: Oxford University Press, 1933.

———. *Evangelical Theology: An Introduction*. Translated by Grover Foley. 1963. Reprint, Grand Rapids: Eerdmans, 1992.

———. *Fragments Grave and Gay*. Edited by Martin Rumscheidt. Translated by Eric Mosbacher. 1971. Reprint, Eugene, OR: Wipf and Stock, 2011.

———. *The Knowledge of God and the Service of God According to the Teaching of the Reformation: Recalling the Scottish Confession of 1560; The Gifford Lectures Delivered in the University of Aberdeen in 1937 and 1938*. Translated by J. L. M. Hare and Ian Henderson. 1938. Reprint, Eugene, OR: Wipf and Stock, 2005.

———. *Letters: 1961–1968*. Translated by Geoffrey Bromiley. Grand Rapids: Eerdmans, 1981.

———. *Theological Existence Today: A Plea for Theological Freedom*. Translated by R. Birch Hoyle. 1933. Reprint, Eugene, OR: Wipf and Stock, 2011.

———. *The Theology of John Calvin*. Translated by Geoffrey W. Bromiley. Grand Rapids: Eerdmans, 1995.

———. *The Theology of the Reformed Confessions*. Translated by Darrell L. Guder and Judith J. Guder. Louisville, KY: Westminster John Knox, 2002.

———. *The Way of Theology in Karl Barth*. Edited by H. Martin Rumscheidt. Eugene, OR: Pickwick, 1986.

———. *The Word of God and Theology*. Translated by Amy Marga. London: Bloomsbury T&T Clark, 2011.

Bell, Daniel M., Jr. *Just War as Christian Discipleship: Recentering the Tradition in the Church Rather than the State*. Grand Rapids: Brazos, 2009.

Bender, Kimlyn J. "Church." In *The Westminster Handbook to Karl Barth*, edited by Richard Burnett, 34-36. Louisville, KY: Westminster John Knox, 2013.

———. *Confessing Christ for Church and World: Studies in Modern Theology*. Downers Grove, IL: IVP Academic, 2014.

———. *Karl Barth's Christological Ecclesiology*. Foreword by D. Stephen Long. Eugene, OR: Cascade, 2013.

Berry, Wendell. *Collected Poems: 1957–1982*. New York: North Point, 1985.

Biggar, Nigel. "Barth's Trinitarian Ethic." In *The Cambridge Companion to Karl Barth*, edited by John Webster, 212-27. Cambridge: Cambridge University Press, 2000.

———. *Behaving in Public: How to Do Christian Ethics*. Grand Rapids: Eerdmans, 2011.

———. *The Hastening That Waits: Karl Barth's Ethics*. Oxford: Clarendon, 1993.

———. "Karl Barth's Ethics Revisited." In *Commanding Grace: Studies in Karl Barth's Ethics*, edited by Daniel L. Migliore, 26-49. Grand Rapids: Eerdmans, 2010.

Billings, J. Todd. *Calvin, Participation, and the Gift: The Activity of Believers in Union with Christ*. Oxford: Oxford University Press, 2007.

The Book of Confessions: The Constitution of the Presbyterian Church (U.S.A.): Part I. Louisville, KY: Office of the General Assembly, 2007.

Brunner, Emil, and Karl Barth. *Natural Theology: Comprising "Nature and Grace" by Professor Dr. Emil Brunner and the Reply "No!" by Dr. Karl Barth*. Translated by Peter Fraenkel. 1946, Reprint, Eugene, OR: Wipf and Stock, 2002.

Burnett, Richard E. *Karl Barth's Theological Exegesis: The Hermeneutical Principles of the Römerbrief Period*. Grand Rapids: Eerdmans, 2004.

Busch, Eberhard. *The Barmen Theses Then and Now: The 2004 Warfield Lectures at Princeton Theological Seminary*. Translated and Annotated by Darrell and Judith Guder. Grand Rapids: Eerdmans, 2010.

———. *The Great Passion: An Introduction to Karl Barth's Theology*. Translated by Geoffrey W. Bromiley. Grand Rapids: Eerdmans, 2004.

Cartwright, Michael G. "Afterword: Stanley Hauerwas's Essays in Theological Ethics: A Reader's Guide." In *The Hauerwas Reader*, edited by John Berkman and Michael Cartwright, 623-71. Durham, NC: Duke University Press, 2001.

Childress, James F. Review of *Ethics from a Theocentric Perspective*. Vol. 1, *Theology and Ethics*, by James M. Gustafson. *Ethics* 94, no. 1 (1983): 392-95.

Clough, David. *Ethics in Crisis: Interpreting Barth's Ethics*. Burlington, VT: Ashgate, 2005.

Collier, Charles M., ed. *The Difference Christ Makes: Celebrating the Life, Work, and Friendship of Stanley Hauerwas*. Eugene, OR: Cascade, 2015.

Collingwood, R. G. *The Idea of History*. Oxford: Oxford University Press, 1956.

Davis, Ellen F., and Richard B. Hays, eds. *The Art of Reading Scripture*. Grand Rapids: Eerdmans, 2003.

DeHart, Paul J. *The Trial of the Witnesses: The Rise and Decline of Postliberal Theology*. Malden, MA: Blackwell, 2006.

Doerge, Halden. "Dueling Ecclesiologies: Barth and Hauerwas in Con-verse." In *Karl Barth in Conversation*, edited by W. Travis McMaken and David W. Congdon, 116-25. Eugene, OR: Pickwick, 2014.

Dorrien, Gary. *Social Ethics in the Making: Interpreting an American Tradition*. London: Wiley-Blackwell, 2009.

Evans, C. Steven. *A History of Western Philosophy: From the Pre-Socratics to Postmodernism*. Downers Grove, IL: IVP Academic, 2018.

Fackre, Gabriel J. "Was Reinhold Niebuhr a Christian?" *First Things* 126 (October 2002): 25-27.

Flett, John G. *The Witness of God: The Trinity, Missio Dei, Karl Barth, and the Nature of Christian Community*. Grand Rapids: Eerdmans, 2010.

Fodor, James. "Postliberal Theology." In *The Modern Theologians: An Introduction to Christian Theology Since 1918*, 3rd edition, edited by David F. Ford and Rachel Muers, 229-248. Malden, MA: Blackwell, 2005.

Frei, Hans W. *Types of Christian Theology*. Edited by George Hunsinger and William C. Placher. New Haven, CT: Yale University Press, 1992.

Gannon, J. F. "MacIntyre's Historicism." *CrossCurrents* 39, no. 1 (1989): 91-96.

Gathje, Peter. "A Contested Classic: Critics Ask: Whose Christ? Which Type?" *Christian Century*, June 19-26, 2002, 28-32.

Givens, Tommy. *We the People: Israel and the Catholicity of Jesus*. Minneapolis: Fortress, 2014.

Goossen, Rachel Waltner. "'Defanging the Beast': Mennonite Responses to John Howard Yoder's Sexual Abuse." *Mennonite Quarterly Review* 89, no. 1 (2015): 7-80.

Grenz, Stanley J. *The Moral Quest: Foundations of Christian Ethics*. Downers Grove, IL: InterVarsity Press, 1997.

———. "Stanley Hauerwas, the Grain of the Universe, and the Most 'Natural' Natural Theology." *Scottish Journal of Theology* 56, no. 3 (2003): 381-86.

Grenz, Stanley J., and John R. Franke. *Beyond Foundationalism: Shaping The-ology in a Postmodern Context*. Louisville, KY: Westminster John Knox, 2001.

Guder, Darrell L. *Called to Witness: Doing Missional Theology*. Grand Rapids: Eerdmans, 2015.

Gunton, Colin, E. *The Barth Lectures*. Edited by P. H. Brazier. London: T&T Clark, 2007.

Guroian, Vigen. *Incarnate Love: Essays in Orthodox Ethics*. 2nd ed. Notre Dame, IN: University of Notre Dame Press, 2002.

Gustafson, James M. *Christ and the Moral Life*. New York: Harper & Row, 1968.

———. "The Sectarian Temptation: Reflections on Theology, the Church and the University." *Proceedings of the Catholic Theological Society of America* 40 (1985): 83-94.

Haddorff, David. *Christian Ethics as Witness: Barth's Ethics for a World at Risk*. Eugene, OR: Cascade, 2010.

Haight, Roger D., SJ. *Christian Community in History*. Vol. 2, *Comparative Eccle-siology*. London: Continuum, 2005.

Hamill, Bruce. "Beyond Ecclesiocentricity: Navigating Between the Abstract and the Domesticated in Contemporary Ecclesiology." *International Journal of Systematic Theology* 14, no. 3 (2012): 277-94.

Harink, Douglas. *Paul Among the Postliberals: Pauline Theology Beyond Chris-tendom and Modernity*. Grand Rapids: Brazos, 2003.

Harnack, Adolf von. *What Is Christianity?* Translated by Thomas Bailey Saunders. 1901. Reprint, Minneapolis: Fortress, 1986.

Hart, John W. *Karl Barth vs. Emil Brunner: The Formation and Dissolution of a Theological Alliance, 1916–1936*. New York: Peter Lang, 2001.

Hart, Trevor. *Regarding Karl Barth: Toward a Reading of His Theology*. Downers Grove, IL: InterVarsity Press, 1999.

Hauerwas, Stanley. *After Christendom: How the Church Is to Behave if Freedom, Justice, and a Christian Nation Are Bad Ideas*. Nashville: Abingdon, 1999.

———. *Against the Nations: War and Survival in a Liberal Society*. Minneapolis: Winston, 1985.

———. *Approaching the End: Eschatological Reflections on Church, Politics, and Life*. Grand Rapids: Eerdmans, 2013.

———. *A Better Hope: Resources for a Church Confronting Capitalism, Democracy, and Postmodernity*. Grand Rapids: Brazos, 2000.

———. "Between Christian Ethics and Religious Ethics: How Should Graduate Students Be Trained?" *Journal of Religious Ethics* 31, no. 3 (2003): 399-412.

————. "Blessed Are the Peacemakers, for They Shall See God: An Interview with Stanley Hauerwas." In *Postliberal Theology and the Church Catholic: Conversations with George Lindbeck, David Burrell, and Stanley Hauerwas*, edited by John Wright, 97-112. Grand Rapids: Baker Academic, 2012.

————. "Can Ethics Be Theological?" *The Hastings Center Report* 8, no. 5 (1978): 47-49.

————. *Character and the Christian Life: A Study in Theological Ethics*. Notre Dame, IN: University of Notre Dame Press, 1985.

————. "Christian Ethics in America: A Promising Obituary." In *Introduction to Christian Theology: Contemporary North American Perspectives*, edited by Roger A. Badham, 103-18. Louisville, KY: Westminster John Knox, 1998.

————. *Christian Existence Today: Essays on Church, World, and Living in Between*. Durham, NC: Labyrinth Press, 1988. Reprint, Eugene, OR: Wipf and Stock, 2010.

————. "Christians Don't Be Fooled: Donald Trump Has Deep Religious Convictions." *Washington Post*, January 27, 2017. https://www.washingtonpost.com /news/acts-of-faith/wp/2017/01/27/christians-dont-be-fooled-trump-has -deep-religious-convictions/?utm_term=.440c14a5eceb.

————. *A Community of Character: Toward a Constructive Christian Social Ethic*. Notre Dame, IN: University of Notre Dame Press, 1981.

————. "Connecting: A Response to Sean Larsen." *Scottish Journal of Theology* 69, no. 1 (2016): 39-45.

————. *Cross-Shattered Christ: Meditations on the Seven Last Words*. Grand Rapids: Brazos, 2011.

————. *A Cross-Shattered Church: Reclaiming the Theological Heart of Preaching*. Grand Rapids: Brazos, 2009.

————. *Dispatches from the Front: Theological Engagements with the Secular*. Durham, NC: Duke University Press, 1994.

————. *Disrupting Time: Sermons, Prayers, and Sundries*. Eugene, OR: Cascade, 2004.

————. "The Ethicist as Theologian." *Christian Century*, April 23, 1975, 408-12.

————. "The Ethics of Black Power." *The Augustana Observer*, February 5, 1969: 3, 7.

————. "Faculty Forum with Stanley Hauerwas: Conrad Grebel University College." *Conrad Grebel Review* 20, no. 3 (2002): 69-80.

————. "H. Richard Niebuhr." In *The Modern Theologians: An Introduction to Christian Theology Since 1918*, edited by David F. Ford with Rachel Muers, 194-204. 3rd ed. Malden, MA: Blackwell, 2005.

————. *Hannah's Child: A Theologian's Memoir*. Grand Rapids: Eerdmans, 2010.

————. *The Hauerwas Reader*. Edited by John Berkman and Michael Cartwright. Durham, NC: Duke University Press, 2001.

———. "Hooks: Random Thoughts by Way of a Response to Griffiths and Ochs." *Modern Theology* 19, no. 1 (2003): 89-101.

———. "The Importance of Being Catholic: A Protestant View." *First Things*, March 1990, 23-30.

———. *In Good Company: The Church as Polis.* Notre Dame, IN: University of Notre Dame Press, 1995.

———. "Karl Barth: *Dogmatics in Outline* (1947)." *First Things*, March 2000, 46-47.

———. *Matthew.* Brazos Theological Commentary on the Bible. Grand Rapids: Brazos, 2006.

———. *The Peaceable Kingdom: A Primer in Christian Ethics.* Notre Dame, IN: University of Notre Dame Press, 1983.

———. *Performing the Faith: Bonhoeffer and the Practice of Nonviolence.* Grand Rapids: Brazos, 2004.

———. "A Place for God? Science and Religion in the Gifford Lectures." *Christian Century*, February 21, 2006, 43-45.

———. *Sanctify Them in the Truth: Holiness Exemplified.* Nashville: Abingdon, 1998.

———. *The State of the University: Academic Knowledges and the Knowledge of God.* Oxford: Blackwell, 2007.

———. *Unleashing the Scriptures: Freeing the Bible from Captivity to America.* Nashville: Abingdon, 1993.

———. *Vision and Virtue: Essays in Christian Ethical Reflection.* Notre Dame, IN: Fides, 1974.

———. *War and the American Difference: Theological Reflections on Violence and National Identity.* Grand Rapids: Baker Academic, 2011.

———. *Wilderness Wanderings: Probing Twentieth-Century Theology and Philosophy.* Boulder, CO: Westview, 1997.

———. *With the Grain of the Universe: The Church's Witness and Natural Theology: Being the Gifford Lectures Delivered at the University of St. Andrews in 2001.* Grand Rapids: Brazos, 2001.

———. *The Work of Theology.* Grand Rapids: Eerdmans, 2015.

———. *Working with Words: On Learning to Speak Christian.* Eugene, OR: Cascade, 2011.

Hauerwas, Stanley, Richard Bondi, and David B. Burrell. *Truthfulness and Tragedy: Further Investigations into Christian Ethics.* Notre Dame, IN: University of Notre Dame Press, 1977.

Hauerwas, Stanley, and Brian Brock. *Beginnings: Interrogating Hauerwas.* London: T&T Clark, 2017.

Hauerwas, Stanley, and Romand Coles. *Christianity, Democracy, and the Radical Ordinary: Conversations Between a Radical Democrat and a Christian.* Eugene, OR: Cascade, 2008.

Hauerwas, Stanley, and Robert Dean. *Minding the Web: Making Theological Connections.* Eugene, OR: Cascade, 2018.

Hauerwas, Stanley, and Chris K. Huebner. "History, Theory, and Anabaptism: A Conversation on Theology after John Howard Yoder." In *The Wisdom of the Cross: Essays in Honor of John Howard Yoder*, edited by Stanley Hauerwas, Chris K. Huebner, Harry J. Huebner, and Mark Thiessen Nation, 391-409. Grand Rapids: Eerdmans, 1999.

Hauerwas, Stanley, Robin W. Lovin, and Emilie Maureen Townes. "Ethics in Our Time: Social Witness for the New Century." *Christian Century*, September 27, 2000, 952-58.

Hauerwas, Stanley, and Samuel Wells, eds. *The Blackwell Companion to Christian Ethics.* Malden, MA: Blackwell, 2004.

———. "Theological Ethics." In *God's Advocates: Christian Thinkers in Conversation*, edited by Rupert Shortt, 175-93. London: DLT, 2005.

Hauerwas, Stanley, and William H. Willimon. "Embarrassed by God's Presence." *Christian Century*, January 30, 1985, 98-100.

———. *The Holy Spirit.* Nashville: Abingdon, 2015.

———. *Resident Aliens: Life in the Christian Colony.* Nashville: Abingdon, 1989.

———. *Where Resident Aliens Live: Exercises for Christian Practice.* Nashville: Abingdon, 1996.

Hays, Richard B. *The Moral Vision of the New Testament: A Contemporary Introduction to New Testament Ethics.* San Francisco: HarperSanFrancisco, 1996.

Healy, Nicholas M. *Hauerwas: A (Very) Critical Introduction.* Grand Rapids: Eerdmans, 2014.

Herdt, Jennifer A. "Alasdair MacIntyre's 'Rationality of Traditions' and Tradition-Transcendental Standards of Justification." *Journal of Religion* 78, no. 4 (1998): 524-46.

Hesselink, I. John. "Law and Gospel or Gospel and Law? Karl Barth, Martin Luther, and John Calvin." *Reformation & Revival* 14, no. 1 (2005): 139-71.

Hobson, Theo. "Ecclesiological Fundamentalism." *Modern Believing* 45, no. 4 (2004): 48-59.

Howard, Thomas Albert. *Protestant Theology and the Making of the Modern German University.* Oxford: Oxford University Press, 2006.

Huebner, Chris K. *A Precarious Peace: Yoderian Explorations on Theology, Knowledge, and Identity.* Scottdale, PA: Herald, 2006.

Hunsinger, George. *Conversational Theology: Essays on Ecumenical, Postliberal, and Political Theology with Special Reference to Karl Barth.* New York: Bloomsbury, 2015.

————. *How to Read Karl Barth: The Shape of His Theology.* Oxford: Oxford University Press, 1991.

————. *Reading Barth with Charity: A Hermeneutical Proposal.* Grand Rapids: Baker Academic, 2015.

Hütter, Reinhard. *Evangelische Ethik als kirchliches Zeugnis: Interpretationen zu Schlüsselfragen theologischer Ethik in der Gegenwart.* Neukirchen-Vluyn: Neukirchener, 1993.

————. *Suffering Divine Things: Theology as Church Practice.* Translated by Doug Stott. Grand Rapids: Eerdmans, 2000.

Jenson, Robert W. "The Hauerwas Project." *Modern Theology* 8, no. 3 (1992): 285-95.

————. "You Wonder Where the Spirit Went." *Pro Ecclesia* 2, no. 3 (1993): 296-304.

Johnson, James T. "Just War in the Thought of Paul Ramsey." *Journal of Religious Ethics* 19, no. 2 (1991): 183-207.

Johnson, Luke Timothy. "Matthew or Stanley? Pick One." *Pro Ecclesia* 17, no. 1 (2008): 29-34.

————. "Unleashing the Scriptures: Freeing the Bible from Captivity to America." *Modern Theology* 11, no. 2 (1995): 283-85.

Johnson, Merwyn S. "Gospel and Law." In *The Westminster Handbook to Karl Barth*, edited by Richard Burnett, 85-87. Louisville, KY: Westminster John Knox, 2013.

Jüngel, Eberhard. *Karl Barth: A Theological Legacy.* Translated by Garrett E. Paul. Philadelphia: Westminster, 1986.

Kallenberg, Brad J. *Ethics as Grammar: Changing the Postmodern Subject.* Notre Dame, IN: University of Notre Dame Press, 2001.

Kelsey, David H. *The Uses of Scripture in Recent Theology.* Philadelphia: Fortress, 1975.

Kerr, Fergus. *Theology After Wittgenstein.* 2nd ed. London: SPCK, 1997.

Kerr, Nathan R. *Christ, History, and Apocalyptic: The Politics of Mission.* Eugene, OR: Cascade, 2009.

Levering, Matthew. *Engaging the Doctrine of Revelation: The Mediation of the Gospel Through Church and Scripture.* Grand Rapids: Baker Academic, 2014.

Lindbeck, George A. *The Nature of Doctrine: Religion and Theology in a Postliberal Age.* Philadelphia: Westminster, 1984.

Little, H. Ganse. "Ernst Troeltsch and the Scope of Historicism." *Journal of Religion* 46, no. 3 (1966): 343-64.

Lorrimar, Victoria. "Christ and Church in the Work of Stanley Hauerwas." *Ecclesiology* 11 (2015): 306-26.

Maddox, Randy L. "John Wesley and Eastern Orthodoxy: Influences, Convergences and Divergences," *Asbury Theological Journal* 45, no. 2 (1990): 29-53.

Mangina, Joseph. "After Dogma: Reinhard Hütter's Challenge to Contemporary Theology; A Review Essay." *International Journal of Systematic Theology* 2, no. 3 (2000): 330-46.

———. "Bearing the Marks of Jesus: The Church in the Economy of Salvation in Barth and Hauerwas." *Scottish Journal of Theology* 52, no. 3 (1999): 269-305.

———. *Karl Barth on the Christian Life: The Practical Knowledge of God.* New York: Peter Lang, 2001.

———. *Karl Barth: Theologian of Christian Witness.* Louisville, KY: Westminster John Knox, 2004.

Massmann, Alexander. *Citizenship in Heaven and on Earth: Karl Barth's Ethics.* Minneapolis: Fortress Press, 2015.

McClendon, James Wm. *Biography as Theology: How Life Stories Can Remake Today's Theology.* New ed. Philadelphia: Trinity Press International, 1990.

———. *The Collected Works of James Wm. McClendon, Jr.* Edited by Ryan Andrew Newson and Andrew C. Wright. 3 vols. Waco, TX: Baylor University Press, 2014–2016.

McClendon, James Wm., and James M. Smith. *Convictions: Defusing Religious Relativism.* Rev. ed. Valley Forge, PA: Trinity Press International, 1994.

McCormack, Bruce L. *Karl Barth's Critically Realistic Dialectical Theology: Its Genesis and Development, 1909–1936.* Oxford: Oxford University Press, 1995.

———. *Orthodox and Modern: Studies in the Theology of Karl Barth.* Grand Rapids: Baker Academic, 2008.

McKenny, Gerald. *The Analogy of Grace: Karl Barth's Moral Theology.* Oxford: Oxford University Press, 2010.

———. "Heterogeneity and Ethical Deliberation: Casuistry, Narrative, and Event in the Ethics of Karl Barth." *Annual of the Society of Christian Ethics* 20 (2000): 205-24.

McMaken, W. Travis. *The Sign of the Gospel: Toward an Evangelical Doctrine of Infant Baptism After Karl Barth.* Minneapolis: Fortress, 2013.

Migliore, Daniel. "Commanding Grace: Karl Barth's Theological Ethics." In *Commanding Grace: Studies in Karl Barth's Ethics*, edited by Daniel Migliore, 1-25. Grand Rapids: Eerdmans, 2010.

Mohler, Albert. "Nearing the End: A Conversation with Theologian Stanley Hauerwas." Albert Mohler website. April 28, 2014. http://www.albert mohler.com/2014/04/28/nearing-the-end-a-conversation-with-theologian -stanley-hauerwas/.

Moltmann, Jürgen. *Ethics of Hope*. Translated by Margaret Kohl. Minneapolis: Fortress, 2012.

Morgan, Brandon L. "The Lordship of Christ and the Gathering of the Church." *Conrad Grebel Review* 33, no. 1 (2015): 49-71.

Mouw, Richard J. "Cultural Discipleship in a Time of God's Patience." *Scottish Bulletin of Evangelical Theology* 28, no. 1 (2010): 80-91.

Murphy, Francesca Aran. *God Is Not a Story: Realism Revisited*. Oxford: Oxford University Press, 2007.

Murphy, Nancey. *Anglo-American Postmodernity: Philosophical Perspectives on Science, Religion, and Ethics*. Boulder, CO: Westview, 1997.

Niebuhr, H. Richard. *Christ and Culture*. 50th anniversary ed. San Francisco: HarperSanFrancisco, 2001.

———. "The Doctrine of the Trinity and the Unity of the Church." *Theology Today* 3, no. 3 (1946): 371-84.

———. *The Kingdom of God in America*. New York: Harper, 1959.

———. *The Meaning of Revelation*. Introduction by Douglas F. Ottati. Louisville, KY: Westminster John Knox, 2006.

———. *The Responsible Self: An Essay in Christian Moral Philosophy*. With an introduction by James M. Gustafson. New York: Harper & Row, 1963.

Nielsen, Bent Flemming. "Theology as Liturgy? The Practical Dimension of Barth's Thinking." In *Dogmatics After Barth: Facing Challenges in Church, Society, and the Academy*, edited by Günter Thomas, Rinse H. Reeling Brouwer, and Bruce McCormack, 67-80. Leipzig: CreateSpace Independent Publishing Platform, 2012.

Nikolajsen, Jeppe Bach. *The Distinctive Identity of the Church: A Constructive Study of the Post-Christendom Theologies of Lesslie Newbigin and John Howard Yoder*. Eugene, OR: Pickwick, 2015.

Nimmo, Paul T. "Actualism." In *The Westminster Handbook to Karl Barth*, edited by Richard Burnett, 1-2. Louisville, KY: Westminster John Knox, 2013.

———. *Being in Action: The Theological Shape of Bath's Ethical Vision*. London: T&T Clark, 2007.

Ochs, Peter. *Another Reformation: Postliberal Christianity and the Jews*. Grand Rapids: Baker Academic, 2011.

O'Donovan, Joan E. "Man in the Image of God: The Disagreement Between Barth and Brunner Reconsidered." *Scottish Journal of Theology* 39, no. 4 (1986): 433-59.

O'Donovan, Oliver. *Ethics as Theology*. Vol. 1, *Self, World, and Time*. Grand Rapids: Eerdmans, 2013.

———. *The Desire of the Nations: Rediscovering the Roots of Political Theology.* Cambridge: Cambridge University Press, 1996.

Paddison, Angus. *Scripture: A Very Theological Proposal.* London: T&T Clark, 2009.

Park, Sung W. "The Question of Deification in the Theology of John Calvin." *Verbum et Ecclesia* 38, no. 1 (2017): 1-5. https://dx.doi.org/10.4102/ve.v38i1.1701.

Pecknold, C. C. Review of *The Blackwell Companion to Christian Ethics*, edited by Stanley Hauerwas and Samuel Wells. *Journal of Theological Studies* 57, no. 1 (2006): 413-18.

———. *Transforming Postliberal Theology: George Lindbeck, Pragmatism and Scripture.* London: T&T Clark, 2005.

Placher, William. *The Domestication of Transcendence: How Modern Thinking About God Went Wrong.* Louisville, KY: Westminster John Knox, 1996.

———. "Postliberal Theology." In *The Modern Theologians: An Introduction to Christian Theology in the Twentieth Century*, edited by David F. Ford, 115-128. 2nd ed. Malden, MA: Blackwell, 1997.

———. *Unapologetic Theology: A Christian Voice in a Pluralistic Conversation.* Louisville, KY: Westminster John Knox, 1989.

Pouivet, Roger. *After Wittgenstein, St. Thomas.* Translated and Introduced by Michael S. Sherwin, OP. South Bend, IN: St. Augustine's, 2006.

Rasmusson, Arne. *The Church as Polis: From Political Theology to Theological Politics as Exemplified by Jürgen Moltmann and Stanley Hauerwas.* Notre Dame, IN: University of Notre Dame Press, 1995.

Ritschl, Albrecht. *The Christian Doctrine of Justification and Reconciliation: The Positive Development of the Doctrine.* Translated and Edited by H. R. Mackintosh and A. B. Macaulay. 2nd ed. Edinburgh: T&T Clark, 1902.

Roberts, Richard H. "The Reception of the Theology of Karl Barth in the Anglo-Saxon World: History, Typology and Prospect." In *Karl Barth: Centenary Essays*, edited by S. W. Sykes, 115-71. Cambridge: Cambridge University Press, 1989.

Siggelkow, Ry O. "A Response to Doerge on Barth and Hauerwas." In *Karl Barth in Conversation*, edited by W. Travis McMaken and David W. Congdon, 125-28. Eugene, OR: Pickwick, 2014.

———. "Toward an Apocalyptic Peace Church: Christian Pacifism *After* Hauerwas." *Conrad Grebel Review* 31, no. 3 (2013): 274-97.

Siker, Jeffrey S. *Scripture and Ethics: Twentieth-Century Portraits*. Oxford: Oxford University Press, 1997.

Smith, James K. A. *Desiring the Kingdom: Worship, Worldview, and Cultural Formation*. Grand Rapids: Baker Academic, 2009.

———. *Who's Afraid of Relativism? Community, Contingency, and Creaturehood*. Grand Rapids: Baker Academic, 2014.

Stendhal, Krister. "The Apostle Paul and the Introspective Conscience of the West." *Harvard Theological Review* 56, no. 3 (1963): 199-215.

Thielicke, Helmut. *The Evangelical Faith*. Vol. 1, *Prolegomena: The Relation of Theology to Modern Thought Forms*. Translated and edited by Geoffrey W. Bromiley. Edinburgh: T&T Clark, 1974.

Thomson, John B. *The Ecclesiology of Stanley Hauerwas: A Christian Theology of Liberation*. Aldershot: Ashgate, 2003.

"Thy Dodd and Thy Niebuhr." *Time*, August 23, 1943.

Tillich, Paul. *Systematic Theology*. 3 vols. Chicago: University of Chicago Press, 1951–1963.

Toulmin, Stephen. *Cosmopolis: The Hidden Agenda of Modernity*. New York: Free Press, 1990.

Vanhoozer, Kevin J. *Biblical Authority After Babel: Retrieving the Solas in the Spirit of Mere Protestant Christianity*. Grand Rapids: Brazos, 2016.

———. *The Drama of Doctrine: A Canonical-Linguistic Approach to Christian Doctrine*. Louisville, KY: Westminster John Knox, 2005.

Wannenwetsch, Bernd. Review of *The Blackwell Companion to Christian Ethics*, edited by Stanley Hauerwas and Samuel Wells. *Journal of Contemporary Religion* 21, no. 2 (2006): 264-65.

Webb, Stephen H. "The Very American Stanley Hauerwas." *First Things*, June 2002, 14-17.

Webster, John. *Barth's Ethics of Reconciliation*. Cambridge: Cambridge University Press, 1995.

———. *Barth's Moral Theology: Human Action in Barth's Thought*. Grand Rapids: Eerdmans, 1998.

———. "Ecclesiocentrism: A Review of *Hauerwas: A (Very) Critical Introduction* by Nicholas M. Healy." *First Things*, October 2014, 54-55.

———. *Holy Scripture: A Dogmatic Sketch*. Cambridge: Cambridge University Press, 2003.

———. *Word and Church: Essays in Christian Dogmatics*. London: Bloomsbury T&T Clark, 2016.

Wells, Samuel. "The Difference Christ Makes." In *The Difference Christ Makes: Celebrating the Life, Work, and Friendship of Stanley Hauerwas*, edited by Charles M. Collier, 5-24. Eugene, OR: Cascade, 2015.

———. *Transforming Fate into Destiny: The Theological Ethics of Stanley Hauerwas*. Carlisle, UK: Paternoster Press, 1998. Reprint, Eugene, OR: Cascade, 2004.

Werpehowski, William. *American Protestant Ethics and the Legacy of H. Richard Niebuhr*. Washington, DC: Georgetown University Press, 2002.

———. *Karl Barth and Christian Ethics: Living in Truth*. Burlington, VT: Ashgate, 2014.

———. "Talking the Walk and Walking the Talk: Stanley Hauerwas's Contribution to Theological Ethics." *Journal of Religious Ethics* 40, no. 2 (2012): 228-49.

Willis, Robert E. *The Ethics of Karl Barth*. Leiden: Brill, 1971.

Yoder, John Howard. "How H. Richard Niebuhr Reasoned: A Critique of *Christ and Culture*." In *Authentic Christian Transformation: A New Vision of Christ and Culture*, edited by Glen H. Stassen, D. M. Yeager, and John Howard Yoder, 31-89. Nashville: Abingdon, 1996.

General Index

postliberalism, 6-10, 57, 62, 86-98, 106-10, 118, 197, 201-2

pragmatism, 106-15, 118-19, 122-23

preaching, 149, 161, 175-76

Ramsey, Paul, 38-39, 41, 97, 102

Rauschenbusch, Walter, 29-31, 32, 35, 40, 42-43

Ritschl, Albrecht, 11-14, 28, 29, 55, 87, 129, 169, 171, 186, 196, 197-98, 203, 208, 210, 213

Ritschl Thesis, 12-14, 16-17, 171-72, 205, 213

sanctification, 33, 167-68, 215

Schleiermacher Thesis, 11-12, 14, 16, 84, 125-26, 157-58, 169

Schleiermacher, Friedrich, 2, 11-12, 15, 28, 51, 55, 78, 87, 129, 177, 197, 201, 210

Scots Confession, 199-200

Scripture, 5, 7-8, 92, 108, 173-186, 197-203
    Barth's doctrine of, x, 53, 60, 171-72, 174-80, 195-96, 206
    Hauerwas's doctrine of, 14, 16, 88, 146, 149, 153-54, 171-72, 180-85, 187-88, 195-96, 197-203, 208

September 11th, 2

simul justus et peccator, 33, 60

Smith, James K. A., 9, 115, 122

social gospel. *See* Rauschenbusch, Walter

sola scriptura, 71-72, 173, 177, 180, 182-83, 185-86, 197-203, 204, 217

Suffering Presence, 63

Theologie Treiben, 119, 121, 209

theology of the third article, 2, 15, 50, 68, 75, 78, 80, 83

Tillich, Paul, 33

Troeltsch, Ernst, 27-28, 29-31, 38, 42, 51, 87-88, 89-98, 101-2, 105, 129, 210

Truthfulness and Tragedy, 63

union with Christ, 167

Unleashing the Scripture, 180, 182-85, 199

Vanhoozer, Kevin, 202-3

Vatican II, 39, 183

war, 2, 35-36, 39, 41-44, 117

Webster, John, 12-14, 37, 58, 132, 169, 171-72, 173, 186, 187, 196, 197-98, 203, 208

Wells, Samuel, 2, 21, 23, 44, 62, 102, 103-4, 105, 146, 147-155, 169, 214

Werpehowski, William, 59-61, 97-98, 162, 164

Westminster Confession of Faith, 148, 199-200

Williams, Rowan, 115, 155

Willimon, Will, 47, 51, 53, 111

With the Grain of the Universe, 64, 73-74, 110, 112-14

witness, 14, 24-25, 54, 56, 64, 80-82, 104-5, 108-18, 122, 149-55, 161, 180, 185, 187, 190-95, 206-8, 215, 216

Wittgenstein, Ludwig, 3, 10, 66, 108, 114-15, 136

Yale Divinity School, 20, 31, 38-39, 50-51, 56, 91, 93, 99, 102, 146

Yoder, John Howard, 2, 20, 23, 38, 40-44, 62-63, 86, 95-96, 98-105, 115-17, 155, 160, 180-81, 184-85, 188, 217